Latin American Politics in the Neoliberal Era

This book offers an outstanding Marxist overview of the turns of the political pendulum in contemporary Latin America, and the shifting fortunes of left in the class struggle. The book is solid and insightful, and unsurpassed in its coverage and depth. An indispensable companion to political economists, trade unionists, community organisers, and activists seeking lessons and inspiration from the most politically active region in the world.

Alfredo Saad-Filho,
SOAS University of London, University of Johannesburg,
LUT University, and Università degli Studi della Campania
'Luigi Vanvitelli'

I highly recommend this profoundly original work. The extraordinary value of this book is that it addresses and dissects the essential dimensions of an exceedingly complex contemporary reality. In this regard it matches works of great importance such as those of Tulio Halperín Donghi or Darcy Ribeiro, who in the past knew how to penetrate appearances to grasp the underlying essence of reality. This book does so superbly in the contemporary context of capitalist development, enhancing a clearly articulated theoretically framed overview of Latin America's historical trajectory with detailed national comparative studies, which range from Mexico and Central America to Brazil and Argentina, Bolivia and Ecuador, Peru, and Colombia. The highlight of the book is an analysis of the dynamics of political change and class struggle in terms of swings to the left and right of the pendulum of electoral politics, and the associated conflict between right-wing neoliberalisms and left-wing progressivisms.

Alberto Bialakowsky,
Instituto de Investigaciones Gino Germani, Universidad de Buenos
Aires; Cofounder, South-South Forum of Social Science;
Founding President, ASET (Argentine Association of Labor Studies)

A refreshing overview and synthesis of past and current happenings in Latin America with attention to neoliberal authoritarianism and progressive politics, social change, and political economy. Emphasis on class and class struggle and includes case studies on Bolivia, Ecuador, Mexico, and Peru. Especially useful as a text for Latin American Studies.

Ronald Chilcote,
Professor Emeritus of Economics and Political Science,
University of California, Riverside

A must-read book on the political crossroads and the dynamics of class struggle in Latin America in the 21st century. The author offers us an in-depth and nuanced analysis of three fronts of the class struggle unfolding in the region, with particular emphasis on the emergence of a progressive cycle of regime change – the so-called 'pink tide' – and the subsequent rise of neo-authoritarian regimes on the radical far right. Added to an analysis of the pendulum swings of electoral politics the book provides an analysis of the class struggles associated with the peasant movement as well as the indigenous communities on the frontier of extractive capital. Highly recommended for scholars and students concerned with the politics of development in Latin America.

Raúl Delgado Wise,
Holder of the UNESCO Chair for Migration and Development at the Universidad Autónoma de Zacatecas, and Emeritus National Researcher with the National Council of Humanities, Science and Technology, Mexico

With customary analytical precision and exacting synthesis Henry Veltmeyer surveys the terrain of class struggle in Latin America within the current world conjuncture of neoliberal authoritarian ascendency and intensifying capitalist extractivism. Assessing advances and setbacks of left projects in the region, across both electoral and social-movement landscapes, Veltmeyer's book is an essential guide through the fault-lines of Latin America in this fraught political moment.

Jeffery R. Webber,
Co-author of The Impasse of the Latin American Left

EMERALD STUDIES IN STATE, POLITICS AND SOCIETY

Series Editor: Berch Berberoglu *University of Nevada, Reno, USA*

At a time of great political turmoil, with state institutions in disarray and the rise of authoritarianism around the world, it is becoming increasingly evident that the study of the relationship between politics, the state, and society will once again take center stage as we move forward in the 21st century.

This series promises to make an important contribution to the study of the class nature of the state and political power as they affect society and social relations on a global scale. The books in this series will aim at examining the nature and dynamics of the state and political institutions that serve particular class interests and are the leading forces that promote prevailing power relations and maintain the established social order.

At the same time, social movements aimed at challenging state power are increasingly taking the lead in confronting the powers of the state through various forms of resistance across the globe. This series will provide an analysis of the class nature and role of the state, hence the relationship between the state and opposing class forces vying for power, in attempting to understand the dynamics of politics and political power in contemporary capitalist society.

EDITORIAL ADVISORY BOARD

Rajendra Baikady — *Central University of Kerala, India*
Patrick Bond — *University of Johannesburg, South Africa*
Rose Brewer — *University of Minnesota, USA*
Christopher Chase-Dunn — *University of California, Riverside, USA*
Adam Fabry — *Universidad Nacional de Chilecito, Argentina*
Walda Katz-Fishman — *Howard University, USA*
Rhonda Levine — *Colgate University, USA*
Ligaya Lindio-McGovern — *Indiana University Kokomo, USA*
Martin Orr — *Boise State University, USA*
Jaroslaw Przeperski — *Nicolaus Copernicus University, Poland*
Larry T. Reynolds — *Central Michigan University, USA*
Alan Jay Spector — *Purdue University Northwest, USA*
Ann Strahm — *California State University, USA*
Henry Veltmeyer — *Universidad Autónoma de Zacatecas, Mexico; Saint Mary's University, Canada*

Latin American Politics in the Neoliberal Era: The Changing Dynamics of Class Struggle

BY

HENRY VELTMEYER
Universidad Autónoma de Zacatecas, Mexico

United Kingdom – North America – Japan – India – Malaysia – China

Emerald Publishing Limited
Emerald Publishing, Floor 5, Northspring, 21-23 Wellington Street, Leeds LS1 4DL.

First edition 2025

Copyright © 2025 Henry Veltmeyer.
Chapter 5 © 2025 Jan Lust.
Published under exclusive licence by Emerald Publishing Limited.

Reprints and permissions service
Contact: www.copyright.com

No part of this book may be reproduced, stored in a retrieval system, transmitted in any form or by any means electronic, mechanical, photocopying, recording or otherwise without either the prior written permission of the publisher or a licence permitting restricted copying issued in the UK by The Copyright Licensing Agency and in the USA by The Copyright Clearance Center. Any opinions expressed in the chapters are those of the authors. Whilst Emerald makes every effort to ensure the quality and accuracy of its content, Emerald makes no representation implied or otherwise, as to the chapters' suitability and application and disclaims any warranties, express or implied, to their use.

British Library Cataloguing in Publication Data
A catalogue record for this book is available from the British Library

ISBN: 978-1-83797-842-7 (Print)
ISBN: 978-1-83797-841-0 (Online)
ISBN: 978-1-83797-843-4 (Epub)

Printed and bound by CPI Group (UK) Ltd, Croydon, CR0 4YY

INVESTOR IN PEOPLE

This book is dedicated to my comrade in (intellectual) arms, James Petras, whose pioneering work, theoretical reflections, and incisive analysis of the changing dynamics of the class struggle in Latin America have paved the way for others in the field. Petras is one of the most important political sociologists of the 20th and 21st centuries, having made significant contributions to a critical Marxist tradition in sociological and political analysis. No one has done as much in shaping and advancing our understanding of the complex dynamics of class and the class struggle in Latin America.

Contents

List of Acronyms	*xiii*
About the Authors	*xvi*
Acknowledgments	*xvii*
Introduction	*1*
Chapter 1 Latin America in the Vortex of Social Change	*13*
Chapter 2 The Politics of Neoliberal Authoritarianism	*29*
Chapter 3 Agrarian Movements and the Land Struggle	*53*
Chapter 4 The Progressive Cycle: A Left Turn in Latin American Politics	*65*
Chapter 5 The Class Struggle in Peru, 2021–2023	*83*
Chapter 6 The Politics of Social Change in Mexico	*103*
Chapter 7 The Turn Back to the Right	*119*
Chapter 8 Populist Authoritarianism: The Bolsonaro Factor	*129*
Chapter 9 The Politics of Extractive Imperialism	*141*
Chapter 10 What Next for Latin America? The Postextractive Transition	*153*
References	*171*
Index	*183*

List of Acronyms

ALBA	Bolivarian Alliance for the Peoples of Our America (Alianza Bolivariana para los Pueblos de Nuestra América)
AMLO	Andrés Manuel López Obrador
APRA	American Popular Revolutionary Alliance (Alianza Popular Revolucionaria Americana)
BRICS	Originally Brazil, Russia, India, China, and South Africa; today also Egypt, Ethiopia, Iran, and the United Arab Emirates
CACEP	Agrarian, Peasant, Ethnic, and Popular Summit (Cumbre Agraria, Campesina, Étnica y Popular)
CDP	Popular Defense Committee of Durango (Comité de Defensa Popular de Durango)
CIMI	Indigenous Missionary Council (Conselho Indigenista Missionário)
CIOAC	Independent Union of Agricultural Workers and Peasants (Central Independiente de Obreros Agricolas y Campesinos)
CND	National Democratic Convention (Convención Nacional Democrático)
COAC	Independent Agricultural Workers and Peasant Center (Central Independiente de Obreros Agricolas y Campesinos)
COB	Bolivian Workers' Center (Central Obrera Boliviana)
CONACAMI	National Confederation of Peruvian Communities Affected by Mining (Confederación Nacional de Comunidades del Perú Afectadas por la Minería)
CONAIE	Confederation of Indigenous Nationalities of Ecuador (Confederación de Nacionalidades Indígenas del Ecuador)
CPAC	Conservative Political Action Conference
CTM	Confederation of Mexican Workers (Confederación de Trabajadores de México)
CUT	Unified Workers' Central (Central Única dos Trabalhadores)
EAP	Economically active population

xiv   List of Acronyms

ECLAC	Economic Commission on Latin America (CEPAL – Comisión Económica para América Latina)
ECUARUNARI	Confederation of Kichwa Nation Peoples of Ecuador (Confederación de Pueblos de la Nacionalidad Kichwa del Ecuador)
ELN	National Liberation Army (Ejército de Liberación Nacional de Colombia)
EZLN	Zapatista Army of National Liberation (Ejército Zapatista de Liberación Nacional)
FAO	Food and Agriculture Organization (United Nations)
FARC-EP	Revolutionary Armed Forces of Colombia – People's Army (Fuerzas Armadas Revolucionarias de Colombia – Ejército del Pueblo)
FDI	Foreign direct investment
FLN	National Liberation Army (Fuerzas de Liberación Nacional)
FTAA	Free Trade Area of the Americas (ACLA – Área de Libre Comercio de las Américas)
FUNAI	National Foundation of Indigenous Peoples (Fundação Nacional dos Povos Indígenas)
FZLN	Zapatista Front of National Liberation (Frente Zapatista de Liberación Nacional)
GDP	Gross domestic product
GEI	Global greenhouse gas emissions (gases de efecto invernadero)
IBGE	Brazilian Institute of Geography and Statistics (Instituto Brasileiro de Geografia e Estatistica)
IMF	International Monetary Fund
INEGI	National Institute of Statistics and Geography (Instituto Nacional de Estadística y Geografía)
ISI	Import substitution industrialization
ITT	Yasuni Ishpingo-Tambococha-Tiputini National Park
IU	United Left (Izquierda Unida)
IVMs	Intentional violent deaths
MAS	Movement toward Socialism (Movimiento al Socialismo)
MESCP	Productive Community Social Economic Model (Modelo Educativo Sociocomunitario Productivo)
MORENA	National Regeneration Movement (Movimiento de Regeneración Nacional)
MRC	The Citizen Revolution Movement (Movimiento Revolución Ciudadana)
MST	Landless Worker's Movement (Brazil — Movimento dos Trabalhadores Rurais Sem Terra)
MUPP-NP	Pachakutik Plurinational Unity Movement – New Country (Movimiento de Unidad Plurinacional Pachakutik – Nuevo País)

NAFTA	North American Free Trade Agreement
NGO	Non-governmental organization
NSP	New social policy
OAS	Organization of American States
OECD	Organisation for Economic Co-operation and Development
PAN	National Action Party (Partido de Acción Nacional)
PCM	Communist Party of Mexico (Partido Comunista Mexicana)
PDVSA	Venezuela State Petroleum Company (Petróleos de Venezuela S.A.)
PNAP	National Agrarian and Popular Strike (Paro Nacional Agrário y Popular)
PRD	Party of the Democratic Revolution (Partido de la Revolución Democrática)
PRI	Institutional Revolutionary Party (Partido Revolucionario Institucional)
PRO	Republican Proposal (Propuesta Republicana)
PROCUP	Clandestine Revolutionary Party Union of the People (Partido Revolucionario Clandestino Union del Pueblo)
PRONASOL	National Solidarity Program (Progama Nacional de Solidaridad)
PSDB	Brazilian Social Democracy Party (Partido da Social Democracia Brasileira)
PSUV	United Socialist Party of Venezuela (Partido Socialista Unido de Venezuela)
PT	Brazilian Worker's Party (Partido dos Trabalhadores)
REM	Mexican Network of Those Affected by Mining (Red Mexicana de Afectados por la Minería)
SELA	Latin American and Caribbean Economic System (Sistema Económico Latinoamericano y del Caribe)
TPP	Trans-Pacific Partnership
UNAM	National Autonomous University of Mexico (Universidad National Autónoma de México)

About the Authors

Henry Veltmeyer is Professor of Development Studies at the Universidad Autónoma de Zacatecas in Mexico and Professor Emeritus in International Development Studies at Saint Mary's University in Halifax, Canada. He also holds a status as Senior Research Fellow with the Maria Sibylla Merian Center for Advanced Latin American Studies in the Humanities and Social Sciences and Emeritus National Researcher with the Mexican Research Council of Humanities, Science and Technology. He is author, coauthor, and editor of over 40 books on issues of Latin American and world development including *From Extractivism to Sustainability: Scenarios and Lessons from Latin America* (2023) and *Buen Vivir and Challenges to Capitalism in Latin America* (2020).

Jan Lust is a Researcher and Professor at the Pontificia Universidad Católica del Perú. He is the author of *Lucha Revolucionaria. Perú, 1958–1967* (2013), a book on the history of revolutionary struggle in Peru in the 1960s; *Capitalism, Class and Revolution in Peru, 1980–2016* (2019), a book that analyzes the political, economic, and social reasons why the Peruvian socialist Left has not been able to carry out its revolutionary project of social transformation; and *Underdevelopment in Peru. A Profile of Peripheral Capitalism* (2023), a study of the structural and systematic nature of underdevelopment in Peru.

Acknowledgments

The author gratefully acknowledges the permission provided by the publishing house Taylor & Francis and the publisher Routledge UK to republish material drawn from several of the author's earlier publications to wit: Petras, J. and Veltmeyer, H. *Class Struggle in Latin America: Making History Today* (London: Routledge, 2018); Petras, J. and Veltmeyer, H. *Latin America in the Vortex of Social Change* (London: Routledge, 2019); and, in particular, Veltmeyer, H. "Populism, Extractivism, and the Social Transformation of Brazil," *Canadian Journal of Development Studies* (2023). This material, substantively rewritten and updated, was useful for the provision of background to the class struggles written about in this book and the pre-2019 context for these struggles.

In addition to acknowledging the permission granted by Routledge UK to republish relevant materials derived from the author's archival notes, the author acknowledges with appreciation the contributions of numerous collaborators in the context of an annual sojourn to different countries in South America and Mexico for field research conducted by the author from 2005 to 2018. These contributions took the form of extensive field notes based on data collected in the research field as well as conversations held with colleagues and collaborators. Among others, these include Raúl Delgado Wise, whose expertise regarding Marxist theory and its application to the political economy of Latin American development is reflected in several chapters. In addition, the author would like to acknowledge the contributions of several other collaborators including Igor Ampuero (re political developments in Bolivia) and Mario Hernandez as well as Norma Giarracca and Miguel Teubal regarding developments in Argentina and Brazil.

But the author would like to particularly acknowledge with deep appreciation and respect the invaluable contributions to the book made by his longstanding colleague, friend, and co-adventurer James Petras, who shared the author's annual sojourn to Latin America and many of the author's research visits to Latin America as well as numerous publications. For many years the two of us would plan and undertake together visits to different countries to collect data and documents on political developments and engage in extensive conversations with social movement leaders, politicians, and activists, as well as colleagues and collaborators.

Finally, the author acknowledges with appreciation the expertise of Mark Rushton in copyediting the manuscript.

Introduction

It is difficult to discern a definitive trend in the pendulum swings of Latin American politics on the stage of electoral politics. Or rather, we can observe a trend in both directions, a trend that began with a left-turn toward a progressive policy agenda in the early years of the new millennium – a decade-long "progressive cycle" of governments and policy regimes that are concerned with moving beyond capitalism in its current form (i.e., neoliberalism/extractivism), a process that played out in South America with a downturn in a primary commodities boom (high export prices for commodities based on natural resources) on capitalist markets. The end of this *progressive cycle* was signaled by the election of Mauricio Macri, a self-proclaimed libertarian free market capitalist and leader of the Republican Proposal (PRO) party since its founding in 2005, as president of Argentina. Macri represented the parliamentary forces of conservative opposition to policies advanced by left-wing progressive forces in the political arena of the class struggle.[1] He served as President from 2015 to 2018, having replaced the center-left regime that featured Cristina Kirschner, who in 2007 succeeded her husband Nestor Kirschner as President and served in this capacity until Macri assumed the presidency. With Macri the pendulum of electoral politics swung from a cycle of left leaning "progressive" policies to right-wing authoritarian populism. This occurred not

---

[1] The term "class," as understood and used in this book refers to the relationship of individuals to production (as opposed to income, occupation, or socioeconomic status). In capitalist systems there are two basic classes so defined: the capitalist class (owners of the means of social production) and the working class, defined by their lack of access to any means of production and who are thus compelled to exchange their labor power for a living wage. The class struggle in this context is based on the capital–labor relation, but most often and in this book, it refers to the social relations of production, exploitation, and political conflict. In the historical context of the capitalist development process the class struggle most often refers to the struggle of workers for higher wages and improved working conditions or (in the agricultural sector) the struggle for land or land reform. But the class struggle involves a very complex multifaceted dynamic, and as this book illustrates all too well, it takes different forms in diverse contexts. In this book, we explore three fronts of the class struggle, although the emphasis is placed on the political arena, which involves the contestation of power and conflicting ideas regarding social change, and the struggle of different class agencies and forces to implement the social and political projects of one class or the other.

only in Argentina, but also in Brazil and in Ecuador, where Rafael Correa, leader of the Citizen's Revolution movement, was succeeded by a series of neoliberal conservative regimes. In this conjuncture, the progressive cycle of Latin American politics sputtered to an end, although generally not as the result of another turn in the swollen tide of electoral politics but as the product of a coup undertaken against a democratically elected regime.

This was notably the case in Brazil with the ouster of Dilma Rousseff, Lula da Silva's successor; and in Bolivia, where Evo Morales, after having served 14 years as the country's president, was ousted by a coalition of right-wing parliamentary forces and the country's armed forces, which withdrew their support from the governing party the Movement Toward Socialism (MAS) after several weeks of political unrest. Morales was succeeded by archconservative, religious ideologue and opposition senator Jeanine Áñez, who played a key role in orchestrating the coup. She served as Bolivia's interim president after Morales was forced to flee the country amid postelection protests in 2019. But after just a few months in office, beset by the activism of the social movements that demanded the holding of new elections,[2] she was charged with the offenses of terrorism, sedition, and conspiracy, before being sentenced to 10 years in prison for orchestrating the coup and for dereliction of duty in making decisions contrary to the constitution. Despite the repression exercised by the government under Áñez's brief stint in the presidency and the devastating impacts of the COVID-19 pandemic, the social movements managed to mobilize effectively to force new elections in October 2020 (Farthing, 2023). Morales's party, The MAS, subsequently returned to power with the election of Luis Arce, Minister of the Economy and Public Finance from 2006 to 2017, and in 2019.

The years 2002–2012 saw a sharp turn away from the neoliberal model of free market capitalism that had served to shape macroeconomic policy for most Latin American governments in the 1990s in response to the Washington Consensus. These years in South America featured what has been described and is generally viewed as a "progressive cycle" of policies oriented toward a more inclusive form of postneoliberal development. The end of this "progressive cycle" and the subsequent emergence of several authoritarian neoliberal regimes were signaled by the election of Macri. But even with this political development – a short interregnum (2015–2019) of conservative governments and neoliberal policy regimes – there were signs of another left turn – a turn to the far left in the case of Chile with the election of Gabriel Boric, a former leader of the progressive student movement;

---

[2] By the mid-1990s, Bolivia's peasant and indigenous movements had forged MAS as a "political instrument" (rather than a political party), which they conceived of as their electoral arm (Farthing, 2023). After 2002, the MAS expanded into urban areas, propelling Morales into office. As documented by Farthing, the social movements went on to play a vital role in the MAS government, including the passage of one of the world's most radical constitutions in 2009. But during Morales's 14 years in office, these movements relinquished much of their mobilization capacity, as their leadership was incorporated into government positions and the MAS party.

Colombia, with the election of a former guerrilla army commander; and Peru with the election of Pedro Castillo, a throwback to the traditional pattern of politics in both Peru and Colombia that featured an endless succession of shifts from the right to the left and back. In the case of Peru, after serving as president for less than a year, Castillo was ousted by forces on the Far Right of the political class. On the political dynamics involved in Castillo's ouster see Chapter 5.

Interestingly, the move by Castillo in December 2022 to dissolve parliament to avoid his impeachment failed, resulting instead in his ouster, which was orchestrated by the conservative forces on the Right. This turn of events was repeated in Ecuador four months later by the neoliberal conservative President Guillermo Lasso, but this time successfully.

Even so, in the case of Ecuador the division in the ruling power bloc and a resurgence of a counter-hegemonic bloc of progressive forces, resulted in an apparent revival of Correism (with reference here to the progressive regime in Ecuador headed by Rafael Correa), manifest in the defeat of the candidates on the Right and the victory of those with close ties to Correa as well as a growing chorus of calls for right-wing President Lasso to step down. The eventual outcome of the correlation of class forces at the time of this writing (September 7, 2023) remained uncertain. But with Luisa González of Correa's Citizen Revolution Movement coming in first place with 33 percent of the vote in the first round of the Presidential elections, and thus advancing to the run-off on October 15, the odds are that the movement started by and associated with Correa will assume power once more.[3] Another related development in the same direction (another turn to the left and a decline in the forces of authoritarian neoliberalism) was a national referendum on banning oil exploitation in the Yasuní National Park – arguably the most biologically diverse spot on earth – that was called for by environmentalists and the indigenous communities. Approval of the referendum, held on the same day as the elections, undoubtedly was a major blow to President Lasso and a major boost to the progressive Left.

But this left turn (a "pink tide" of progressive regime change) – neither Peru nor Colombia having participated in the progressive cycle formed at the turn into the 21st century – also included the advent of Andrés Manuel López Obrador (a left populist popularly known as AMLO) as President of Mexico; the re-election in 2022 of Lula da Silva, who was restored to power at the head of a broad center-left coalition; and the electoral victory of progressive forces in regional elections in Ecuador. This second "pink tide" of regime change, which was kicked off in

---

[3]The October 15 vote called for by President Lasso to avoid his impeachment for corruption was not, as widely expected, won by the RC candidate, Luisa González. It was won by the National Democratic Alliance (AND) candidate Daniel Noboa, a conservative but inexperienced politician and an heir to a fortune built on the banana trade, who will serve as president until the end of Lasso's mandate in May 2025. Noboa was supported by conservative forces on the right. Noboa himself, although bizarrely proclaiming himself to be on the center-left, is clearly situated on the right wing of Ecuadorian politics.

2018 by Mexico, washed ashore in Bolivia in 2020, and in 2021 in Peru, Honduras, and Chile, and then Brazil and Colombia – Colombians having elected the first left-wing president in their history. We have here another turn to the left after several short-lived conservative authoritarian regimes from 2015 to 2019.

As for Mexico, after the state visit in February 2023 of Cuban President Miguel Díaz-Canel, Lopez Obrador took advantage of TA convergence of left-leaning regimes by proposing a summit of progressive governments in the region as a means of creating a common agenda of progressive policies. To date (early September 2023) the governments of Argentina and Brazil have agreed to participate in the summit, but it is expected that Cuba, Colombia, Chile, Honduras, and Venezuela, as well as Bolivia, would also join this gathering of progressive forces. Meanwhile, in a blow to President Biden's efforts to bring together governments across the region to concert action regarding the thousands of migrants seeking to enter the United States along the southern border, Lopez Obrador informed Biden that he planned to skip his Summit of the Americas. At issue here was the US government's refusal to invite Cuba and Venezuela.

But to add an element of ambiguity and confusion to these crosscutting trends and developments, in the midst of this second left turn that raised hopes on the political left of another progressive cycle, the Far Right appeared to be on the rise again with the emergence of both a traditional variety of right-wing politician and politicians in the populist-authoritarian mold of Jair Bolsonaro, who represented a new type of conservative politics – radical right authoritarian populism – versions of which also emerged and has spread across the world in recent years (Berberoglu, 2020).[4] And it would appear it is still trending in Latin America. This surge of authoritarian populism represented a backlash against both libertarian developmentalism and the new conservatism of the 1980s which at the time was disguised as neoliberal globalization (Haggard & Kaufman, 2021; Hunter & Power, 2019; Sanahuja & López Burian, 2021).

After the capture of the presidency by Bolsonaro, right-wing candidates and parties with an authoritarian bent have emerged in several countries, notably José Antonio Kast in Chile, Guido Manini Ríos and his party Cabildo Abierto (CA) in Uruguay – and, most recently, Javier Milei in Argentina, a populist in the mold of Bolsonaro. In El Salvador the pendulum of electoral politics brought

---

[4] Authoritarian populism – what Kestler (2022) describes as "radical right populism" (RRP) – is a subcategory of right-wing populism. As noted by Kestler, it is specified by Mudde (2007) through the ideological features of authoritarianism and populism as well as radicalism, defined by Mudde (2007, p. 25) as "opposition to some key features of liberal democracy," what some views as a benevolent more humane form of capitalism, ignoring the inner secret or scatalogical fact or truth of capitalism: that regardless of its specific form it is fundamentally based on exploitation and thus crisis-ridden. Initially, this categorization of populist antielite authoritarian was understood to apply mainly to European cases, but with the rise of such figures as Rodrigo Duterte in the Philippines, Donald Trump in the USA, Bolsonaro in Brazil, and now Milei in Argentina, RRP seems to have become a global phenomenon (Berberoglu, 2020; Zanotti & Roberts, 2021).

to power Nayib Bukele, a businessman and a very unconventional representative of the trend toward right-wing populist authoritarianism, who like Bolsonaro and Trump, has no use for the niceties and institutional trappings of liberal democratic politics, evidently prepared to bypass these institutions if need be in asserting his presidential power and taking direct actions against the ultra-violent criminal gangs that have plagued El Salvadorian and regional politics, even spilling into the United States. In March 2022, following a sudden spike in violence, he declared open war on these gangs. Bukele and his allies quickly established a state of exception, allowing law enforcement agencies and courts to bypass due process guarantees and other constitutional protections, taking the criminal gangs off the streets, suspending their constitutional rights. Since March almost 60,000 people have been arrested, some because of arbitrary detentions. In Peru, a similar proposal to suspend an institutional proceeding (in this case, an effort of Pedro Castillo, the recently elected leftist president, to dissolve the legislature to avoid his impeachment) failed because his opponents on the Far Right of a sharply divided and polarized legislative chamber greatly outnumbered his allies on the center-left and were in a position and able to take revenge for having lost the presidency by charging him with "rebellion" ("breaching the constitutional order") and deposing him.

As for the defeated but not necessarily down and out Bolsonaro,[5] who has been frequently referred to as a kind of "tropical Trump" and often mentioned in the same breath as Hungary's Victor Orban or Italy's Matteo Salvini (Weizenmann, 2019), he has returned from self-imposed exile to renew the class struggle. In Chile, first round winner of the 2021 presidential election (he ended up losing to the leftist candidate Gabriel Moric), José Antonio Kast, the far-right founder of the Republican Party, evidenced strong sympathies not just for the right-wing populist Jair Bolsonaro in Brazil but also for other right-wing extremists like the Spanish party Vox. Noting that Chile "might have a future after all" (anticipating his winning the elections), he vowed to join the class struggle with a right-wing populist agenda (Rama et al., 2021). His success in the first round of the 2021 presidential election was commented on enthusiastically by the Argentine populist outsider and recently elected Javier Milei, who declared himself a natural ally of Donald Trump and adopted the claim "Don't tread on me" known from the US's Tea Party movement (Figueiredo, 2021). Regardless of whether these politicians have managed to capture the reins of political power, right-wing populism evidently is an ascendent force in Latin American politics.

Other examples of an emergent right-wing populism, what some have labeled "radical right authoritarianism" (Kestler, 2022), is Uruguay's Guido Manini Ríos, who declared his intention of bringing about a "moral renewal" of his country,

---

[5]Upon his defeat Bolsonaro, who, like Trump refuses to countenance the idea that he lost the election (echoing Trump in his declaration that the elections to had been "rigged"), went into self-imposed exile in Miami but has since returned to Brazil to promote and plot to his return in command of the right-wing forces that brought him to power and renew the fight against Lula's centrist regime.

and the far-right libertarian Milei, who against all odds has captured the *Casa Rosada* (Pink House), the Argentine Republic's official workplace. Like other right-wing populists, both Manini Ríos and Milei, like Donald Trump, also oppose universalism and the politics of inclusion. These commonalities suggest that there exists a kind of populist contagion, leading some observers to conclude that the new right-wing populism in Latin America fits the category of neoliberal or radical right populist authoritarianism known from its appearance in Europe and North America (Berberoglu, 2020; Cannon & Rangel, 2020; Kestler, 2022; Luna & Rovira Kaltwasser, 2021; Zanotti & Roberts, 2021).

Setting the Agenda for the Latin American Class Struggle

In this book, we seek to gauge the prospects of the Latin American Left caught in the headwinds of right-wing authoritarian or neoliberal populism. The situation in which the political Left finds itself is not unique to Latin America. What some observers have termed "right-wing populism," or the politics of neoliberal globalization, has manifested itself all over the world. Berberoglu (2021), for example, edited a collection of 12 essays on the crisis of neoliberalism and the surge of postneoliberal right-wing authoritarianism all over the world, with case studies from Putin's Russia, China, and the United States as well as Latin America, Africa, and Asia.

David Collier, in 1979, had edited a collection of essays on what was then described as "bureaucratic authoritarianism" (O'Donnell et al., 1986), in Latin America and Southern Europe, with reference to the politics of the "new conservatism" that originated with the concern in some policy circles for the excessive power of unions and organized labor, and the emergence in Brazil and the southern cone of South America of military dictatorships oriented toward the National Security Doctrine fabricated by the US imperialist state (O'Donnell, 1979).

The neoconservative project is to halt or reverse the gains made by the working class in the United States and elsewhere (the United Kingdom and Europe, in particular) in increasing their share of national income, which, to the chagrin of conservatives and the capitalist class, reduced the pool of available capital for investment and threatened their capacity to accumulate capital.[6] The solution to this problem as proposed by the advocates of the new conservatism was to reduce the role or take the State out of the development process (its responsibility for economic and social development) and turn it over to the market – to release the "forces of economic freedom" from the regulatory constraints of the

---

[6]Capital, as understood and used in this book refers to productive resources such as money used to expand production or accumulate wealth. Capital comes in diverse forms – financial, natural, physical, and social – but most often is used in its financial form – money or other financial resources available for investment in the expansion of production or the generation of wealth. Although one form of capital might predominate in a particular context, in actuality – in the capitalist development process – the development of the forces of production – different forms of capital are usually combined in practice.

welfare-developmentalist state. To bring this about they turned to the ideas established by a group of scholars associated with the Pellerin Society in the 1930s who elaborated the doctrine of free market capitalism or neoliberalism.[7]

The ideas of this school, based on the ideology and economic doctrine of free market capitalism in the 1970s were converted by the "Chicago School" of neoliberal thought into policies and structural reforms – *globalization* (integration into the world market) the *privatization* of state enterprises, *deregulation* of markets, and the *liberalization* of both commerce and the flow of capital – into a doctrine and policies that were implemented in the first instance by Pinochet and his "Chicago Boys" in the wake of his takeover of the state apparatus in the context of a military coup launched against the democratically elected socialist regime of Salvador Allende. In the 1980s, the neoliberal "structural reforms" proposed by these Chicago Boys were imposed on the heavily indebted countries in Latin America – especially the big three – the MBA (Mexico, Argentina, Brazil) – whose industrial import-substitution policies had helped push these countries into a debt crisis. The outcome was the installation of a new world order based on neoliberal globalization, which effectively launched a new era in the history of capitalist development in the region.

The focus of this book is on the politics of this advanced phase of capitalist development, which has been characterized as "extractive capitalism," with reference here to the massive flows of investment capital mobilized under the rules of the new world order, that is, investments in the extraction of natural resources (minerals and metals, fossil fuels, and agri-food products) for the purpose of exporting them to capitalist markets in primary commodity form. For the development and resistance dynamics of extractive capitalism see Chapter 10.

The Class Struggle, Chapter by Chapter

The opening chapter provides a framework for understanding the dynamics of capitalist development and the forces of social change associated with the class struggle in Latin America, a struggle that is rooted in *the capital–labor relation*, a relation of *production, exploitation, and political conflict* that is reproduced *in the center–periphery relation of dependency between countries at the center of the world capitalist system and those on the periphery*. As we see it, this cente–periphery structure of international relations, and the associated conditions of economic exploitation and dependency, has given rise to forces of resistance that has taken the form

---

[7]The Mont Pelerin Society (MPS) is a neoliberal international organization composed of economists, philosophers, historians, intellectuals, and business leaders. Its founders included Frank Knight, Karl Popper, Ludwig von Mises, George Stigler, Milton Friedman and Friedrich Hayek who, in 1947, invited 39 scholars, mostly economists, to a meeting to discuss the fate of classical liberalism, his goal being an organization which would resist interventions and promote his conception of classical liberalism. Thus, the Mont Pelerin Society was born, although it was not until the 1980s that the neoliberal doctrine espoused by it would achieve hegemony regarding economic policy.

of a class struggle for land and labor – and equality. Each advance of capital(ism) in the development process, each phase in the development of the forces of production, it is argued, generates new forces of resistance that can be mobilized to either the left or the right, from above or from below. The chapter elaborates on this point with reference to recent political developments in Latin America.

Chapter 2 provides a framework for understanding the politics of capitalist development in the current context. This framework centers on what we describe as the geoeconomics and politics of capital, with reference to the relative advance of "extractive capital" (foreign investments in the large-scale acquisition of land – "landgrabbing," in the parlance of Critical Agrarian Studies) (Borras et al., 2012), and the extraction of raw materials and natural resources for export in primary commodity form. The geopolitics of capitalist development has to do with what in the Latin American context is understood as a "pink tide" of "progressive" regimes formed in the wake of a decline in the legitimacy of neoliberalism as an economic doctrine and policy framework (Barrett et al., 2008). It could be argued (see Petras & Veltmeyer, 2011) that the apparent demise of neoliberalism can be traced back to the political activism of the peasant movement and indigenous communities in the 1990s (in Bolivia, Brazil, Ecuador, Paraguay, and Mexico).

Chapter 3 turns to a second front of the class war focused on the politics of agrarian change. The class struggle throughout the 20th century took two fundamental forms – a struggle for higher wages and better working conditions waged by workers against the capitalist class; and a struggle for land and land reform protagonized by the peasantry of small-scale agricultural producers. The land struggle over the years took diverse forms, but in this chapter, the focus is on the activism of the peasant-based agrarian movements in the neoliberal era. It is argued that the activism of these movements generated conditions that led to a progressive cycle in Latin American politics – a left turn on the front of democratic electoral politics.

Chapter 4 explores the political dynamics of the so-called pink tide that took form as a "progressive cycle" – a succession of regimes concerned with moving beyond neoliberalism toward a more inclusive form of national development. This cycle of progressive regimes, which paralleled not coincidentally a primary commodities boom on capitalist markets, unfolded primarily in South America.

Chapters 4–8 explore the political dynamics associated with various left and right turns in the dynamics of electoral politics in recent years. At issue in these dynamics is the emergence of left-leaning postneoliberal regimes facilitated by the political activism of the peasantry, or what was left of it after several decades of capitalist development in the neoliberal era (a semiproletariat of rural landless workers – the "rural poor," in the development discourse of the World Bank). This left turn came to an end after a 10-year cycle of progressive policies oriented toward inclusive development, or "neodevelopmentalism" – a model promoted by economists in the structuralist tradition of the Economic Commission on Latin

America and the Caribbean (Bresser-Pereira, 2007).[8] At issue in these political developments is the emergence of a new type of conservatism and right-wing activism, neoliberal or populist authoritarianism – as well as a second left turn.

Chapter 5 analyzes the dynamics of class struggle in Peru, in the context of what has emerged as a second left turn in Latin American politics after a short interlude of conservative governments and neoliberal authoritarian regimes formed in the years 2015–2019. This second left turn in Latin American politics is associated with a cycle of presidential elections in Chile, Colombia, and Peru, where the electoral process brought forth the presidency of Pedro Castillo, Peru's first truly left-wing Peruvian president. The election, which took place in the context of a series of battles between forces on the Right and the Left, came as a surprise for society in general, and the author (Jan Lust) argues, for the political forces on the Right, notwithstanding its evident internal political crisis. The chapter provides a detailed look at the political dynamics of the class struggle in these years with particular reference to conditions that help explain the victory of the Left and the aftermath of the impeachment and imprisonment of President Castillo, which gave rise to massive protests against the government of the first female president in the history of Peru – Dina Boluarte. The chapter emphasizes the role of the regional grassroot organizations in mobilizing the forces of resistance and the protest movement, the electoral Left having manifestly demonstrated its inability to organize the masses and mobilize the resistance. Thus, Lust argues that "if the communities in the regions would not have started to protest, there would not have been any protest movement." On this point he quotes Béjar, the former Minister of International Relations in the Castillo government: "it is a popular, grassroots movement, much broader than the political left. It is also true," Béjar adds "that the majority of militants of the different leftists existing in Peru are fully committed to supporting this popular movement."[9]

Chapter 6 turns to developments in Mexico arising from and associated with the election of López Obrador in 2018, as the President of Mexico. Mexico did not participate in the progressive cycle: all the prior governments as of Carlos Salinas de Gortari (1988–1994) committed to the neoliberal ideology of free market capitalism. The election of López Obrador resurrected hopes of Latin America's political class on the Left for another progressive cycle. The chapter assesses the significance of the López Obrador regime with reference to the class struggle both in Mexico and Latin America.

Chapter 7 reconstructs the end of the progressive cycle in the context of a worldwide political turn toward the hard right in the form of authoritarian populism. This trend in the neoliberal era has taken diverse forms in different parts of the world. In Latin America, the political turn toward the hard right took place

---

[8]This model also provided a policy framework for the alternative model of agricultural developed elaborated by Via Campesina and the peasant movement writ large in the new millennium. On this, see in particular Vergara-Camus, & Kay (2017a).
[9]Source: Perú. Héctor Béjar: Perú vive momento constituyente de un nuevo sistema (*Resumen Latinoamericano*, January 18, 2023).

in the ebbing tide of a progressive cycle of left-leaning regimes espousing postneoliberal policies aimed at moving countries in the direction of inclusive and sustainable development. In this context, the chapter identifies and discusses the forces of change that have emerged on the political landscape over the past three decades of the neoliberal era. The chapter then turns to the political dynamics of several development-resistance cycles that have unfolded on the changing frontier of capitalist development in the region – what we describe as the new geoeconomics of capital, characterized by the advance of resource-seeking "extractive" capital, that is, foreign investments in the acquisition of land and the extraction of natural resources to the purpose of exporting them in primary commodity form to capitalist markets.

Chapter 8 elaborates on this phenomenon of right-wing populist authoritarianism in Brazil, highlighting the role of Jair Bolsonaro, an outsider vis-á-vis the political establishment of class politics whose role and impact on Latin American politics has been likened to the role played by Donald Trump in the United States. The chapter reflects on the significance of the Bolsonaro factor in the Latin American political process.

Chapters 5–8 provide case studies (Bolivia, Ecuador, Mexico, and Peru) of the left and right turns that have characterized Latin American politics and the class struggle in the late neoliberal era, an era, which it could be argued is fast coming to an end in a transition provoked by forces of transformative change. These forces have emerged on two fronts of the class struggle: electoral politics, the central focus of Chapters 5–8; and the extractive frontier in the countryside, the major concern and central focus of Chapters 9 and 10, and the epicenter of the resistance today. As for the short-lived swing to the Far Right that brought the progressive cycle to an end, it featured the emergence of Jain Bolsonaro and the politics of authoritarian populism, a new brand of conservatism that Bolsonaro brought from the shadows into the mainstream of South American politics. The emergence of Bolsonaro as a major political factor in this development (authoritarian populism) – akin to Trumpism in the United States – resonates with what has emerged as a global trend (Berberoglu, 2020).

The class struggle in Latin America as elsewhere within the capitalist world system is based on the capital–labor relation. The major front of this struggle has to do with various turns in the tide of regime change and the dynamics of democratic electoral politics regarding the capital–labor relation. However, the emergence of Bolsonaro as a political factor not only highlighted a swing to the right in the pendulum of Latin American politics but the emergence of another front in the class war on the frontier of extractive capital in the Amazon, the largest repository of biodiversity in the world, and a key factor in the global fight against carbon emissions and the global environmental crisis caused by carbon emissions. On this front, the class struggle no longer revolves around the question of land and labor, as was the case in the postwar period of developmentalism (the 50s–70s), and indeed throughout the 20th century. Nor is this struggle fundamentally concerned anymore with the neoliberal policy agenda, as it was in the 1990s. In the current phase of capitalist development (extractive capitalism in the neoliberal era), which can be dated from the turn into the new millennium in conditions of a surge in the global demand for natural resources on capitalist markets, the class struggle has taken a different form, primarily as a territorial struggle waged by indigenous and non-indigenous communities on the extractive frontier to regain their access to the global commons in a demand for respect of their territorial rights. It has been argued that the communities on the extractive frontier constitute a force for transformative change in the postcapitalist, post-development transition toward an alternative future in which people can live in conditions of social solidarity and harmony with, as opposed to dominion over, nature. Some analysts and theorists associate this development with what they view as Hugo Chávez would have it: the socialism of the 21st century. Others, including the authors, would highlight instead the importance of the social and popular rebellions – the territorial resistance movements from below – that have emerged on the extractive frontier in a struggle of communities for a recovery of their territorial rights.

Chapter 9 takes a closer look at the form taken by the class struggle on the extractive frontier. In the current conjuncture, the territories and communities on this frontier are the host to the largest outbreak of environmental conflicts in the world – conflicts that are intrinsically connected to the neoextractivist development model that has been embraced throughout the continent as of the early 2000s. The aggressive expansion of extractivist operations in recent years has generated a cycle of new political conflicts as Indigenous communities assert their claims to territory and resources. The class struggle in this context revolves around the resistance of local communities on the extractive frontier against the advance of extractive capitalism in the countryside, and the assault on rural livelihoods and the lives and health of people in the thousands of local communities across the world on the margins the world capitalist system – an assault that has taken the form of environmental destruction and contamination, the poisoning and pollution of the land and waterways, adding pressures on local communities to abandon their way of life and their communities.

The concluding chapter addresses the question of whether natural resource extraction, or extractivism, has a role to play in the postcapitalist transition – perhaps in neodevelopmentalist form as articulated by the pink tide governments (see Svampa, 2011) – and whether the forces of anticapitalist resistance and the class struggle on the extractive frontier help move us forward on a pathway toward a more inclusive and sustainable form of postcapitalist or socialist development – a pathway that prioritizes social and environmental justice, sovereignty, sustainable and inclusive development, democratic governance, and the well-being of both humans and non-humans. At issue here is the question as to whether resource extractivism is a blessing, as argued by the economists at the World Bank, or a curse, as argued by the advocates of living well (*buen vivir*); and the question of a coalescence of the forces of progressive change found on the arena of democratic electoral politics as well as the extractive frontier.

Chapter 1

Latin America in the Vortex of Social Change

This chapter provides a framework for the arguments advanced in the following chapters that might be used to explain the dynamics of recent political developments in the region. The argument is constructed as follows: First, we review the dynamics of the new geoeconomics of capital in Latin America and the corresponding politics.[1] We then elaborate on certain dynamics associated with the political economy of two types of capitalism, with reference here to the way in which two forms of capital are combined in the current context of capitalist development in the region. The third part of the chapter provides a brief review of the economic and political dynamics that led to the pink tide of regime change in South America. We then provide a brief review and analysis of the policy dynamics of the governments formed in the wake of this sea tide of regime change and the associated progressive cycle in Latin American politics (Bebbington, 2009; Burdick et al., 2009; Grugel & Riggirozzi, 2009; Levitsky & Roberts, 2011). The chapter then turns toward the recent pendulum swing of electoral politics toward the hard right of neoliberal policy reform, before turning to another front of the class struggle opened by the advance of extractive capitalism in the countryside. The chapter ends with a brief discussion of the forces of resistance mounted by the indigenous communities on the extractive frontier against the forces mobilized in the advance of resource-seeking "extractive" capital and various contradictions of capitalist development. It is argued that in the current context this resistance provides the best hope for transformative change.

The New Geoeconomics and Geopolitics of Capital[2]

By the "new geoeconomics of capital" (Shazad, 2022) reference is made to the confluence and interaction of two types of capital(ism), two modalities

---

[1]On this see Veltmeyer (2013).
[2]This section leans heavily on, and uses material referred to in, Novkovic and Veltmeyer (2018) and presented and discussed in detail in Petras and Veltmeyer (2019, pp. 40–46).

of accumulation: (i) industrial capital(ism) based on the exploitation of the "unlimited supply of surplus labor" generated by the capitalist development of agriculture – what we might regard as "normal capitalism" – and (ii) the advance of extractive capitalism based on the exploitation of both labor and nature (Giarracca & Teubal, 2014; Gudynas, 2011; Svampa & Antonelli, 2009; Svampa, 2015; Veltmeyer & Petras, 2014). These two modalities of accumulation – one based on the advance of industrial capital and the other of extractive capital – do not exist in isolation and in many conjunctures of the capitalist development process are combined in one way or the other. The point is that each form of capital, and both modalities of accumulation, generate distinct development and resistance dynamics that need to be differentiated and clearly distinguished for the sake of analysis and political action.

A second feature of the geoeconomics of capital in the current conjuncture has to do with a reconfiguration of global economic power over the past three decades, with reference here to the emergence of a new power bloc (the BRICS) and the advent of China's voracious appetite for natural resources and commodities, particularly industrial minerals and metals and fossil fuels (Bond & Garcia, 2015). This "development" implicates not just rapid economic growth and the Chinese demand for natural resources but also the "emerging markets" of the BRICS, which helped fuel the growth of a demand for these resources on capitalist markets and a primary commodities boom. This boom in the demand for natural resources, and an associated decade of rapid economic growth in Latin America,[3] fueled by record commodity prices spurred by Chinese demand and consumer demand in the BRICS, coincided in Latin America with a progressive cycle of governments formed in the so-called pink tide, governments with a policy regime oriented toward a postneoliberal model of inclusionary activism and neodevelopmentalism (Arbix & Martin, 2010; Bresser-Pereira, 2007, 2009; Friedman, 2018; Macdonald & Ruckert, 2009). As for the geopolitics of this development process, the chapter focuses on the cycle of postneoliberal policy regimes formed in this changing of the political tide. The policy regime of these "progressive" or left-leaning regimes has been described as neoextractivism, with reference to the use of the fiscal revenues derived by these governments from the exportation of raw materials and natural resources, both nonrenewable (oil and gas, industrial minerals and metals, etc.) to finance their poverty reduction programs (Burchardt & Dietz, 2014; Gudynas, 2010; Svampa, 2017; Veltmeyer & Petras, 2014). In short, the economic model used by them to make public policy

---

[3]From 2002 to 2012 Latin America experienced a decade of rapid economic growth at an annually averaged rate of at least five percent (Ocampo, 2007). Over this period – dubbed by some as the "decade of Latin America" – the region almost doubled its share of world economic output to eight percent (Rathbone, 2013). The IMF estimated that the windfall from the commodity boom was equivalent to an extra 15 percent of output a year. At the same time, the middle class grew by an estimated 50 million while inequality in the distribution of income (i.e., the rate of poverty) shrank from 40 to 50 percent (ECLAC, 2012).

in development has two pillars: neodevelopmentalism (i.e., the post-Washington Consensus on the need for a more inclusive form of development) and an extractivist strategy of capital accumulation.

The Political Economy of Extractive Capital(ISM)[4]

An extractivist strategy based on the export of natural resources in primary commodities form has long been the dominant approach of governments in the region toward national development, an approach that is reflected in the emergence of an international division of labor in which countries on the periphery of the world system serve as suppliers of raw materials and natural resources with little to no value-added processing or industrialization (Veltmeyer, 2012, 2013).[5]

As for the geoeconomics and geopolitics of capital in the current context of neoliberal globalization, it can be traced back to the 1980s, to conditions and forces generated by the establishment of what was at the time a "new world order" of free market capitalism. This world order entailed a series of policy guidelines or "structural reforms" in macroeconomic policy such as *privatization* of the means of production, *deregulation* of markets, and the *liberalization* of trade and capital flows. Implementation of these reforms resulted in the destruction of forces of production in both agriculture and industry that had been built up in previous decades under the aegis of the development state. It also unleashed a massive inflow of capital in the form of foreign direct investment (FDI), particularly resource-seeking extractive capital, which by the end of the 1990s dominated the flows of capital into the region (Veltmeyer, 2012).[6]

At the turn of the new millennium, the service sector still accounted for almost half of FDI inflows. However, the preeminence of extractive capital in FDI inflows either held steady or trended upward in the years 2002 to 2008 of the commodities boom (ECLAC, 2012). Despite the global financial and economic

---

[4]This section relies on material discussed in Petras and Veltmeyer (2019, pp. 46–51).
[5]A generation of structuralist and dependency theorists described this approach as the structural source of uneven capitalist development or the "development of underdevelopment" (Kay, 1989). The same economic structure was taken by Lenin as a defining feature of what he described as "imperialism," the highest stage of capitalism as he understood it at the time.
[6]The "real FDI boom in Latin America and the Caribbean," according to ECLAC (2012, p. 72), took place in the second half of the 1990s when many State-owned assets were privatized and many sectors, which until then had received little FDI, were opened and deregulated. It was during this period that transnational corporations began to expand their role in the region's economies. The 1990s saw a six-fold increase in the inflow of capital in the form of FDI in the first four years of the decade and then another sharp increase from 1996 to 2001, which in less than 10 years tripled the foreign capital accumulated in the region (ECLAC, 2012, p. 71). As a result of these trends from 2002, at the beginning of the commodities boom, to 2008, barely six years in, the share of natural resource extraction in total FDI inflows increased from 10 to 30 percent (Arellano, 2010).

crisis at the time, FDI flows toward Latin America and the Caribbean in 2008 reached a record high (US$128.3 billion), an extraordinary development considering that FDI flows worldwide at the time had shrunk by at least 15 percent. This countercyclical trend signaled the continuation of the primary commodities boom and the steady expansion of extractive capital in the region – until 2012, when the prices of many key commodities began to fall or collapse, heralding the beginning of the end of the boom (Harrup, 2019; Wheatley, 2014).

In 2009, barely a year into what morphed into a "global financial crisis," Latin America was the recipient of 26 percent of the capital invested globally in the extraction and exportation of industrial minerals and metals. And, according to the Metals Economics Group, a 2010 bonanza in world market prices led to another increase of 40 percent in investments related to mineral exploration, with governments in the region, both neoliberal and postneoliberal, competing fiercely for this capital. In 2011, on the eve (the year before) of an eventual collapse of the primary commodities boom, South America attracted 25 percent of global investments related to mining exploration, the production of fossil and biofuels, and agro-food extraction (Kotze, 2012).

Large-scale investments in the acquisition of land and the extraction of natural resources (in the form of metals/minerals, fossil fuels, and agro-food products) was a defining feature and a fundamental pillar of the model used by the progressive governments to make public policy in the arena of development (Gudynas, 2010). The other pillar was extractivism, or to be precise, neoextractivism, which led to a process of rapid economic growth, averaging 5–6 percent over the progressive cycle, which coincided almost precisely with the progressive policy cycle and a process of primarization (Cypher, 2010) – or, to be more precise, reprimarization, inasmuch as the exports of most of the countries in the region long involved the export of commodities in primary form. But this fundamental long-term structural trend (see Table 1.1), as well as the commodities boom-bust cycle, was accentuated in a new development-resistance cycle that emerged with the advance of extractive capital in the Latin American development process.

The policy dynamics of the "pink tide" and the associated cycle of development and dynamics – each cycle generating a corresponding development in the forces of resistance – has been analyzed at length over the past decade (Svampa, 2019).[7] In addition to the question as to the fundamental pattern and dynamics

---

[7]The concept "extractivism," as Gudynas (2018) among others understands the term, can be traced back as far as the 1970s as a means of describing developments in the mining and oil export sectors of the economy in the neoliberal era. Although Chiasson (2016), in a systematic review of the literature, notes that one of its very first appearances in academic and political discourse was in a chapter written by Bunker in 1984. In any case, Gudynas (2018) notes that the term *extractivism* was promoted by large transnational corporations in what we would today describe as the "extractive sector" of capitalist development (mining, fossil fuels) as well as by multilateral banks and governments. However, groups and organizations and civil society, as well as environmentalists and political activists opposed to extractivism or different "modes of extraction," for their negative social and environmental impacts, also use the

Table 1.1. The Structure of Latin American Exports, 1990–2011.

	2011	1990	2000	2004	2006	2008
Argentina	70.9	67.6	71.2	68.2	69.1	68.0
Bolivia	95.3	72.3	86.7	89.8	92.8	95.5
Brazil	48.1	42.0	47.0	49.5	55.4	66.2
Chile	89.1	84.0	86.8	89.0	88.0	89.2
Colombia	74.9	65.9	62.9	64.4	68.5	82.5
Ecuador	97.7	89.9	90.7	90.4	91.3	92.0
Mexico	56.7	16.5	20.2	24.3	27.1	29.3
Peru	81.6	83.1	83.1	88.0	86.6	89.3
Venezuela	89.1	90.9	86.9	89.6	92.3	95.5
Latin America	**66.9**	**40.9**	**46.2**	**51.3**	**56.7**	**60.9**

Sources: ECLAC (2004, 2012).

of capital inflows in the form of FDI, at issue in this analysis are problems to which we will make only brief reference, problems such as:

1. The policy outcomes of the economic development model used to formulate policy in the development arena – a combination of *neodevelopmentalism* (the quest for inclusive development – a strategy formulated in the Post-Washington Consensus formed in the 1990s) and *extractivism*. One of the main policy outcomes, which relates to both this consensus and a protracted war fought by the World Bank and the United Nations since at least the mid-1970s, is the dramatic reduction in the rate of poverty achieved by these governments over the course of the decade-long cycle of progressive policies – up to 40–50 percent in the case of a number of progressive regimes (see the discussion in Chapter 2).
2. When added to the fundamental contradiction of labor and capital and the secondary contradiction of center–periphery relations within the world capitalist system, the advent of extractive capitalism introduces an entirely new dynamic in the resistance to the advances of capital in the development process. This dynamic relates particularly to the contradiction between the strategy pursued by the progressive postneoliberal regimes in the region, which, in the case of Ecuador and Bolivia, implicates the eco-socialist idea of

---

term. This scenario became more complex as of the mid-2000s, particularly in South America where a series of left-leaning postneoliberal regimes formed in what has been described as a "progressive cycle" (or a "pink tide" of regime change) in Latin American politics – also opted for the extraction of minerals and metals, hydrocarbons (oil and gas), and agro-food products, and the export of these "natural resources" in primary commodity form (Gudynas, 2010; Svampa, 2019; Veltmeyer, 2012).

"living well" in social solidarity and harmony with nature (*Sumak Kawsay*, or *Vivir Bien*) in opposition to the destructive and negative impacts of extractive capital (Acosta, 2012).[8]

3. The forces of resistance and the class struggle formed in response to the advance of extractive capitalism: a struggle of indigenous and nonindigenous communities on the extractive frontier to reclaim their territorial rights to the commons (of land, water, resources for production, and subsistence), and in protesting the negative socioenvironmental impacts of extractive capital and its destructive operations (Svampa, 2015). On the complex and diverse social and political dynamics of this resistance see, inter alia, Barkin & Sánchez (2019); Bebbington and Bury (2013); Bollier (2014); Dangl (2007); and Petras and Veltmeyer (2005).

The Contradictions of Capitalism

Marx's theory regarding capitalism is that it is beset by contradictions that are reflected in a propensity toward crisis and class conflict (Marx, 1975 [1866]). The source of this conflict is an economic structure based on the capital–labor relation and the exploitation of workers (labor) by capitalists (capital). The capitalist class, it is argued, is driven by the need to accumulate – to profit from the labor power of workers. The developmental dynamics of this relation of capital to labor – the driving force of capitalist development – are both structural and strategic. The structural dynamics of the system are manifest in conditions that are, Marx argued, "independent of our will" and thus not of our own choosing and objective in their effects – an objectivity that accords with everyone's class position. The political dynamics of the capital–labor relation, the foundation of the social structure in capitalist societies, are reflected in class consciousness, a matter of workers becoming aware of their exploitation and acting on this awareness. In this context, each advance of capitalism in the development process generates forces of resistance and social change.

Marx's theory of capital, as well as most studies by Marxist scholars on the contradictions of capitalism, are predicated on the capital–labor relation and the capitalist development of agriculture – the dispossession and proletarianization of the direct producers, the peasantry of small-scale peasant farmers, and the exploitation of the "unlimited supply of surplus labor" generated by the capitalist development process (Araghi, 2010; Hall, 2013). As mentioned above, each advance of capital in the development process generates forces of resistance, social relations of conflict, and contradictory outcomes in which Capital appropriates the social product of cooperative labor. The result, at the level of the capital–labor relation, is a protracted class struggle over land and labor – a struggle that dominated the political landscape in the 20th century – and a propensity toward crisis.

---

[8]On *vivir bien/buen vivir* as eco-socialism in the context of Andean indigenous thought re: ethno-territorial rights, class, and resource governance, see Lalander and Lembke (2018).

At the level of international relations, this fundamental contradiction has manifested itself in the uneven development of the forces of global production and a relation of dependency between the center and the periphery of the world system – between the imperial state in its quest for hegemony over the system and the forces of anti-imperialist resistance (Borón, 2012).

The 1970s was a decade of structural and strategic responses to a systemic crisis, which put an end to what some historians have dubbed "the golden age of capitalism." One of these responses was the construction of a "new world order" based on the belief in the virtues of free market capitalism. The installation in the 1980s of this new world order by means of a program of "structural reforms" in macroeconomic policy (globalization, privatization, deregulation, and the liberalization of the flow of goods and capital) gave rise to a new development dynamic on the Latin American periphery of the system – the advance of extractive capital – and with it new forces of resistance that brought to the fore what we might conceive of as the "contradiction(s) of extractive capitalism."

The advance of extractive capital in the form of large-scale foreign investment in the acquisition of land, or landgrabbing, and the extraction of natural resources took form as a primary commodities boom from 2002 to 2012, and what Svampa describes as the "commodities consensus" and what others (e.g., Gudynas, 2010) understand and have described as "neoextractivism" (the combination of neodevelopmentalism and extractivism) – the export of natural resources in primary commodity form to capitalist markets and the use of the resource rents appropriated in the process to finance a program of inclusive development or poverty reduction.

The fundamental contradiction of extractive capitalism is manifest in a pronounced tendency for the accumulation process to exceed the ecological limits of sustainable development (O'Connor, 1998; Redclift, 1987). This contradiction takes several forms, including what some economists have described as a "resource curse" – that resource-rich economies tend to be poor and underdeveloped, while many resource-poor countries have managed to achieve high levels of economic and social development (Auti, 2001; Berry, 2010). Dimensions of this resource curse include what has been described as the "Dutch disease" (with reference to the negative effect of commodity exports on other export sectors) and what Latin American economists in the structuralist tradition have described as "dependency" – a reliance on the export of unprocessed raw materials and primary commodities in exchange for value-added processed and industrialized goods produced in the center of the system.

A fundamental dimension of the contradictory nature of extractive capitalism is an exaggerated form of the capital–labor relation of economic exploitation. Extractive capital typically employs relatively little labor – relative to capital and technology. As a result, while the share of labor in national income for a regime based on industrial capital might be as high as 40–60 percent, in a regime based on extractive capital (particularly in the mining sector) the share of labor typically oscillates around 10 percent. With the State appropriating from 20 to 25 percent of the surplus in the form of resource rents (royalties, export taxes), well over 60 percent of the value of the social product on capitalist markets is appropriated by capital (foreign investors, multinational corporations, and commodity traders),[9] while the brunt of the destructive and negative socioenvironmental impacts of the operations of extractive capital are borne by the indigenous and nonindigenous communities contiguous to the sites of extraction. Needless to add, this feature of extractive capitalism has generated powerful forces of resistance and relations of conflict between the companies and the communities, with the governments – even the most progressive ones such as Ecuador under Correa, and Bolivia under the presidency of Evo Morales – often taking the side of the companies against the communities in this conflict. This is a fundamental dimension of the contradictory nature of extractive capitalism, which, in the current context on the extractive frontier, is taking the form not of a class struggle but a territorial struggle, viz. the demand of communities to reclaim their fundamental human and territorial rights to the global commons as well as the rights of Nature (Acosta & Machado, 2012).

Another fundamental contradiction of extractive capitalism in the current context is manifest in the actual policies of economic development that some progressive governments have pursued in contradiction with the constitutionally defined aim of bringing about a social condition of *living well*.

Resource Nationalism, Left-wing Populism, and Poverty Reduction

The progressive governments that seized state power in the pink tide of regime change have been widely criticized for the failure to use the additional fiscal revenues derived from resource exports to bring about lasting structural change and sustainable development (Acosta & Machado, 2012). And these criticisms might be warranted, at least as regards the contradictions of an extractivist model of economic development. However, these criticisms should not lead to a failure to acknowledge the considerable progress made by these so-called "progressive" regimes in the direction of poverty reduction, the principal policy instrument of a neodevelopmentalism strategy oriented toward the goal of bringing about a more inclusive form of development based on a social redistribution of income, the hallmark of progressivism.

The evidence is clear enough. The progressive governments formed in the pink tide pursued a neoextractivist strategy of channeling additional fiscal revenues

---

[9]As for the financial returns to external entities and interests, foreign investors, etc., the *Financial Times* on April 18, 2013, published an article (Blas, 2013) that documented the fact that traders in commodities have accumulated large reserves of capital and huge fortunes in the context of the primary commodities boom and the financialization of capitalist development. As the author of the article observed: "The world's top commodities traders have pocketed nearly $250 billion over the last decade, making the individuals and families that control the largely privately owned sector big beneficiaries of the rise of China and other emerging countries" – and, we might add, beneficiaries of the turn towards extractivism and export primarization.

Table 1.2. Latin America: Poverty Rates, 2002–2021 (Percent).

	2002	2008	2010	2012	2014	2015	2021
Poverty	43.9	33.5	31.1	28.2	28.2	29.2	32.3
Extreme poverty	19.3	12.9	12.1	11.3	11.8	12.4	–

Sources: ECLAC (2015) and ECLAC (2023, Table 16.1).

derived from commodity exports into programs of poverty reduction (Gudynas, 2018). Table 1.2 provides a graphic representation of this strategy, which revolved around the policy of "conditional cash transfers" – transferring to poor households, on condition that children of the households would be sent to school and clinics to attend to their healthcare, sufficient income to automatically lift them out of a condition of extreme poverty as defined by the World Bank's measure of $1.25 a day ($37.50/month). Regarding this policy, see Valencia (2023). The table also suggests that the downward trend in the rate of poverty has stalled and to some extent has been reversed in the postboom/progressive cycle context.

Taking Bolivia as an exemplar of the policy subsequently pursued by up to 19 governments in the region, including Mexico, which (until the election of AMLO) had continued to pursue a neoliberal policy line, the percentage of people living in poverty fell or was reduced from 59.9 percent in 2006, when Morales came to power, to 34.6 percent in 2017 (Lalander & Lembke, 2018). Extreme poverty, in the same timeframe, according to official figures was reduced from 38.3 to 15.2 percent. The reduction in Bolivia's poverty rate and the associated drop in inequality in the distribution of national income tallied with a trend that held across all the regimes formed in the progressive cycle – the average reduction in the poverty rate somewhere between 40 and 50 percent. This trend was in stark contrast with the situation in countries like Mexico that continued to hoe the neoliberal policy line throughout this progressive cycle. In the case of Mexico, the poverty rate throughout a succession of neoliberal regimes oscillated from between 53 and 44 percent; but under López Obrador's more progressive policy regime it fell from 43.9 percent in 2020 to 36.3 percent just two years later, three years into López Obrador's progressive social liberal regime (BNN Bloomberg, August 23, 2023).[10]

One of the few governments to resist the restoration of conservatism or the rise of right-wing populism in the wake of the collapse of the commodities boom was Bolivia.[11] It was one of very few countries in which economic growth, driven

---

[10]Porter, Eduardo. (2023). AMLO's anti-poverty success in Mexico has a dark side. *Bloomberg*, August 23. Available at https://www.bloomberg.com/opinion/articles/2023-08-23/amlo-s-anti-poverty-success-in-mexico-has-a-dark-side.

[11]The economic model used by the pink wave governments to guide policy was constructed on the base of two pillars (neodevelopmentalism and neoextractivism), which exposed a dependence on continuing high prices for commodity exports and thus a fundamental vulnerability evident in the negative response to the collapse of the commodities boom by other progressive regimes. However, regarding this model Bolivia was no different than Argentina, Brazil, and other progressive governments. Thus, the

by the demand for resources on capitalist markets, continued well past the collapse of the commodities boom. Evo Morales' policy regime was the only one in the progressive cycle able to sustain a relatively high rate of economic growth (at an annually averaged rate of 4.9 percent) in the face of the collapse in the commodity boom, which perhaps explains in part the failure of the right-wing opposition to take power by means of democratic electoral politics. Export revenues grew sixfold during Evo's first term in office, from an average of $1.14 billion a year over the previous two decades to US$7 billion. Another partial explanation of Morales' continued popular support, despite several scandals and opposition from indigenous groups concerned about his government's extractivist strategy, was continued support from the social movements, the regime's social base (Dangl, 2007).

Toward the end of his tenure as president, there were coca-producing peasant farmers (*cocaleros*) both in support of the government and in opposition, but while President Morales was able to manage the fraught relationship between the government and the social movements, this was in sharp contrast to other progressive regimes such as Correa's "Citizens Revolution" in Ecuador where, once the regime was consolidated, the social movements that helped propel it to state power were subsequently pushed aside (Farthing, 2023).

However, the relationship between the Morales regime and the social movements was not all rosy. It required a process of strategic management and tactical manipulation. In its early years, some union members were appointed to various positions, including parliamentary and civil-service roles. The opposition was a neoliberal-right determined to block the functioning of Bolivia's Constituent Assembly. Until 2009, halfway through Evo Morales' mandate, MAS managed to maintain a popular unity not seen since the struggles against military dictatorships in the 1970s and 1980s. But this ended with the December 2009 referendum that approved Bolivia's new constitution. Although the political Right was crushingly defeated at the polls, the Left's internal divisions resurfaced. Even so, Morales managed to contain these opposition forces both within the neoliberal hard right and within his own social base. And this was no small part due to Evo Morales' ability to manage or manipulate the social forces in his social movement base, but it also reflected the government's ability to deliver on the promise of progressive development in the direction of socialism (or communalism, as Evo Morales defined it).

---

likely explanation of Bolivia's continued high growth is likely the government's "recipe for economic recovery": public investment in "productive community social economic development." It is telling that after a recession caused by the coronavirus crisis and a period of turbulence, Luis Arce, on regaining state power for the MAS, reverted to the "Productive Community Social Economic Model (MESCP)," which had made Morales' public investment policy regime "stand out" from other progressive regimes at the level of economic growth, low inflation, reduction of the fiscal deficit, as well as the reduction of poverty and unemployment, despite an adverse international context (https://lacrus.org/2021/04/15/bolivian-recipe-for-economic-recovery/).

Bolivia under Morales' two mandates, which spanned 14 years (2006–2019) demonstrated an exceptional capacity for sustaining a relatively high rate of economic growth, securing re-election, and neutralizing the opposition by combining a radical-left foreign policy with a moderate, mixed public–private export economy. In this regard, while the government continued to condemn US imperialism, the multinational corporations in the extractive sector (fossil fuels, metals and minerals, and lithium, as well as soy), together with the stock market's biggest "vulture funds,"[12] continued and continue to invest heavily in Bolivia. Notwithstanding Evo Morales' rhetoric regarding resource nationalism (the country's "wealth of natural resources belongs to the people"), toward the end of his tenure the actual extraction, or looting one could say, of the country's vast oil and gas reserves of hydrocarbons were under the control of 29 multinational companies. Given the government's continued dependence on these and other multinational companies in the extractive sector, Morales over time moderated his ideological posture from communal socialism to a local version of liberal democratic multiethnic and plurinational cultural politics.

Morales' embrace of a mixed economy neutralized any overt hostility from the United States and the new far-right neoliberal authoritarian regimes in the region formed when the progressive cycle came to an end. Thus, while remaining politically independent, Bolivia has integrated its exports with the far-right neoliberal regimes in the region. Morales's moderate economic policies, diversity of mineral exports, fiscal responsibility, incremental social reforms, and support from well-organized social movements has led to political stability and social continuity despite the volatility of commodity prices.

Even the professional groups and other segments of the country's middle class, clear beneficiaries of the policies pursued by the regime, have struggled to contest the proposition that life has gotten demonstrably better over the past decade. As reported by *The Guardian Weekly* (March 15, 2019), Morales' policies have not only resulted in greater social equality in the distribution of income, or at least reduced poverty as well as improvements in conditions of work and the minimum wage, but also in conditions of greater concern and interest to the country's growing middle class – a stable currency, subsidized petrol, asphalt highways, shopping centers, access to affordable housing and university education (Lewis et al., 2019).

---

[12]Blackrock and Vanguard, two of the world's largest US-based "vulture" investment funds, and US bank JPMorgan and Britain's HSBC, effectively are the main owners of the lithium extracted and exported from the 'lithium triangle' (Argentina, Bolivia, and Chile) that accounts for 75–80 percent of world reserves of lithium. The effective if not nominal "ownership" by these multinationals is reflected in the extremely low royalty payments made in the export of the mineral that average some 3–3.5 percent of its exported value – indeed, only 1–2 percent after deductions and bonuses are accounted for (*Resumen Latinoamericano*, September 9, 2023). This compares to the 30–35 percent withheld for payment by the companies to the government for the extraction of soybeans, the darling (*niña mimada*) of the Southern Cone's economy.

The End of the Progressive Cycle? Another Turn of the Tide

The origins of the progressive cycle in Latin American politics can be attributed to the political activism of the social movements in the 1990s directed against the neoliberal policies of the governments at the time. Whereas the social movements in the 1960s and 1970s were concerned with land and labor, the movements formed on the extractive frontier were fundamentally concerned to reclaim their territorial rights and access to the commons (Bollier, 2014; Bollier & Silke, 2012).

In recent years there have been diverse attempts at explaining the end of the progressive cycle. Theories have ranged from structural explanations (the contradictions of extractive capitalism and the consequent loss of an important segment of progressive forces), the collapse of the commodities boom and/or the fall in the international prices of oil, and the resulting loss of fiscal revenues to finance social and development programs), to widespread corruption as well as fundamental mistakes in designing and executing development policies (particularly in the case of Venezuela), as well as shifts in the correlation of class power at the level of electoral politics. But whatever the reason or the forces involved, there is no doubt that the pendulum of electoral politics has swung back toward the right – restoring to power politicians who are oriented toward what might well be described as "authoritarian neoliberalism." In this regard, recent political developments in Latin America reflect what appears to be a global trend (Berberoglu, 2020).

The beginnings of this trend – a change in the correlation of force in the class struggle at the level of electoral politics – can be traced back to the ascension of Macri to political power in the case of Argentina, and in Brazil the "soft coup" perpetrated against the PT regime of Dilma Rouseff),[13] and then the election of the far-right populist Bolsonaro in March 2019. In addition, up to 14 presidential contests were scheduled to take place in the years 2018–2019.

The exception to this pattern was the election in December 2018 of López Obrador in Mexico, which did not participate in the progressive cycle in Latin American politics but that continued to hoe the neoliberal macroeconomic policy line in alignment with the United States. As for the so-called "progressive" regimes, most of them, including Ecuador under the post-Correa regime established by Lenin Moreno, succumbed to the forces of electoral change. The one exception – apart from Venezuela, which is a special case of a progressive regime (in not having its origins in the activism of the social movements) – is Evo Morales, whose survival against the opposition forces ranged against it, can also be attributed to the social movements. In other cases, where the social movements were directed against the State (the government's neoliberal policies), but on the center-left's ascension to state power were to all intents and purposes sidelined or demobilized, the policies of the progressive regime lost its social base in the movement, thus rendering it vulnerable to forces of reaction. In the case of Bolivia, however, the movements

---

[13]The irony was that Temer, who, as Dilma Rouseff's second in command, took power as the result of machinations focused on removing her from office, and ensuring the imprisonment of Lula, was charged (April 2019) with high crimes and corruption.

were neither demobilized nor shunted aside. Rather, Evo continues to mobilize the movements in continuing support of his progressive policies.

Conclusion

Although the social programs of the postneoliberal compensatory states formed in the pink tide of regime change managed in several cases to significantly reduce the incidence of poverty, they did not anywhere lead to structural change. The resulting improvement in income redistribution did not fundamentally alter the class structure and the social inequalities associated with it. The poverty reduction and social development programs implanted by these "progressive" regimes merely compensated the least well-off strata with resource rents derived from the export of natural resources within the context of a short-lived commodity boom on capitalist markets. Even so, there were undeniably positive outcomes of the progressive cycle. On the one hand, there is much to admire in the progressive policies and accomplishments of these postneoliberal compensatory states. For example, in the case of Bolivia and Ecuador (see Table 1.2) the rate of poverty was reduced by as much as 40–50 percent, lifting millions out of poverty as well as incubating an incipient middle class.

Behind this accomplishment these progressive regimes or postneoliberal compensatory states – especially Venezuela, Bolivia, and Ecuador, countries that represented a more radical form of regime change oriented toward not inclusive development but socialism – were able to capture the profits and resource rents derived from the sale of commodities on capitalist markets, and by means of a New Social Policy designed for "inclusive development" (conditional cash transfer programs accompanied by state investments in healthcare and education), achieve significant social gains. But an assessment of these gains must be balanced against the limits of progressive change under regimes tied to extractive capital and rentier capitalism. For example, social compensation provided an internal momentum for economic expansion based on the expansion of the consumption capacity of the popular classes – what economists associate with the growth of a "middle class" – but the underlying structure of social inequality and power, as well as the associated rights and privileges, as already mentioned remained fundamentally unchanged.[14]

The improvements in income redistribution and the few benefits flowing to the bottom or poorest strata in the current context are a function of a model that allowed and have led to a disproportionate appropriation of the wealth generated by the model by foreign investors, obliging the indigenous and peasant farming

---

[14]Machado and Zibechi (2016), for example, point out that although progress in the Pink Wave was made in reducing poverty through the implementation of redistribution policies, the same did not happen in terms of inequality. They distinguish two types of inequality – structural and conjunctural – and argue that during the decade of progressive governments there were improvements in terms of the second type of inequality but that the indicators of structural inequality were not modified. See also Dávalos and Albuja (2014) regarding Correa's Ecuador.

communities that make up what the World Bank describes as the "rural poor" to bear the exceedingly high social and environmental costs of the extractive model. This is to say, the social gains of the progressive policies implemented by some governments in recent years are limited by the contradictions of extractive capitalism and global markets tied to rentier capitalism.

A conclusion drawn by several analysts is that the apparent end of the progressive cycle and a pendulum swing in the arena of electoral politics toward the neoliberal hard right can be explained in large part in terms of what some economists have described as a "resource curse" but that we, to the contrary, understand as an outcome of the contradictions of extractive capitalism. This is to say, the erosion in popular support suffered by left-leaning governments such as Argentina and Brazil that combined extractivism with neodevelopmentalism, and by Ecuador under the presidency of Rafael Correa committed to a more radical form of postneoliberalism, can be attributed to the pursuit and commitment of these governments to an extractivist development strategy – a strategy fraught with contradictions.

These "contradictions" include a dependence on large-scale foreign investments in the extraction and export of natural resource wealth. Conditions of this dependence – the "new dependency" according to some theorists (Borón, 2008; Martins, 2011; Sotelo, 2000, 2009) – implicate:

1. A reliance on these foreign investments and associated resource rents to finance the government's poverty reduction and development programs, subjecting the domestic economy to the boom-bust cycle of commodity exports on capitalist markets.
2. Consolidation of an export structure with a built-in tendency toward uneven development, with a resulting "underdevelopment" of the region's forces of production.[15]
3. Externalization of the benefits of economic growth, leading to a decapitalization of domestic production and the national development process, and a degradation in the conditions of social existence of communities on the extractive frontier, forced to bear all the negative socioenvironmental costs and destructive impacts of extractivism while being virtually totally excluded from its questionable economic benefits.

---

[15] López Segrera (2016), for example, analyzes the weaknesses that remain despite the progress made based with respect to the policies implemented by the post-neoliberal governments, with reference to the dependence of the region's economies on the price of raw materials and associated problems. In this regard he points out that in addition to the dependence generated by the economy being linked to the international prices of exported goods, many of these sectors depend on the importation of technologies and products from the central countries. At the same time, they have a social impact in terms of the devastation of some regional economies, the expulsion of populations, and the impact on the health of those exposed to the destructive and negative socioenvironmental impacts of extractive capital and its operations.

4. Dependence of the State on access to global capital, resulting, inter alia, in these states (including Bolivia and Ecuador, both classified as progressive) taking the side of capital in the struggle of local communities on the extractive frontier to resist the destructive forces of capitalist development; and, at the level of electoral politics.
5. The propensity of rentier regimes on both the Left and the Right toward endemic corruption, resulting in widespread deception and disillusionment among the electorate with politics as usual by the political class.

This disillusionment was undoubtedly a factor in the correlation of force in the class struggle and the restoration of the Right as a political force. But the evidence, which includes the ability of Evo Morales in the case of Bolivia to resist the rightward turn in the political fortunes of the political class suggest that the most recent change in the pendulum swing of electoral politics can be found in the contradictions of extractive capital as well as the inability of the center-left pink tide regimes to hold onto a social base for their progressive policies.

A dramatic case in point is Venezuela, where the urban and rural poor, the social base of the regime's progressive or socialist policies, continue to support the socialist regime despite the enormous pressures placed on it in the current economic and political crisis and by the heavy hand of US imperialism. Under Chávez and Maduro's radical populist policies and socialist regime not only were millions lifted out of poverty but over two million houses were built for the shantytown dwellers; and over two dozen universities and educational centers were built for the poor – all free of charge. Public hospitals and clinics were built in poor neighborhoods as well as public supermarkets that supplied low-cost food and other necessities which sustain living standards despite subsequent shortages. How did the regime manage to survive such pressures and these conditions when the other regimes formed in the recent progressive cycle succumbed to them, and the Chávez-Maduro regime was also a clear and obvious victim of at least one of what we have described as the contradictions of extractivist capitalism (dependence on the boom-bust cycle of commodity markets)? The answer is not unambiguously clear, but it might well include the fact that unlike the other pink wave governments, the Chávez-Maduro regime did not pursue a policy of class conciliation; and in regard to the urban and rural poor the regime went well beyond the new developmentalist model by including the poor themselves in decision-making in the form of cooperativism and community development, and popular militias and community councils, that mobilized and gave voice to the mass of the poor and facilitated their active participation as well as their representation. It turns out that the state-led project initiated by Chávez to bring about the "Socialism of the 21st Century" has effectively been transformed into a communitarian socialist project advanced by a broad popular Chavista movement. The capacity of this and other instances of an emerging popular movement in the region to resist the advance of capital in the development process, and to take over from the State the responsibility and project of constructing and alternative form of society, is one of several lessons that the Left can draw from an analysis of the vortex of social change in which the region is currently embroiled.

Chapter 2

The Politics of Neoliberal Authoritarianism

Today what we see all around us in Latin America is a political swing toward the hard right and the emergence of regimes brought to power in a wave of populist or authoritarian neoliberalism. Although it is tempting to see this as a worldwide phenomenon, it is also evident that the conditions of this authoritarian tide are different in different parts of the world. As for Latin America, the turn toward the hard right has taken place in the ebbing tide of a progressive cycle in Latin American politics which was brought about by the activism of antineoliberal peasant-based social movements in the 1990s. But in other parts of the world, the conditions that led to the (re)emergence of authoritarian or right-wing neoliberal regimes are undoubtedly different. In this book, we concern ourselves with the dynamics of right-wing neoliberal authoritarianism in Latin America, with reference to Argentina, which, together with Brazil under the presidency of Jair Bolsonaro, represent the most dramatic instances of this phenomenon. The argument advanced is that authoritarian neoliberalism in Latin America can best be understood in terms of the dynamics of US imperialism in supporting the advancing capitalism in the development process. We construct this argument as follows: First, we identify and review the forces of change that have emerged on the political landscape over the past three decades of the neoliberal era. We then discuss the dynamics of several development-resistance cycles that have unfolded on the changing frontier of capitalist development in the region – what we might describe as the new geoeconomics of capital, characterized by the advance of resource-seeking "extractive" capital. As we see it, the powerful forces of resistance mounted by the peasant movements in the 1990s, together with several epoch-defining changes in the configuration of global economic power, created the conditions of a progressive cycle in Latin American politics. We then provide a detailed analysis of the forces of change associated with the end of this progressive cycle and the return to state power of several right-wing regimes that reflected the reemergence of neoliberal authoritarianism. We end the chapter with some reflections on the likely outcome of this political development.

Latin American Politics in the Neoliberal Era:
The Changing Dynamics of Class Struggle, 29–51
Copyright © 2025 by Henry Veltmeyer
Published under exclusive licence by Emerald Publishing Limited
doi:10.1108/978-1-83797-841-020241003

Setting the Stage for a Progressive Cycle in Latin American Politics

Neoliberal authoritarianism is not new to Latin America.[1] In 1964, Brazil pioneered what turned out to be the first round of experimentation with what would materialize in the 1970s (with Pinochet in Chile and Videla in Argentina) and then more generally on a global scale in the 1980s as neoliberalism. In the Latin American context, neoliberalism invoked in Brazil and the Southern Cone the formation of military dictatorships that were described by political scientists in the democratic liberal tradition as "bureaucratic authoritarianism." These authoritarian regimes – or, not to put too fine a point on it, fascist military dictatorships – were formed with the aim and promise of halting and reversing the tide of revolutionary change associated with and epitomized by the Cuban Revolution. To prevent a similar development taking hold in Brazil, members of the armed forced led by Medici took power with the full backing and collaboration of the US imperial state, which, in the person of President Johnson, telephoned the military junta within four hours of their coup to congratulate them for having "restored democracy." The military coup overthrew the administration of President João Goulart – who had assumed the office of president upon the resignation of the democratically elected president Jânio Quadros – and ended when José Sarney took office on March 15, 1985, as President.

On September 11, 1973, a similar development unfolded in Chile with a military coup led by Augusto Pinochet, with the full support and active participation of the US State Department, perpetrated against a democratically elected socialist regime formed by Salvador Allende, with the promise to "teach the world a lesson in democracy." The lesson, by Pinochet's own account (see Veltmeyer in Leiva & Petras, 1994), rested on the institution of a neoliberal policy regime of structural reforms such as privatization and administrative decentralization. This policy regime was predicated on a belief in the virtues of free market capitalism. With the help of the "Chicago Boys," economists trained in the doctrine espoused by Milton Friedman at the University of Chicago, Pinochet set about to restructure the economy, putting its commanding heights at the disposal of both domestic and US multinational capital. By 1989, after 18 years of undisputed power when through a miscalculation of the political support of his policies and his regime, Pinochet lost control of the state apparatus. The economy and society had been totally restructured, including all the strategic heights of the economy which were privatized, except for copper, the export proceeds of which were directed by the dictatorship's constitution toward support of the armed forces.

With the region-wide implementation of the National Security Doctrine, a pillar of US imperialism at the time (the 1970s), in the form of a war waged against the forces of "subversion" (subversives, i.e., all opponents of government policy), the dynamics of class war, hardline conservative politics and neoliberal

---

[1]The following discussion of neoliberal authoritarianism relies substantively on material written by the author in a book on the class struggle in Latin America and published by Routledge (Petras & Veltmeyer, 2017).

economics, were extended from Brazil to Argentina, Bolivia, and Uruguay, creating in the Southern Cone a broad zone of authoritarian politics where a cluster of right-wing military dictatorships – and what both liberal and illiberal political scientists described as "bureaucratic authoritarian" regimes – held sway (Linz & Stepan, 1978; O'Donnell, 1973).

The irony is that the very factor that was meant to consolidate the advance of capital in the region – the displacement and its weakening of the state in terms of its policy-making and regulatory powers – resulted in a reawakening of the forces of anti-imperialist resistance which had been defeated by means of a two-pronged strategy of repression and rural development (Veltmeyer, 2005). This strategy had succeeded in both undermining the power of the labor unions and destroying the forces mobilized in the land struggle – a struggle for national liberation and revolutionary social change (Moyo & Yeros, 2005).

During the 1980s, the popular resistance rebounded in a concerted effort to reject the imposition of free market reforms, understood at the time as "IMF Reforms," and rally the forces of social mobilization led by the urban poor in defending poor neighborhoods against the forces of capitalist development. The agency of this resistance included the neighborhood associations of the urban poor, but also a myriad of nongovernmental organizations (NGOs) that occupied the space left by the retreating state. This emerging "civil society," misunderstood by a new generation of European and American social scientists as "new social movements" that eschewed class politics (on this see Veltmeyer, 1997), took aim not only against the IMF austerity measures but also the military dictatorships formed in the 1970s (1964 in the case of Brazil) in the Southern Cone countries (Chile and Uruguay in 1973, Argentina in 1976) in response to widespread social unrest. These military regimes continued to wield state power until the mid-1980s – except for General Augusto Pinochet, de facto dictator of Chile who finally surrendered to the growing demand in the region for the restoration of democracy in December 1989 as the result of a plebiscite.

A renewal of the class struggle in the 1990s took the form of resistance against the neoliberal "structural reform" policy agenda imposed on heavily indebted countries in the region (Mexico, Argentina, Brazil, Jamaica) by the IMF and the World Bank as a requirement and condition for renegotiating their debts (Leiva & Petras, 1994). This resistance was led by a series of newly formed sociopolitical movements with their social base in what remained of the peasantry after the onslaught of forces generated in the capitalist development process. The theory, advanced by both mainstream development economists and orthodox Marxists, was that capitalist development of the forces of production would result in the transformation of the peasantry into an industrial proletariat with its reserve armies of surplus labor. To some extent this did indeed occur. But the dominant pattern was the formation of a semiproletariat of dispossessed peasants or landless rural workers with one foot in the urban economy (in the informal sector, on the margins of the capitalist system) and the other in the rural communities.

As in the 1950s and 1960s, in an earlier development-resistance cycle, this semiproletariat – the "rural poor" in the World Bank's development discourse – essentially had two options: (1) to resist the forces of capitalist development, as many did with the formation of social movements directed against the neoliberal policy agenda (Petras & Veltmeyer, 2005, 2009) or (2) to adapt or adjust to these forces by abandoning agriculture and their rural communities, and taking the development pathway out of rural poverty, namely, migration and informal labor (World Bank, 2008). However, in the mid-1990s the "rural poor" had available to them a third option, which was to stay in their rural communities under conditions of a "new rurality" (Kay, 2008), this with reference to a subsistence strategy of the rural poor in the form of diversifying the sources of their household income – adding to agriculture and labor income, the proceeds of migrant remittances and micro development projects – and, in response to a policy initiative of Luís Inácio Lula da Silva, leader of the Workers' Party and President of Brazil at the time, direct cash transfers to the poor households (Valencia Lomeli, 2013). By the end of the decade the rural exodus, which had dramatically expanded in the neoliberal era, had begun to slow down. And the neoliberal policy agenda, pursued by most of the governments in the region was forcefully resisted by the peasant movements, was on the defensive, creating conditions for the emergence of a progressive cycle in Latin American politics based on a search for a postneoliberal alternative to development.

The Geoeconomics of Extractive Capital

The neoliberal policy agenda, based on the Washington Consensus, facilitated a massive flow of investment capital to the periphery of the world system in the search for natural resources needed for industrial development. Table 2.1 provides a glimpse into the dynamics of these capital flows, particularly as regards the expansion of capital in the form of foreign direct investment (FDI). The data points toward the reverse outward flow of capital associated with this inflow, which, according to Saxe-Fernandez and Nuñez (2001), worked somewhat like a siphon, resulting for the region in a net loss of capital over the course of the decade in the order of some US$100 billion. Petras describes this "development" as the "golden age of US imperialism" (i.e., "right-wing-imperial plunder").

Another feature of the capital flows stimulated by the neoliberal policy agenda is a preference for and a pronounced tendency toward resource-seeking "extractive" capital – capital invested in the large-scale acquisition of land and the extraction of natural resources such as minerals and metals, fossil fuels, and biofuels (Veltmeyer & Petras, 2014). As it turns out, FDI in the extraction of natural resources for the purpose of exporting them in primary commodity form would become a major feature and a fundamental pillar of the economic model used by the *progressive* regimes formed in the first decade of the new millennium. Over the course of the primary commodity boom (2002–2012) from 30 to 90 percent of regional exports took the form of primary commodities. But given the coincidence in the time frame of this progressive policy cycle and the primary commodities boom, which collapsed at almost the same time as the progressive cycle came to an end (2012–2015), the extractive model proved to be the Achilles heel of progressive (postneoliberal) politics. When the commodities boom collapsed (also in 2012) the capacity of the postneoliberal progressive regimes to finance their poverty reduction programs also evidently collapsed.

This purported pink tide of regime change was stimulated by two developments: (1) a reconfiguration of global economic power, leading to the rise of China

Table 2.1. Capital Inflows and (Net) Outflows, Latin America 1985–2002.

	1985–1990	1991–1992	1993	1994	1995	1996	1997	1998	1999	2000	2001	2002
Capital inflows	–	105	124	126	67	99	104	109	97	97	83	50
Foreign aid	38	10	5	6	6	6	–9	11	2	11	20	13
Private flows	95	118	120	61	93	112	98	95	85	63	37	–
FDI	43	29	17	29	32	44	66	73	88	76	69	42
Portfolio	–	45	74	63	5	12	13	–2	–4	02	1	–
Loans	642	127	28	24	38	33	27	11	10	–9	–6	–
Returns to capital	142	74	73	79	79	83	99	108	91	100	97	–
Profit	–	62	35	37	41	43	48	51	52	53	55	53
Interest	211	76	38	35	36	35	33	46	54	35	43	42
Royalty fees	5	2	1	2	2	1	2	2	2	2	2	2
Net resource transfer	–150	31	32	10	19	23	32	27	–3	–0	–5	–39
Accumulated capital stock												
Debt	420	480	520	564	619	641	667	748	764	741	728	725
FDI	–	–	168	186	226	321	375	397	191	207	216	270

Sources: ECLAC (1998), UNCTAD (2007), US Census Bureau (2002), and World Bank (1997, 2000, 2022).

and several "emerging markets" (the self-styled BRICS) for natural resources in primary commodity form and (2) widespread rejection of neoliberalism as an economic doctrine and a policy agenda, a "development" that can be attributed directly to the activism of the peasant social movements in the 1990s (Petras & Veltmeyer, 2011; Vergara-Camus, 2023).

Over the last 30 years, social movements for agrarian reform have struggled to keep up with the profound changes in the structures of land and agricultural production that swept across the continent (Brent, 2015). What was once a struggle for redistribution (land to the tiller, land and income redistribution, dignity, and social justice in the context of national liberation), Brent argues, in the neoliberal era shifted toward construction of a model of "market-led land reform" focused on increasing productivity, privatization, and opening land markets. Today, she adds, in *both* the global South and North on the periphery and the center of the world capitalist system, landgrabbing and the financialization of land and development have contributed to processes of capitalist development and territorial restructuring, which constitute broad threats to rural communities and livelihoods, indigenous peoples, and small-scale producers for local markets, and peasants. Consequently, the peasant sociopolitical movements and broad alliances that emerged in this context shifted their traditional concerns regarding a class struggle for land and land reform toward opposition to the neoliberal policy agenda and a territorial perspective on autonomous local development, access to the global commons, and respect for their territorial rights (Bretón et al., 2022).

The Development Dynamics of Extractivism

Over the past three decades of the neoliberal era, Latin America experienced a notable increase in the inflow and volume of direct foreign investments in the extraction of natural resources for the purpose of exporting them in primary commodity form. This expansion in the flow of "extractive capital" was largely the result of three interrelated factors: (i) lack of dynamism in the industrial sector; (ii) the buoyancy of commodity prices for regional raw materials and an associated increase in the demand for resource-based commodities; and (iii) the turn of many governments in the region toward both the neoliberal policy agenda and an extractivist development strategy in order to take advantage of the region's comparative advantage in its wealth of natural resources and the growing demand for these resources on capitalist markets. In this orientation toward extractivism, governments either welcomed or actively sought to attract foreign investments in a coincidence of economic interest (profits for the companies, resource rents, and additional fiscal revenues for the governments). This shared economic interest is a major factor in the possible explanation of the dramatic expansion and sectoral distribution of foreign investment inflows in the 1990s, and the pronounced tendency in the direction of resource-seeking "extractive" capital, a trend that can also be traced out indirectly in a growing trend toward (re)primarization of exports (see the discussion below).

As for the almost exponential increase and the sectoral distribution of FDI inflows to Latin America in the neoliberal era, the data are startling as well as revealing. Research conducted by Rivera-Batiz (2000) shows that six of the twelve countries receiving the highest FDI in the world in the 1990s and the new millennium came from Latin America, the destination point for more than 80 percent of this flow of capital – and half of these inflows were received by Brazil. In addition, while the share of the extractive industries in inward FDI stocks globally declined throughout the 1990s, Latin America actually experienced a sixfold increase in the inflows of capital in the form of FDI in the first four years of the decade; this was followed by another sharp increase from 1996 to 2001, which in less than 10 years tripled the volume of foreign capital accumulated in the region in the form of foreign-company subsidiaries (ECLAC, 2012, pp. 71–72).

Another major inflow occurred in the first decade of the new millennium, in conditions of a primary commodities boom (Ocampo, 2007). Toward the end of this boom, Latin America received 26 percent of the capital invested globally in mineral exploration and extraction. Most of these investments were directed toward four countries, with Brazil once again accounting for the lion's share.

These trends in the inflow of capital in the form of FDI in the 1990s were manifest in or paralleled by a pattern of export primarization, which represented an increase in the production for export of low value-added goods based on raw materials and natural resources and an increase in the ratio of primary products to total exports (as well as an increase in tax revenues derived from the primary commodity exports). The primarization of Latin American exports is deeply embedded in the center–periphery structure of international relations, which Lenin identified as a fundamental feature of what at the beginning of the 20th century he regarded as "imperialism, the most advanced stage of capitalism." However, the integration of Latin America into the new world order gave an additional impetus and a new twist to primarization.

Whereas exports of primary products as a percentage of total exports for Latin America declined from 1990 to 2010, it increased – from 48.1 to 66.2 percent in the case of Brazil. This trend, which was also manifest to a lesser extent in Colombia, Peru, and Venezuela, represents the impact of several structural factors discussed above. However, it also reflected a reorientation of Brazilian politics from developmentalism toward neoliberalism. Despite their modernization rhetoric, both the Brazilian Social Democracy Party (PSDB) and Worker's Party (PT) governments that preceded the Bolsonaro regime stimulated an accelerated process of reprimarization of the Brazilian export agenda. This undoubtedly represented a commitment to neoliberalism, but it was also in part a response to the limitations and instabilities of the global financial crises that increased in frequency and intensity in the 1990s, and that led President Lula, at the threshold of primary commodities boom on capitalist markets, to turn toward a progressive neoextractivist strategy as a source of additional fiscal revenues that could be used to finance a neodevelopmentalist program of poverty reduction.

Neodevelopmentalism or Neoextractivism?

The policies of the center-left governments formed in the progressive cycle were based on what the economists at ECLAC (the UN Economic Commission for Latin America) have conceptualized and described as "neo-developmentalism," a model constructed on the base of two pillars: (1) "inclusionary state activism" and (2) extractivism – the extraction of natural resources for the purpose of exporting them in primary commodity form (Bresser-Pereira, 2006, 2007, 2009). The policy aim with this model is to use the proceeds (extra or windfall fiscal revenues) of exporting these commodities (resource rents collected in the form of royalties and export taxes) to finance their programs of poverty reduction – the policy means of achieving or bringing about a more "inclusive" form of national development. And indeed, the policy has been widely lauded regarding these progressive regimes having in fact effectively reduced the rate of poverty in some cases by as much as 50 percent over the course of the "progressive cycle" (2003–2012). In Brazil, the national poverty rate fell by more than 25 percentage points from 1992 to 2013 – from 45 to 19 percent. This was in stark contrast to regimes such as Mexico that steadfastly held to the neoliberal policy agenda. In the case of Mexico, the rate of poverty went up – to 57 percent of the population, according to official figures released by the government. This compares with progressive postneoliberal regimes such as Bolivia and Brazil where the number of people living in poverty from 2002 to 2016 fell or was reduced by 15 percent in the former and 25 percent of the population in the latter.

The problem with this interpretation of the facts related to poverty is that it ignores the political pact formed by most of these regimes with the transnational companies in the extractive sector as well as business, agro-mineral, and banking elites (Petras, 2020, p. 11). The deal struck by these governments with the corporations in fact did not lead to the growth and sustainable development of new productive forces needed to sustain rising incomes for workers and farmers or to sustain the poverty reduction process. For example, according to a report commissioned by ECLAC, the rate of poverty and extreme poverty, in decline in almost all the governments over the course of the progressive cycle (2003–2012), began to rise in 2015 and has been on the increase since. Nor did the pact resolve major structural problems in the economy; indeed, it tended to exacerbate them under conditions in which up to 70–80 percent of the value of the exported commodities on the world market is appropriated by Capital (the transnational corporations, the commodity trading houses) while the local communities contiguous to the open pit mines and other sites of extraction have had to bear all of the socioenvironmental costs – and they are onerous and many (Acosta, 2012; Gudynas, 2010).

In addition, implementation of the extractive model led to a fundamental contradiction between this model and the commitment of the most progressive governments (Bolivia, Ecuador) to bring about an inclusive form of development based on a policy of poverty reduction (Dávalos & Albuja, 2014; Gudynas, 2014).[2]

---

[2]Based on the worldview or cosmovision of the Quechua peoples of the Andes, *sumak kawsay* – or *buen vivir*, to give it its Spanish phrasing – describes a way of doing things that is community-centric, ecologically balanced and culturally sensitive (Oviedo Freire, 2017). Other words that capture the concept of *buen vivir* (Ecuador) or *vivir bien* (Bolivia, which is a far cry from the market-is-king model of capitalism, include *Allin Kawsay/Suma Qamaña/Küme Mongen/Teko Kavin*. The concept of *buen*

Furthermore, the dependence of the model on FDI has generated new forms of "dependency," including the fact that because of their reliance on extractive capital for funding their social programs, the governments – even the more "progressive" ones like Ecuador – have tended to side with these companies in their conflicts with the local communities that are negatively impacted by the destructive operations of extractive capital.[3] For example, environmental activists in the struggle of these communities against the depredations of extractive capital are regularly branded by these governments as "environmental terrorists" who are willing to sacrifice the common good (development, the fight against poverty) in their personal interests.[4]

The Politics of Neodevelopmentalism

The turn into the new millennium witnessed the emergence of what is described in the periodical and academic literature as a pink tide of regime change. This pink tide, and the resulting progressive cycle, can be attributed to the activism of the peasant movements in the 1990s that led to widespread discontent and the rejection of neoliberalism as an economic doctrine in policy circles.

However, not everyone on the Left were, or are, either sanguine or enthusiastic about this progressive cycle. For one thing, while the Left in the academic world celebrated the "rising pink tide" the emerging leaders of the "progressive left" replaced the "old neoliberal Right" as the new partners of the business, agro-mineral, and banking elite in their positive response to the high and growing demand on capitalist markets for the natural resources needed for industrial development in the global North – resources that Latin America has in great abundance. It is estimated that Latin America, with seven percent of the world's population, has 42–45 percent of the world's reserves of fresh water, half of its biodiversity, and immeasurable reserves of oil, gas, and minerals. It also commands 80 percent of the world's known reserves of lithium, 93 percent of lithium reserves, 61 percent of fluorspar, 59 percent of silver, 56 percent of rhenium, 54 percent of tin, and 44 percent of platinum (Katz, 2023b). And the region is an important source of agri-food and agro-fuel products such as soybeans (see the discussion below of Latin America's soy complex).

---

vivir/vivir bien (to live well in solidarity and harmony with nature) inspired the new Bolivian constitution and the recently revised Ecuadorian constitution, which now reads: "We ... hereby decide to build a new form of public coexistence, in diversity and in harmony with nature, to achieve the good way of living" (Acosta, 2012).
[3] A report of the Observatory of Mining Conflicts in Latin America (OCMAL, 2017), which provided a snapshot of mining conflicts in 2017, shows that in 2017 there were 219 conflicts in the mining sector (229 projects involving 234 communities in 20 countries). Peru had the largest number of conflicts (39), followed by Mexico and Chile with 37 each, then Argentina with 27, Brazil with 20, and Colombia with 14. In these conflicts, the State sought to mediate between the companies and the communities, but ultimately sided with the companies.
[4] In the case of Bolivia, Alvaro García Linera, the former Vice-President, has characterized the activists in the struggle over the rights of nature and associated nongovernmental organizations as stooges of US imperialism, provocateurs or environmental terrorists (Rojas, 2015).

Given the coincidence of economic interest shared by the multinational companies and foreign investors (opportunities to accumulate capital and generate profits) and the progressive governments (additional fiscal resources to finance their development and social programs), the new political left turned their "inclusionary activism" toward extractivism as a strategy of national development, combining it with the search for a more inclusive form of postdevelopment found in what economists at ECLAC have termed "neodevelopmentalism" (adding to a neoliberal macroeconomic policy of private sector-led growth a new social policy of poverty reduction). On this neodevelopmentalist model – otherwise known as neoextractivism – see Bresser-Pereira, 2007, 2009; Svampa, 2017, as well as our discussion of neodevelopmentalism in Chapters 1 and 2.

This neodevelopmentalist model used by the progressive governments was in part based on an extractivist strategy of capitalist development, which in turn was predicated on an undeclared political pact between Capital (corporate transnational agribusinesses, the multinational companies in the extractive sector) and the political left. This pact was predicated on a coincidence of economic interest between the companies that were concerned to protect their investments and the policymakers who were reliant on the resource rents derived from commodity exports.

Notwithstanding the efforts of some progressive governments like Bolivia to demand that the multinational companies in the extractive sector invest in technology and the processing of the extracted source of minerals and metals, nowhere were there any new technological inputs in the economy over the course of the progressive cycle. Instead – to quote James Petras, in his trenchant critique of both the extractive capitalists and those on the political left prepared to strike an unsavory deal with these capitalists – these progressivists on the political Left "mounted flashy pharaonic prestige projects linked to corrupt contracts to crony capitalists who devoured the growing public revenues derived from the commodity boom" (Petras, 2020, p. 12). In fact, he observes, "the patronage machine had never functioned more smoothly."

Predictably, Petras adds, uncritical left academics celebrated these new "progressive" regimes while ignoring the corruption scandals. Even the Workers' Party in Brazil, which at its foundation had strong roots among the masses and the working class, and that had pioneered the inclusive development strategy and *Bolsa Família*, the new social policy of direct cash transfers to the poor, were disposed to form tactical alliances with the *Ruralistas*, a powerful congressional bloc that represented the interests and reactionary politics of the country's most powerful agribusiness elite.

The Tragedy of the Left: 2015–2018[5]

In Brazil and Argentina, the "democratic electoral" transition meant simply that the klepto-left – to employ a term used by Petras (2020, p. 13) – was replaced by a more "efficient" kleptocratic regime. Brazilian President Dilma Rousseff was

---

[5]The discussion in this section is based on material in the author's research archives, some of which was previously published in Petras and Veltmeyer (2017).

impeached by what Petras (2017) has described as "a congress of thieves" while her coalition partner Vice-President Michel Temer assumed power. Similarly, Argentine President Cristina Fernandez Kirchner was succeeded by Macri.

Throughout these changes, the banking, petroleum, construction, and meat-packing klepto-oligarchs continued to operate with the same mafia principles regardless of the tint of the presidency. Lucrative contracts, captured markets and record profits, allowed for the uninterrupted flow of payoffs to the right-wing presidents and their entourage of business cronies.

According to James Petras, a Marxist sociologist who has dedicated his entire academic career to a critical study of capitalism, imperialism, and the class struggle – predominantly in the Latin American context – leftist academics for the most part have ignored the workings of what Petras 2020) describes as the klepto-state and its pervasive networks of corruption. As Petras (2020, pp. 13–14) put it:

> many held their noses while diving right into the lie-factories in exchange for privileged access to the mass media (publicity, talk shows, intellectual and cultural "round tables," etc.), invitations to fancy gatherings at the presidential palace, speaking engagements abroad and an ever-expanding source of sideline income as professors, columnists, advisers, and publicists.

When the agro-mineral extractive model collapsed as it did in Brazil in 2012 and elsewhere a few years later, many of their voters abandoned the political Left and turned to street protests – and the politicians on the hard authoritarian right who promised to rein in the widespread corruption and "drain the swamp," to use former US President Donald Trump's language. The oligarchs and the right-wing parties knew the time was ripe for the people to dump the political class and those who had ridden the wave of regime change to power. In the judgment of Petras, the left seized the instruments of political power and the opportunities provided by corruption to further concentrate their own economic wealth, property, and social control over labor. This view by Petras (2014) regarding what he terms "kleptocracy" (viz. "the kleptocratic leanings of the political left"), and its susceptibility in regard to corruption that had captured state power in the wake of the pink tide might be somewhat purist and harsh, but then there is a plethora of evidence regarding the widespread and even rampant corruption associated not only with authoritarian right-wing regimes, as emphasized by the political Left, but, as argued by Petras, with some regimes formed in the progressive cycle. In any case, these progressive regimes did not substantially change the relationship between business, economics, and politics forged in earlier years and decades under diverse liberal, neoliberal, and conservative regimes.

The Return of Right-wing Neoliberal Authoritarianism

The collapse of the primary commodities boom precipitated another swing in the pendulum of Latin American politics – this time toward the Hard Right. The first sign of this development was the election of Macri, which many observers (see, e.g., Aznárez, 2016) saw as the beginning of the end of the progressive cycle. And indeed, it seems to be the case, with a similar political development in Brazil, Peru, Chile, Colombia, Paraguay, Guatemala, and Honduras, and even Ecuador with the ascension to the presidency of Lenín Moreno in 2017, which some observers have painted as a struggle for the soul of the country's (and Latin America's) Left.

Apart from Argentina, regimes that have moved decisively from the center-left to the center-right in recent years include Tabare Vazquez's "Broad Front" government in Uruguay and Ecuador with the election of Lenín Moreno to replace Rafael Correa's "Citizen's Revolution" and the PAIS Alliance. In both cases, the groundwork was established via accommodations with oligarchs of the traditional right parties. The centrist regimes of José Mujica and Rafael Correa had succeeded in pushing for public investments and social reforms (Avila Nieto, 2017). Capitalizing on the commodities boom on the world market and the high demand for agromineral exports to finance their reforms they combined their leftist rhetoric with progressive policies oriented toward an "inclusive" form of development based on poverty reduction. However, with the decline in world prices and the public exposure of corruption, the center-left parties of Mujica and Correa changed direction, nominating and electing center-right candidates who turned anticorruption campaigns into vehicles for embracing neoliberal economic policies. Once in power, the center-right presidents marginalized the leftist sectors of their parties and rejected economic nationalism, encouraging large-scale foreign investment, and implementing fiscal austerity programs that appealed to the upper-middle class and ruling class.

Interestingly, one of the few countries that appears to have escaped this restoration of conservatism – apart from Bolivia and Costa Rica – is Mexico, one of the few countries in the region that had continued to hoe the neoliberal policy line. What changed was the election of López Obrador, a populist center-left politician who led a progressive coalition to victory in the 2018 presidential elections. His mandate was limited to six years, which should have provided ample opportunities and time to implement a progressive agenda, which included an assurance that ensure that the "poor come first," increasing financial aid for students and the elderly, provide amnesty for some drug war criminals, universal access to public colleges, a referendum on energy reforms that would end Pemex's monopoly in the oil industry, and provide a stimulus to the country's agricultural sector, increase social spending and slash politicians' salaries and perks. As it turned out, by September 2023 – five years into his presidency, Lopez Obrador has indeed made considerable progress in implementing at least in part most of these reforms and progressive policies.

Perhaps not so progressive was his campaign promise and actions taken over the past five years to construct more oil refineries, a promise that reflects a rather incoherent energy "security" policy that relies on extracting already waning fossil fuel reserves and accepting natural gas imports from the United States. Another of López Obrador's policies that has raised questions on the Left has been to decentralize the executive cabinet by moving government departments and agencies from the capital to the states. This policy is seen by some as "progressive," but it smacks of a policy implemented by the Chilean dictator Augusto Pinochet in his overtly neoliberal proposal to decentralize the administration of government services to "bring the government closer to the people" and to "teach the world how to practice democracy."[6]

Another challenge to López Obrador's progressivist credentials was his controversial decision to pass a law that would authorize construction of the "Mayan Train," a project – estimated to cost from US$ 6 billion to US$ 8 billion – that has come under fire and has been fiercely protested by environmentalists and the indigenous communities on route who have pointed out the likely degradation of critical habitats of stunning biodiversity (Mexico is one of the 17 megadiverse countries, hosting the world's second largest number of ecosystems. But its forests and mangroves are disappearing at an alarming rate).

The project, which López Obrador intended to complete by the end of his six-year mandate in 2024 (the Campeche-Cancún section began operation on December 15, 2023), was evidently implemented without meaningful consultation with the indigenous communities impacted by it. The project, it turns out, has divided the population and many communities, some hopeful of the promised economic and development benefits it would bring (jobs, infrastructure, etc.), but others, especially environmentalists and the indigenous community leaders and other people living along its route, who are fearful of the environmental damage and eventual negative impacts, including deforestation and destruction of the second largest rainforest in the Americas after the Amazon.

Sara López González, a member of the Regional Indigenous and Popular Council, bemoans the way that the project has divided both the local and the wider community (Morris Xpujil, 2023). The project, she says, is supposed to bring development, but the opposite is the case. "It is," she says, "a megaproject of death. It is an ecocide." This view of the megaproject has been substantiated by the International Tribunal of the Right of Nature, which met in September 2023 to consider the case of the Mayan Train. The tribunal, as it turned out, "held the Mexican State responsible for ecocide and ethnocide for the violation of the fundamental rights of nature, the Mayan people, Mother Earth and the right to life and to exist" (López y Rivas, 2023). It also "condemned the Mexican authorities," [demanding] "the immediate suspension of the megaproject, as well as the demilitarization of indigenous territories and the suspension of the processes of dispossession of ejido land."

Notwithstanding such protests, López Obrador evidently has no intention of abandoning his pet megaproject. As for the more progressive policies and measures that his administration has touted over the years in the name of López Obrador's so-called "fourth transformation," they await a systematic review of how many and which have been implemented, and what changes have resulted from this turn to the Left in Mexico in a period that saw the rise of right-wing neoliberal authoritarian governments elsewhere in the region.

---

[6]This policy of administrative decentralization was reflected in one of the two neoliberal "structural" reforms ("the law of administrative decentralization") that was implemented by Gonzalo Sánchez de Lozada, the President of Bolivia (1993–1997), as part of a neoliberal model of governance under the aegis of the guardians of the new world order.

Several partial reviews of AMLO's policies and actions taken over the past five years of his *sexenio* (Tetreault et al., 2023; Toledo, 2023; Tornel, 2023a) have concluded that López Obrador's national development plan, elaborated as a means of advancing the "fourth transformation," is mistakenly regarded as "antineoliberal." As argued by Carlos Tornel, a PhD candidate in Human Geography at Durham University with research interests in energy transformations beyond capitalist modernity, it is entirely consistent with a modernist traditional conception of economic development (Tornel, 2023b). Like the development plans formulated by mainstream development economists to advance variations of a theory of modernization, it is predicated on the active participation of foreign investors and transnational corporations in the extraction of both renewable and nonrenewable resources for export to the market. And like these earlier modernist studies, López Obrador's national development plan does not include a clearly articulated environmental policy. This is perhaps understandable in the context of state-led development, but it is totally unacceptable, not to mention regressive, in terms of Lopez Obrador's progressive credentials, in the current context of a broad consensus in the literature on the need for inclusive and sustainable resource development.

As noted in a study by Montaño and Tornel (2022), a response to the climate crisis does not just imply acting to reduce drastic and accelerated global greenhouse gas emissions but transforming radically actually existing society. This means independence and energy security rather than progressively eliminating the addiction to economic growth, recognizing the geological-technical limits of hydrocarbon extraction and propose an equitable reduction and redistribution energy on a national scale. A real "fourth transformation" would have to start by asking for what, how, and for who is the energy produced by extracting the resource and polluting and damaging the environment is it produced?

Is Latin America Moving Toward Another Progressive Cycle?

The most recent cycle of electoral politics in Chile, Peru, and Colombia brought to the fore a new bloc of progressive forces. Regardless of whether these forces will win the popular vote in the next election they might well augur another turn in the tide of electoral politics, apart from Lopez Obrador, this progressive bloc includes Gustavo Petro of the progressive movement *Colombia Humana*, who captured over 25 percent of the vote for President in the July 2018 elections, coming a close second to Iván Duque, a conservative banker and lawyer who ran as the candidate of Uribe's right-wing Democratic Center Party. It also included Verónika Mendoza of New Peru (*Nuevo Perú*), and Gabriel Boric as well as Giorgio Jackson of the Broad Front (*Frente Amplio*) in Chile.

None of these personalities are new to politics. Each has their own peculiarities, reflecting the historical context of each country. Even so, they share certain traits, to wit:

1. The new progressive regimes emerged in countries that had neoliberal regimes for decades – countries found on the Pacific coast from Chile to Mexico. Until 2020 these countries – with the exception of Ecuador – constituted a

neoliberal axis dubbed the Pacific Alliance, in contrast to the progressive cycle that encompassed Brazil and the Andean countries. But it is precisely in what had been the neoliberal regimes of the Pacific Alliance (Chile, Colombia) where an alternative program of progressive policies was advanced in the context of what appears to be another left turn at the level of politics. After years of living with the normalization of poverty and poor living and working conditions for the working classes, the new political options have emerged in harmony with basic demands for the improvement of education, health, employment, wages, and opportunities for youth.

2. The "progressives" and "progressive regimes" that emerged in the latest turn in the political tide (from 2020 to 2023) for the most part is the product of democratic elections rather than social and political mobilization. These are not times of road blockades and mass marches – although Macri's far right neoliberal policies in 2018 mobilized hundreds of thousand workers to take to the street. But on the Pacific Rim the still-silent majority has not protested vehemently, yet their discontentment has grown in spades as evidenced by the acts of everyday resistance that surround working class neighborhoods. Notwithstanding the volatility of electoral politics, it is evident that the populace is distrustful of politics as usual.

Popular support for change – for abandoning neoliberalism – is not visceral; it is not accompanied with party loyalty. For now, it appears to be temporary, cyclical, everything hanging by a thread. But slowly, as progressivism retreats and neoliberal policies advance, and inequality and exclusion grow, the possibility to put an end to the old becomes tangible; and the vote for change in the electoral process might be expected to grow. In this context, the electoral path to social change – as opposed to the revolutionary road of social mobilization and political protest – might very well appeal to the working classes as a way of bringing about social change by stealth, channeling widespread discontent into a force for change without the need to hit the barracks or invade the plazas. What this might mean as regards social change is unclear.

3. The emerging progressive forces originate in the left-wing of the political class. All the current representatives of this emerging or new progressive Latin-American wave come from the same political locus, but each with its own nuances. For one thing, they have all served in the trenches of a subterranean class war, which, with the passage of time they abandoned; and they have all experimented with various left-wing proposals. For example, Gustavo Petro, recently elected President of Colombia, had years of experience with left M19, an urban guerrilla movement active in the late 1970s and 1980s as well as the left-wing political party Alternative Democratic Pole; in Mexico, López Obrador left the Party of the Democratic Revolution before forming a center-left coalition to contest the presidential elections; Veronika Mendoza, a Peruvian social democratic politician situated somewhere between the left and the center-left, left the *Frente Amplio*, a political coalition of parties, political organizations, social movements, and activist citizens whose objective is to unify and different sectors (progressive, socialist, and communist) of the Peruvian Left; and Gabriel Boric, the leftist President of Chile who left left-wing university politics behind to take the leap into national politics.

4. All the leading forces in an incipient revival of the political left had a starting point in left-wing politics, but over the years they transformed themselves according to their circumstances without abandoning what they were, but updating proposals and political projects that they are now defending. In other words, they moved toward a progressive political project that is still very much under construction. The outcome of this move will depend on the range of possibilities for opening political space and depends on what the people want. For one thing, they do not seek to make revolutions or political change from a preconceived agenda or crafted by any software. Not that everything is in flux. Everything is based on the maturation of objective conditions and emerging subjectivities. In this situation, the first task is to adjust to the people's current demands. Later, everything else will be taken care of, whether they will govern and under what conditions. There are multiple factors that will mark the life of each political project. But thus far they do coincide in the following: a demand for basic social rights, more inclusive policies, more equal opportunities, and food sovereignty.

5. The new progressives seek to maintain equidistance between the old right-wing disguised-as-new and the left-wing variety of politicians born and formed at the beginning of the turn into the 21st century. They are situated in the antipodes of a right-wing conservative offensive. However, they evidently are also trying to maintain a certain distance from the left-wing politics of the former progressives – Chávez, Maduro, Evo Morales, Correa, the Kirschners, and Lula and Rousseff. They do not want to inherit the assets and liabilities of other processes that are alien to them, even though they have had a certain impact on their thinking; at least a lesson: they need to take power to change things. The postmodern idea of bringing about change without taking power is seen as a utopian dream if not misguided politics. At the same time, it is like a shadow that haunts them because it is used by their opponents to stigmatize them as quickly as the New Left attacked the old way of doing politics. This is a dilemma that still needs to be resolved.

Even as some right-wing parties and politicians took power in the short four-year (2015–2019) interlude between two left turns in Latin American politics – and the ouster of Castillo in 2022, as well as the emergence on the political stage of the far-right self-proclaimed libertarian Javier Milei[7] – signals the likelihood of another rightward swing in the pendulum of electoral and extra-parliamentary politics – they fell victim to the very contradictions of the structural reforms and policies that they sought to impose. Their reliance on debt financing, accompanied by rising interest rates undermined any efforts to stimulate an industrial recovery. In addition, economic fundamentals were ignored, and their dependence on speculators attracted the wrong capital at excessive cost with virtually

---

[7]Milei won the primaries in the 2023 presidential election and was touted as the likely winner of the October 22 elections. The prospect of Milei, a right-wing populist in the mold of Bolsonaro and Donald Trump, winning what has been described as a potential catastrophe and the most transcendental elections in Argentina's history sent a shockwave throughout the country. This shockwave was followed by another, when Milei ended up winning the presidential election in November 2023.

no multiplier effects. In addition, the economies of Argentina and Brazil, the countries that headed the right turn or white tide in Latin American politics, are stagnating, and both countries are mired in deepening political and social conflicts and economic crises. However, it is Lula who, having defeated Bolsonaro in the voting booths, will have to deal with this crisis, which, in the case of Argentina, has proven to be endemic. In any case, Wall Street expectations of stable markets and large-scale investments by the regimes that vehemently pursued the neoliberal policy agenda in this conservative interlude did not materialize. Thus, the launching of a new cycle of neoliberal ascendancy was stillborn and was abruptly aborted. The neoliberal tide, predicated on a north-south convergence, failed to materialize.

This abrupt end to the anticipated neoliberal revival opened prospects for a new progressive cycle that will presumably reverse the regressive socioeconomic measures introduced in the short interlude of right-wing regimes. Indeed, as recent developments in Brazil, Chile, and Colombia attest, a second left turn seems to be well under way (see the discussion below). Although the Armed Forces across Latin America have exhibited no appetite for coups or to otherwise intervene in the political process, Petras (2020) opines that the ousting of the neoliberal regimes formed in the recent right-wing turn could yet cause the business elite and Washington once more to turn toward the military as their "last best hope." In turn, the survival or prospects of another progressive alliance survival would depend on its ability to recapture the State and change the direction of public policy to preserve and deepen consequential structural socioeconomic change.

A Right-wing Interlude or the Demise of Neoliberalism?

Business writers, neoliberal economists, and politicians in North America and the EU heralded Latin America's embrace of a "new wave of free markets and free elections" that swept across Latin America toward the end of both the primary commodity boom and the progressive cycle in the years 2012—2015. With reference to developments in Argentina (the election of Macri) and Brazil (the soft coup that removed Dilma Rousseff, Lula's successor as President, from power), they predicted a new era of growth, stability, and good government free of corruption and progressive policies and run by technocratic policymakers. However, by early 2018, barely two years into the hoped-for return to normalcy, the neoliberal edifice constructed by forces on the near- or far-right had crumbled, the promises and predictions of a neoliberal success story forgotten (Petras, 2020). With the election of the left-of center populist politician, Obrador Lopez, to a six-year term as President of Mexico in December 2018 it was the political Left, rather than the forces assembled on the neoliberal Right, that began to dream of taking over the reins of state power.

To conclude this analysis of the politics of capitalist development in Latin America in the latest development-resistance cycle, we need to critically re-evaluate the initial claims and the fragile foundations of a return to neoliberal orthodoxy. We do so below, before concluding with some reflections on the reasons why neoliberalism has always been a crisis-ridden project, a regime whose fundamentals are structurally unstable and based on capitalism's easy entry and fast departures. On this see Petras (2020).

From the onset of 2015 and extending into 2018 with the Brazilian general elections on October 7, several right-wing neoliberal regimes came to power in some of the most important countries of Latin America. This included Argentina, Brazil, Ecuador, and Colombia. With this political development (a sharp turn to the Right) these countries joined a cluster of existing "free market" regimes in Mexico, Peru, Honduras, and Paraguay. Wall Street, the financial press, and the White House hailed this development as a "right-wing wave," a return to "normalcy," and the rejection of (left) populism, corruption, and economic mismanagement. Leading investment houses looked forward to technocratic economists' intent on following the precepts of neoliberalism. Bankers and investors looked forward to long-term stability, dynamic growth, and lucrative opportunities.

The formulae applied by the neoliberal regimes at the time included deregulation of the economy, lowering tariffs, elimination of subsidies on energy, fuels and public utilities, the firing of thousands of public employees and the privatization of entire sectors of the mining, energy telecoms, and infrastructure sectors. Debt moratoriums were brought to end, and bankers were rewarded with lucrative billion-dollar payments for loans they had purchased, pennies on the dollar.

The neoliberal regimes promised that foreign investors would flock through the "open doors" with long-term large-scale investments. Lucrative capital gains, benefiting from tax exemptions, would encourage the return of overseas holdings of domestic speculators. These regimes claimed that privatized firms would end corruption and increase both employment and mass consumption. They argued that deficits and unemployment would decline and that the "neoliberal wave" would last a generation or more. However, within months of coming to power, most of these neoliberal regimes entered a period of instability and what might yet turn out to be a terminal crisis. First, most of these regimes did not come to power by the institutional means of democratic elections. For instance, in Brazil Michel Temer took over the presidency by means of a congressional "soft" coup based on President Dilma Rousseff's alleged administrative mismanagement. In Honduras a US-backed military coup ousted the progressive liberal government of President Jose Manuel Zelaya, as was the case in Paraguay with President Fernando Lugo. In Argentina, Macri had exploited the provincial patronage machine capitalized by a banker-media-agro-mineral alliance to take power based on a Mexican-style "electoral" process. In Ecuador newly elected President Lenín Moreno followed a "Trojan Horse" ploy – pretending to follow in the footsteps of national populist President Rafael Correa, but once elected embracing the Guayaquil oligarchs and the Wall Street bankers. As noted by Petras (2020), neoliberalism's democratic credentials are of dubious legitimacy.

As for the socioeconomic policies adopted by these regimes, they undermined their optimistic promises, and in each case led to what can be described as a socioeconomic disaster.[8] In Argentina, Marci's neoliberal regime led to a doubling

---

[8]The following analysis of the political dynamics associated with the turn to the neoliberal far right after a decade of center-left relatively "progressive" policies is based on information provided by Aznárez (2016), Hernandez (2018), and Petras (2017).

of the rate of unemployment and under-employment, while living standards declined precipitously. In addition, tens of thousands of public employees were fired. Interest rates rose to a high of 65 percent, effectively eliminating business loans and financing. Initially, many business enterprises were eager to back the neoliberal regime, but faced with devaluation, debt, and depression, investors fled to safer havens after pocketing windfall profits (Aznárez, 2016).

In Brazil, a truckers' strike paralyzed economic activity in the major cities and forced the Temer regime to retract its policy of letting petrol prices float upwards in response to market forces. In addition, widespread popular discontent and massive street demonstrations that mobilized hundreds of thousands of workers effectively blocked the regime's regressive privatization and pension programs. As a result of the forces mobilized by this popular resistance against his neoliberal policies, Temer's standing in the polls fell to single digits, lagging 30 percent below the level of popularity in the polls of Workers' Party leader Lula da Silva, who was still in jail, having been framed by the forces of right-wing opposition to his candidacy for the presidency. At the beginning of September, only weeks before another round of elections, the PT finally removed Lula as its Presidential candidate, having recognized and accepted the ability of the right-wing congressional opposition to prevent the release of Lula from jail. In this circumstance, with none of the established political parties able to garner sufficient electoral support to gain the presidency, Trump-like populist and proto-fascist candidate for President, Jair Bolsonaro, a federal deputy for three decades (but presenting himself as antisystem), and a former army captain and defender of the erstwhile military dictatorship who was advised by military personnel and economists funded from foreign sources, won the presidential elections and assumed the levers of state power – a stunning reversal of the progressive cycle.

Turning to Colombia, regime corruption led to a popular referendum that was opposed by the Far Right. The leaders of the social movements and a left-wing coalition that came a close second to then-candidate Duque in his successful bid for the presidency have charged the new neoliberal President and his predecessors with ignoring and indeed encouraging the assassination of over three hundred social activists over the past three years.

In Ecuador, Moreno's embrace of the business elite and IMF-style "adjustments" led to widespread disillusionment. As President Moreno laid the groundwork for privatizing the mines, telecoms, and the banks, his austerity measures reduced the GDP to barely one percent, resulted in a dismantling of the robust social programs that under President Correa had brought about a 50 percent reduction in the official poverty rate.

The only progressive regime formed in the wake of the commodities boom and widespread rejection of the neoliberal policy agenda that managed to resist a turn to the neoliberal authoritarian Right was Bolivia, and this most likely because Morales' MAS regime (el Movimiento al Socialismo) was the only one that had the backing of the social movements. In the case of Ecuador, the Citizens Revolution regime established by Rafael Correa never did manage to get the backing of the indigenous movements. Indeed, the government labeled indigenous resistance to large-scale mining and oil exploitation in the country as "terrorism and sabotage" (cited in Webber, 2010, p. 1). The government's support of the regulated operations of mining companies and the extraction industry over the protests of the indigenous nationalities and communities led the representative organization of these nationalities (CONAIE) to break with the government in open resistance against and opposition to its policies.

Conclusion

Several neoliberal regimes formed in the wake of the most recent progressive cycle in Latin American politics took power with Wall Street cheers and plaudits, but these cheers were notably dampened by evidence of failure and imminent crisis – and in the case of Argentina, according to *Financial Times* possible economic collapse. While financial journalists and private investment consultants express surprise and attribute the ensuing crises to regime "mistakes and mismanagement," obfuscating the real reasons for the predictable failure of neoliberal regimes because of forces released by fundamental contradictions and major policy flaws intrinsic to the neoliberal policy agenda (Aznárez, 2016).

For example, the policy of deregulation undermines local industries that cannot compete with Asian, US, and EU manufacturers. Increases in the costs of utilities bankrupt small and medium producers. Privatization deprives the state of revenues for public financing. Austerity programs reduced deficits but undermined domestic consumption and eliminated fiscal financing. The resulting capital flight and rising interest rates increased the cost of borrowing and devalued the currency. Devaluations and capital flight during the Macri regime deepened the recession and increase inflation. Finance ministers raided reserves to avoid a financial crash. And austerity, stagnation, unemployment, and social regression – all conditions and outcomes of neoliberal policies – provoked labor unrest and public-sector strikes. Consumer discontent and bankruptcies led to a deep decline in regime popularity and the election of Alberto Fernandéz, a member of the Justicialist Party but representing the center-left Patriotic Union coalition, also bringing back the center-left Justicialist Party's Cristina Fernandez de Kirschner, who had served with her husband and then by herself as president from 2003 to 2015, but this time as vice-president. The pendulum of electoral politics had swung back toward the left (the center-left, to be precise) after a short interlude of Macri's right-wing administration and neoliberal policies. But this time, according to *The Economist*, elevating to the Casa Rosada a "president without a plan" and a "weak administration," alluding to the Kirschners' 12-year administration from 2003 to 2015.

As the political crisis continued to unfold, the regime reshuffled ministers, increased repression and sought salvation with IMF financing. But financiers balked at sending good money after bad. Thus, Macri's neoliberal regime entered what threatened to be a terminal crisis (Hernandez, 2018).

While the neoliberal regimes formed in what turned out to be a four-year interlude appeared to be close to moribund, some of them they still retained state power, a modicum of elite influence, and a capacity to exploit internal divisions among their adversaries. Meanwhile, the antineoliberal opposition in many countries challenged the swing to the Right and a return to neoliberal orthodoxy at the level of macroeconomic policies but had trouble in formulating an alternative political economic strategy. In addition, the business and financial press expressed concern, particularly regarding Argentina, that despite the IMF's bailout to the tune of US$57 billion, pressure seemed to be building up for a social explosion – and a possible return to 2001 when the President was forced into exile.

The decisive electoral victory of far-right Brazilian presidential candidate Jair Bolsonaro was met with dismay and startled both politicians and analysts of the traditional parties on both the Left and the Right. It also raised several fundamental questions as to whether it represented a "model" or possible pathway for other countries in the region (what might be described as "right-wing populism," "neoliberal fascism," or "authoritarian neoliberalism"), or whether it was the result of the circumstances specific to Brazil and thus not necessarily the face of the near future.

In this regard, several considerations are in order. First, Bolsonaro's populist politics and neoliberal policy regime undoubtedly resonated with some politicians in Latin America, namely Javier Milei, the extreme far-right politician who shocked the political left in Argentina by winning the 2023 presidential election on November 19, 2023. But in Colombia, large-scale-militarization and deathsquads' collaboration in support of neoliberalism were in place for decades prior to Bolsonaro's rise to power. Moreover, Colombia's oligarchic and fascistic regime under the administration of Ivan Duque Márquez (2018–2022) did not have a mass base or the charismatic leadership of Brazil's Bolsonaro. As for Macri, the dependence of his regime on the IMF and its mandated austerity program precluded the formation of any "mass base" which could have been mobilized at the start of his neoliberal regime. In any case, strictly speaking he was not a right-wing populist in the Bolsonaro mold.

A second consideration relates to the possibility of Bolsonaro's return to power as he has threatened to do, and thus the prospect of Brazil in another swing to the right of the pendulum of electoral politics once again having to endure and fend off implementation of his authoritarian neoliberal policy agenda. First, Bolsonaro's embrace of radical attacks on wage earners, salaried employees, pensioners, debtors, small farmers, and businesspeople over the course of his four years in power eroded his mass appeal and charisma. The mass electoral fervor that catapulted Bolsonaro into the presidency did not withstand the deterioration of basic socioeconomic living standards. Second, Bolsonaro's lack of a congressional majority obligated him to form alliances with the same corrupt parties and politicians that he denounced, and the inevitable postelection political deal-making disillusioned many of his supporters, who are not likely to back another bid for the presidency.

Third, if Macri's free-market policies deepened social polarization and advanced the class struggle, the result – even under Fernandez's more pragmatic policy regime – was disillusionment, protest and general strikes, conditions that almost catapulted a radical right-wing libertarian populist into the presidency (Hernandez, 2018). As it turned out, the presidential election was ultimately won by the Sergio Masse of the ruling Union for the Homeland. In any case, the centrist Masse will have to contend with a rebellious working class. He is unlikely to deploy the state's repressive apparatus against the rebellious workers and the turbulent waters that await him. As for Brazil it lacks Argentine's working-class tradition of class struggle, so the capitalist class and Lula's right-wing parliamentary opponents are unlikely to engage the Workers' Party regime in a class struggle. In any case, with the solid backing of the working class and the unions Lula da Silva is likely to prevail in an open class war.

Fourth, the agro-mineral elite, the military and the bankers backed Bolsonaro's "war on crime" and even benefited from the war prosecuted by the Bolsonaro regime in the slums. In any case, despite a political and policy regime that was biased and open to private sector and foreign investments in the exploitation of the country's natural resource wealth, including the Amazon, while President Bolsonaro was unable to stimulate productive foreign investments on a large scale; with a policy regime that favored extractive rather than industrial capital and innovative technology, Brazil under Bolsonaro was well on the way to being reduced to becoming merely an agro-mineral economy run by oligarchs and warmed-over corrupt politicians. Fifth, Bolsonaro's hostility to blacks, women, gays, trade unions, and urban and rural social movements may have helped him win votes, but it did not lead to an improvement in economic conditions. Furthermore, this hostility generated outbursts of political and personal violence that turned many working-class and middle-class voters away from neoliberal or authoritarian populism, causing Bolsonaro to lose his bid for a second term. In many countries across the region, neither the Left nor the Right has a solid electoral majority, and very often the election could go either way and is won by just a few percentage points. For example, despite Bolsonaros' defeat by the leader of the centrist Workers' Party he still commands the support of perhaps forty percent of the potential electorate.

A conclusion that can be drawn from the conservative regimes formed by Macri and Bolsonaro is that a program of reactionary policies may attract amorphous working class and middle-class voters, but it is not a governing strategy, nor does it serve as a coherent economic strategy. One possible outlier to this conclusion is the election in February 2019 of Nayib Bukele, a conservative businessman and politician, as El Salvador's youngest ever President of El Salvador. On assuming office in June of that year he proceeded to implement a thoroughly right-wing policy agenda that has evidently garnered the support of most of the population. A recent poll conducted in 2024 shows that his policies, which include a frontal assault on the political gains made by the feminist movement,[9] have the support of an incredible 85 percent of the population (Freeman & Perelló, 2024).

---

[9] A major target of the right-wing populists (Milei, Kast, Bukele) who gained state power in the brief interlude in progressive policies that Petras describes as the tragedy of the Left' (2015–2019) are the gains made by the feminist movement over the past decade. Milei led this assault, but Bukele and Kast joined him in this "cultural war" against what Bukele described as "the feminist ideology" (El Pais, 2024). After denying the existence of the wage gap between men and women, which official statistics put at 25 percent, and having demoted the Ministry of Women, Gender, and Diversity to an undersecretary, Milei for his part announced that the government would ban the language of social inclusion and "everything related to the gender perspective" in the national administration.

On the other hand, it is evident that this support is based not on his economic policies but on a radical anticrime program, a "war on gangs" launched in March 2023 that dismantled the infamous street gangs that terrorized the population for decades and that has led to the incarceration of up to 58,000 people rounded up by the police and the armed forces, a resoundingly popular policy measure that has led to serious concerns by human rights activists regarding the state of exception (AP News, November 24, 2024).

Another conclusion that we might draw from the swings to the right and the left of the pendulum of electoral politics is that the defeat of right-wing neoliberal authoritarianism depends on the scope and depth of organized resistance. For example, Bolsonaro's ability to implement his assault on the living standards of the popular classes was limited by the scope and intensity of the class struggle as well as electoral politics. Bolsonaro and Bukele, as well as Milei, another libertarian populist, successfully navigated the morass of democratic electoral politics to gain the presidency, obviating the need for right-wing politicians to resort to a coup or the support of the armed forces, but even so it has yet to be determined whether neoliberal authoritarianism is a viable alternative to neodevelopmentalism or populist nationalism and social democracy. Also, it is not evident whether the Left, fragmented and discredited in certain circles or elements of the electorate, can regroup and offer an alternative policy agenda. What this means is that the outcome of current developments in Argentina and elsewhere where the Right has returned to power with the intention of consolidating power and their neoliberal policy agenda, depends on the correlation of forces in the class struggle. On this see Katz (2012), who has argued that the main threat confronting the conservative restoration is the wave of popular movements that have hit the region in recent years. In any case, the dynamics of this correlation cannot be predicted in advance of the forces of resistance formed in response to the advance of capital in the development process.

Chapter 3

Agrarian Movements and the Land Struggle

Throughout the 20th century, there were two main fronts in the class struggle. One involved the struggle of organized labor for higher wages and improved working conditions, a struggle that pitted Capital against Labor. The other was a predominantly rural struggle for land, a movement based on the concerns of the small- or medium-scale agricultural producers and the peasants whose productive activity was oriented toward local markets. In the first three decades of the postwar era of the development state and developmentalism the agrarian movement and associated class struggle was predominantly concerned with land reform, reclaiming the land and access to means of agricultural production, and the movement on the Latin American periphery of the world capitalist system took the form of a movement for revolutionary change and "armies of national liberation" from the power of corporate capital. By the end of the 1970s, this struggle and these movements were decapitated and defeated, their forces of resistance against the advance of capitalism in the agricultural sector weakened to the point of defeat. In the 1990s, the land struggle was renewed in the context of a new world order based on free-market capitalism. In this context, the struggle of the peasantry, or what was left of it after decade of capitalist development, the dispossessed rural landless workers, shifted from a demand for land and reform to opposition to the neoliberal policy agenda of many governments in the region.

With a weakened and defeated working class, which had lost its capacity to mobilize the forces of resistance, leadership of the popular movement against the advance of capitalism in the development process shifted to the peasant social movements. The activism of these movements in the 1990s not only brought down several governments but it also created conditions – widespread discontent and the rejection of neoliberalism – that allowed the political Left to capture the state, initiating what was widely viewed and we have studied in this book as a "progressive cycle" of macroeconomic and social policies.

In this context, the class struggle has three major fronts. One involves the dynamics of electoral politics and contestation of the policy-making power vested in the state. The second relates to a protracted land struggle in the countryside and the social movements mounted by the rural landless workers in a struggle to bring about transformative social change. The third front in the class struggle has been formed by the resistance of the communities located on the extractive frontier in the rural areas. This chapter reconstructs the dynamics of the class struggle on these three fronts.

The Classes of Labor in Rural Society

Over the years, after more than a century of capitalist development of agriculture and industry, the economy and the population have been increasingly urbanized. By the turn of the new millennium in Latin America, most of the population was in a small number of cities and a larger number of urban centers. At the time of the World Bank's seminal reports on the state of development (World Bank, 2007) many societies in the region had been urbanized; and only two countries at the time, Paraguay and Guyana, could be classified as rural. By 2021, up to 81 percent of the total population in Latin America and the Caribbean lived and worked in the urban areas and cities. As for the primary sector (including here agriculture, forestry, and the fisheries) it continued to be a critically important factor in total production, although in all but two countries in the region agriculture contributed less than 10 percent of value added to total production, a far cry from the 20 percent criterion used by the World Bank to define an "agriculture-based society." Although critically important, primary agriculture (including the forestry and the fisheries) accounts for only around eight percent of the GDP in Latin America and the Caribbean, but the regional average masks considerable differences across countries (in Bolivia and Guyana, for example, agriculture accounts for 12.9 and 11.3 percent of the GDP).

Another fundamental feature was the growing complexity of the social structure of rural society in the agricultural sector (Bernstein, 2010). Although much of the rural population still self-identified as "peasants" this designation was more of a political than an economic category. Whereas agrarian society at the turn into the 20th century could be and was described as the peasantry, which was differentiated into three categories (poor, medium, and rich), by two decades into the neoliberal era, the "peasantry" was a much more diverse and complicated analytical category that included low-income and poor small- and medium-scale farmers who produced for the local market, and a small number of higher income earning (even relatively "rich") famers, but the social structure of rural society was predominantly composed of a semiproletariat of landless or near-landless rural workers, who for their reproduction and livelihoods depended on a combination of four sources of income: the sale of their agricultural products on local markets, wage labor (over 50 percent of peasant households depended on wage labor – the sale of their labor power), small income-generating development projects and migrant emittances, and conditional cash transfers by the government (Valencia Lomeli, 2013).

The most numerous "class of labor" in Latin America's rural society, to use a term contributed by Bernstein, constitutes a semiproletariat in that members of this class are dependent on combining direct agricultural production with wage labor. Bernstein's concept of "classes of labor" refers to the growing proportion of the population that is compelled to reproduce itself through various forms of petty production and wage-labor that is increasingly scarce, informal, and precarious. In addition to this social structure, large numbers of the displaced and dispossessed rural population – categorized as "the rural poor" by the World Bank – have exited or taken the road out of rural poverty offered by the agencies of international cooperation, namely, labor and migration (World Bank, 2007). As a result, although rural poverty accounts for most of the poor in Central America, poverty in the aggregate today is principally urban. Eighty-one percent of the population in Latin America today lives in urban areas (O'Neill, 2024).

The Politics of Agrarian Change

The agrarian movements have always been fundamentally concerned about land and land reform, with an overall focus on peasant concerns: access to land and land control (recognition of existing land rights, redistribution of large landholdings, private or public, or restitution of previously lost lands), as well as demands for lower prices for farm inputs, lower costs of social reproductive needs (food, clothing, and shelter), and fairer prices for farm produce (Vergara-Camus & Kay, 2017b). But because of the advance of capital in the development process and crosscutting interests, etc. the struggle today is much broader than regaining access to the land.

Apart from the issue of land tenure, that is, reclaiming access to the land as a means of production, a major dimension of the class struggle over land today is the demand of peasants and rural workers for a larger and fair share in access to productive resources and the distribution of national income. The lion's share of the vast wealth that rural zones produced and continue to produce has accrued to shareholders in corporations and financial institutions headquartered in a handful of distant, economically dynamic urban centers (Edelman, 2021, pp. 512–513). Here, the land struggle pits the agrarian producers, the productive classes in the agrarian sector, against the hegemony of international finance capital.

Another dimension of the agrarian class struggle is the question of property rights and what Borras has described as "land sovereignty" – "the right of working peoples to have effective access to, use of, and control over land and the benefits of its use and occupation, where land is understood as resource, territory, and landscape" (Borras, 2023).

A third dimension of the agrarian class struggle relates to the importance of movements of the working class that straddle the rural–urban corridor (Borras, 2023). The key challenge here, Borras argues, in analyzing the intra-agrarian class dynamic is the process of building agrarian, rural and rural–urban anticapitalist movements, and alliances within and between these spheres, which calls for more attention to agrarian movements seen from the inseparable domains of the rural–urban continuum. What has complicated analysis of this dimension of the struggle is "the challenge of understanding the agrarian component of productive and social reproductive activities of this social category, and the importance of their access to and control of the means of social production (land, among others)" and reproduction (Borras, 2023).

Another dimension of the politics of land reform and agrarian change, as Borras and his colleagues in critical agrarian studies (Scoones et al., 2022) see it, relates to the struggle against "populist authoritarianism," which implicates a political struggle against the encroachment of agribusiness interests in the countryside and the rural–urban corridor, and the demand by peasant farmers for the redistribution of large landholdings or the restitution of previously lost lands (Scoones et al., 2022). In the case of Brazil, this struggle included the demand for legal title to land occupied and settled by the Landless Workers Movement, the MST (*Movimento dos Trabalhadores Rurais Sem Terra*), formed by rural workers and by all those who want to fight for land reform and against injustice and social inequality in rural areas (Sauer, 2020). On the dynamics of this struggle see Vergara-Camus (2009) and the discussion below.

Notwithstanding the diverse form taken by what we can describe as the politics of land reform, the resistance of the peasant movement in the current context goes well beyond what we might describe as the politics of land reform to a search for and ideas about an alternative agricultural model – to counter the dominance of the agribusiness model with a model based on what amounts to a fourth agricultural revolution – to incorporate more sustainable "green" eco-technologies into the production process (agro-ecology) and the demand by peasant farmers for lower prices of farm inputs, lower costs of social reproductive needs (food, clothing, and shelter), and fairer prices for farm produce (Rosset & Martínez-Torres, 2012).

Agrarian Movements in the Class Struggle

Throughout the 20th century, the agrarian movements in the class struggle were focused narrowly on the land question. However, in the wake of the Cuban Revolution in the immediate postwar period (1960s–1970s) the land struggle merged with the resistance against the incursions of capital into the countryside and the broader anticapitalist struggle for systemic or revolutionary social change. In this context, the peasant movement – based on the peasantry but often led by elements of the political left (the FARC in Colombia the exception in its having a peasant leadership) – engaged both the capitalist agribusiness enterprises in the agricultural sector and the State, which confronted the revolutionary movements for national liberation and revolutionary change with programs of social reform and rural development – and when required with its repressive apparatus of armed force.

By the end of the 1970s, on the threshold of a new world order, all these antisystemic (anticapitalist) peasant movements ("armies of national liberation"), except for the FARC–EP (*Fuerzas Armadas Revolucionarias de Colombia – Ejército del Pueblo*), had been defeated, their forces of resistance brought to ground. However, in the crucible of neoliberal "structural reform" in the 1980s some of these movements, notably the EZLN (Zapatista Army of National Liberation) that timed its resurrection and insurgency with the enactment on January 1, 1994, of NAFTA (the North American Free Trade Agreement (among the United States, Canada, and Mexico), which the Zapatistas regarded as the destruction of the indigenous peasant small-scale local and national economy. Another antisystemic social movement, the MST, was formed in the 1980s by the rural landless workers in Brazil to press their demand for land and land reform, and their opposition and rejection of the neoliberal policy agenda of the government. The MST, like the Zapatistas, saw the neoliberal policy agenda as a trojan horse for the advance and expansion of capitalism in the countryside.

In addition to EZLN and the MST, a confederation of some 24 indigenous nationalities in Ecuador (CONAIE), challenged state power and led the popular movement against the advance of capitalism in the form of the neoliberal policy agenda. In 1990, and then again in 2000, the indigenous communities and peasant organizations that formed the social base of CONAIE, the country's most powerful indigenous group, revolted against the 1964 agrarian reform which was designed to integrate the indigenous population into the rest of society, and the neoliberal policy agenda of the government, which they saw as responsible for impoverishing them and dislocating them from their indigenous culture (the multicultural and multiethnic nature of their society and traditional way of life).

The 2000 insurrection deposed then-President Jamil Mahuad, replacing him with a short-lived junta composed of Antonio Vargas, who represented CONAIE; Lieutenant Colonel Lucio Gutiérrez, who represented a group of junior military officers that sympathized with the concerns and demands of the indigenous communities; and former supreme court president Carlos Solórzano, who together with Vargas and Gutiérrez formed a *junta* of National Salvation (Petras & Veltmeyer, 2005).

For the first time in the history of Latin America, an alliance between elements of the military and an indigenous people's organization conspired to overthrow an elected president. On January 21, 2000, hundreds of thousands of Ecuadorians, mobilized by CONAIE, flooded the streets and squares of the capital, Quito, to protest the newly proposed dollarization of the economy and other neoliberal policies. But Colonel Gutiérrez promptly deferred to his superior, General Carlos Mendoza, who took his place on the ruling council but soon succumbed to pressures from the United States.

The United States expressed its vehement disapproval of the nonelected government and most industrialized nations followed suit. In this context, General Mendoza announced his resignation from the *junta* and threw his, and the military's, support behind Vice-President Gustavo Noboa. Noboa, who, upon assuming the office of the presidency, announced that the dollarization program would continue as part of the government's economic restructuring plan. Hours later, the indigenous people went back to their highland towns feeling betrayed by the military high command and put the new government on notice that it was being watched and judged. They reaffirmed their right to return to the capital should the government's performance fall short of their expectations.

The Rural Landless Workers Movement (MST) in Brazil

The formation of a rural landless working class derives from several processes. Large families of small farmers, for example, create a labor surplus composed of sons and daughters who do not have access to land; in other cases, sharecroppers, renters, and tenant farmers are displaced by farmers engaged in converting to new crops, introducing mechanization, or cultivating capital intensive crops. In many cases, the government's neoliberal trade policies result in the importation of cheap foodstuffs that bankrupt small farmers, while cutbacks in agricultural credits and loans, together with high interest rates, have also resulted in an enforced and massive exodus of small family farmers, driving many to migrate to the cities or beyond in the search of work. The theoretical point is that, while the segments of the rural laborforce that remain in the countryside are formally "propertyless rural workers," their ties to the land are still relatively strong, their "lineage" and extended family networks are "rural," and their "class consciousness" is still bound up with access to land, particularly arable land in regions familiar to them (Mendes Pereira, 2005).

There are several reasons for considering the MST as a modernizing social movement (Mendes Pereira, 2005). In the first place, their program is directed toward modernizing agriculture, converting fallow estates into productive units incorporating credits, technical assistance, and innovative marketing strategies (Robles & Veltmeyer, 2015). In the four decades since its creation, the MST has organized and settled on the land more than 350,000 families to create new communities, cooperatives, farms, small-scale food processing enterprises, and farmers markets that are increasingly based on a sustainable method of food production (agro-ecology), which is good for both the climate and biodiversity (Desmarais, 2007). The great majority of these farmers, many of them settled in cooperatives, have increased the cultivation of land, improved living standards (including health, education, and housing) and produced a marketable surplus for sale on local markets, and even significant coffee exports to overseas markets.

The national and regional leadership of the MST has passed through advanced training programs, many sponsored by the organization, where invited lecturers, including university professors and technical experts, teach courses on modern agricultural farming, cooperative management, and contemporary political economy (Petras & Veltmeyer, 2002). The organization of MST activities and its strategies and tactics of struggle have evolved into a highly sophisticated (if mixed) structure. The strategy of land occupations is based on an elaborate structure of self-governance, dealing with food, security, negotiations with the state, etc. During the 1990s, the MST engaged in direct action protests, demanding greater credits and financing to stem the outflow of bankrupt smallholders and impoverished landless rural workers fleeing to the cities in pursuit of low paid, unproductive urban employment.

The MST has been and remains a leading force in organizing urban alliances to counteract the neoliberal agenda of privatization and budget cuts, in the process mobilizing trade unions, political parties, universities, and religious groups through a campaign called "Consulta Popular." In the late 1990s, the MST led a march of over 100,000 urban and rural workers to Brasilia, drawing urban support along the parade route across the country. The organization, leadership, productive units, and activities of the MST have been and are directed toward modernizing agriculture on the one hand and against unproductive landlords and land speculators on the other; and neither tend to invest in increasing productivity and producing a marketable surplus (Stédile & Frei, 1993). The MST has also counterposed its modernization strategy against large agribusiness enterprises that have expelled smallholders and farm workers. In this context, the MST has pursued a "modernization from below with equity" strategy, in opposition to the elite modernization strategy favored by the government and its World Bank sponsors.

Within the institutional framework of the broader and dominant capitalist system, the MST has widened its agenda from agrarian reform to include issues such as banking and credit reform, a moratorium on foreign debt, the conservation of the Amazon, and the protection of domestic producers. It has called for greater social spending on public health and education as part of a national project toward greater national autonomy within the global economy.

The MST has been an active participant in many of the most important national and international conferences dealing with globalization, environmental issues, gender, and minority rights (Sauer, 2020).

The effectiveness and prominence of the MST in national and Third World politics, Petras (2020) argues, is based precisely on its "modern" character, and its capacity to build a modern program and adapt it to the primary demands of the landless rural workers and impoverished small landholder. In addition, the MST has been and remains in the vanguard of a search for a noncapitalist or postcapitalist alternative to the dominant corporate model.

National Confederation of Indigenous Nationalities (CONAIE) – Ecuador

In 1990, a significant sector of Ecuador's indigenous peasants launched an uprising against the State and its neoliberal policies (Paige, 2020).[1] Over the subsequent decade, the conditions that had led to this uprising generated an antisystemic social movement of significant proportions, with a series of concerted actions that included the storming in 2000 of Congress and a brief take-over of the presidency. At issue in these actions are a seriously deteriorating economic situation and a series of drastic economic reforms and policies of adjustment that include adoption of the US dollar as the country's currency. Other issues include

---

[1] The indigenous uprising of the mid-1990s is still considered the largest revolt of Ecuadorian indigenous peoples (*Resumen Latinoamericano*, October 8, 2019). Since this first major "uprising" in 1990, indigenous movements have been constantly involved in key moments in Ecuadorian politics related to the economic measures implemented by diverse governments. In less than 30 years, they overthrew a president, participated in a failed triumvirate [in conclusion to the 2000 uprising], upended alliances with three other presidents [including Rafael Correa and Lenin Moreno]. On June 25, 2015, ECUARUNARI, one of three major regional groupings that constitute the Confederation of Indigenous Nationalities of Ecuador (CONAIE), announced a *National Indigenous UPRISING for Life, Education, Land, Justice, and Liberty*.

concessions to transnational corporations of permits to construct oil pipelines and engage in economic development projects to the detriment of the country's indigenous peoples, their communities, the environment, and their local economy.

Behind these concerted actions can be found an impressive organization of indigenous communities from across the Andean highlands that are politically represented by CONAIE (Petras & Veltmeyer, 2005). By the turn of the new millennium, this peasant-based indigenous movement had clearly taken the lead of a nation-wide social movement advocating social transformation and opposition to the government's IMF-mandated policies, a movement aimed at changing not only the relationship between the country's indigenous peasants, the state and economy, but also the overthrow of the whole system (Macas, 2000). To this end, the peasant communities organizing the movement joined with other social forces in a concerted program of direct action, while itself remaining the most dynamic social force for systemic social change in the country. On this point, there is a wide agreement among scholars and observers, notwithstanding the existence of a parallel indigenous discourse on identity politics and the plurinational character of the state which bears comparison with similar developments in Bolivia and Mexico.

The beliefs and ideas used to mobilize collective action by Ecuador's peasant and indigenous peoples are clearly articulated in a series of programmatic statements made by the movement's leaders and spokespeople as well as in other forms of discourse. There is no room for misinterpretation here. Although the discourse is indigenist in nature, and couched in the language of identity politics, such as a "return to the good times" (*Pachakutik*), the "reaffirmation of our historical roots," and the "plurinational character of our society and the state," on the basis of their own accounts, the series of uprisings and the overall movement of the country's indigenous peoples and peasants are based on a clearly modernist development project.

The critical dimensions of this are clearly reflected in the discourse associated with both the *Inti Raymi* uprising and the creation of MUPP-NP (United Plurinational Pachakutik Movement – New Country). Both are oriented ideologically and politically toward three issues: The first is development, as embodied in the aim to bring about a "profound social transformation (in) the lives of the people." The second is the "construction of democracy," in order "to profoundly and radically change the structures of the Ecuadorian state and existing forms of class domination." And the third is social justice, as projected in the intention "to determine in a manner that is ... participatory, just ... the destiny of each people" (Macas, 2000). In terms of this modernist anticapitalist political project, the associated discourse addresses issues of national economic development and the need for a new politics centered on community-based relations and forms of power. In other words, what is sought is Another Development that is constructed from below, participatory, people-led and centered, inclusive, equitable, and just – and empowering.

Zapatista Army of National Liberation (EZLN) – Mexico

In Mexico, it is estimated that the indigenous peoples comprise some 15.7 million, most of them peasants, landless workers or jornaleros, a subproletariat of seasonal or permanent migrants, refugees from what Marcos termed *bolsillos de olvido* ("forgotten pockets"), which in official discourse are defined as "marginal zones" of subsistence production, exclusion, and poverty (Gunderson, 2013; Veltmeyer, 2000).

There is nothing purely "discursive" about these categories – marginality, exclusion, poverty, etc. – as argued by postmodern theorists of the new social movements. Rather, they reflect conditions that are structural and objective in their effects according to their location in the capitalist system. In terms of the directives and communiques of the movement, the armed rebellion and uprising of indigenous peasants in Chiapas were directed against the Mexican State and the capitalist system supported by it (Veltmeyer, 1997; Vergara-Camus, 2009). In the poetic language of subcomandante Marcos, the official spokesperson of the movement, the cause of the uprising was "the wild beast" (imperialism) whose "bloody jaws" and teeth have sunk deeply into the throat of south-eastern Mexico, drawing out large pools of blood (tribute in the form of "petroleum, electrical energy, cattle, money, coffee, banana, honey, corn") through "[as] many veins – oil and gas pipes, electrical lines, train-cars, bank accounts, trucks and vans, clandestine paths, gaps and forest trails" (Marcos, 1994). As far as the EZLN is concerned, the enemy is imperialism and the Mexican State that sustains its globalizing neoliberal project. This was made clear by Marcos himself as early as 1992, a year and a half before the 1994 uprising and soon after the Zapatistas' first skirmish with the government's armed forces. And the point is made, not as eloquently but as clearly, both at the time of the EZLN's unexpected irruption and subsequently in the convocation of a series of national and tricontinental encounters and forums that the Zapatistas have organized against neoliberalism and for humanity.

With reference to the imperialist and class nature of the oppressive state and rapacious capitalist system, the Zapatista uprising coincided with the inception of NAFTA, viewed by Marcos as "the deathknell of the peasant economy." And in similar terms, the Zapatista discourse, in the form of a series of communiques and reflections and calls for solidarity, speaks consistently of the need to combat (structural and political) relations of oppression and exploitation; and to establish new relations of power with the state and the economy, based on "independence, democracy and justice" – a modernist project if there ever was one.

At the outset, the Zapatistas spoke or wrote clearly in class terms. Over time, however, this language transmuted into terms that have given rise to misinterpretation by an international array of postmodernist intellectuals tuned into cyberspace and anxious to establish the presence of the "first postmodernist" movement in history. Accordingly, historians like Florencia Mallon speak of the postmodern condition of the postcolonial peasantry and the political (discursive) struggle for ethnic or national identity. In this poststructuralist reading of EZLN discourse, objectively real or existent relations of cause/effect involving imperialism/capitalism/the state on the one hand, and Zapatista actions on the other, are reduced to a meaning derived from their discourse: namely, relations of power and hegemony arising from and consisting of discursive activity. The objective thus becomes not to act on and change reality, as Marx had it in the 11th thesis on Feuerbach, but simply to reinterpret it.

In the process of forming itself into a national force, the Zapatistas were concerned to establish a new form of power and politics that is reminiscent of the theoretical discourse initiated by Foucault and reproduced by Mallon and other members of the subaltern group of historians (Veltmeyer, 1997). However, it takes a perversely poststructuralist reading of this discourse to convert its categories into purely discursive phenomena with a socially constructed meaning. As for the Zapatistas themselves, there is a question about the meaning attached to their words. They reflect class-based conditions that are grounded in a modernist project – to bring about change in the lives of the country's indigenous peasants.

Agrarian Social Movements as a Force of Social Transformation

Agrarian social movements, formed in the vortex of capitalist development, have been in the forefront in the resistance against the advance of capitalism in the development process throughout the 20th century. First, they constituted the agency of the peasant wars, the dynamics of which were studied and reconstructed by the Marxist anthropologist Eric Wolf (1971). Second, in the era of developmentalism (the 1950s–1970s) these movements were the backbone of the revolutionary movements, formed as "armies of national liberation" in the Latin American countryside. In the subsequent neoliberal era, when these movements were brought to ground, their forces of resistance dispersed, the agrarian or peasant movements mobilized the diverse forces of resistance in the countryside against the advance of capitalism in the form of the neoliberal policy agenda. As noted above, the activism of these movements was directly responsible for creating a condition (a generalized discontent with, and the rejection of, neoliberalism as an economic doctrine and as a policy agenda) that allowed and led the political left to assume the reigns of state power in a pink tide of regime change. Subsequently (over the past two decades of the new millennium) the agrarian or "peasant" movement, or movements, throughout the region have taken the lead in confronting the "capitalist hydra" (to use the Zapatistas' evocative term for capitalism) not just in mobilizing the forces of resistance in both the countryside and the main cities, but in constructing an alternative economic model for a different postcapitalist society (Scoones, et al., 2001).

As for mobilizing the forces of popular resistance, the role played by the contemporary sociopolitical peasant movements in the politics of social transformation can be ascertained in the diverse encounters and conferences orchestrated by peasant-based organizations across Latin America (Vergara-Camus & Kay, 2017b). One of these quite typical "social mobilizations for rurality" took place in Colombia in 2013, a "significant year for social mobilization for rurality in Colombia." It involved a National Agrarian and Popular Strike (PNAP), which brought together small and medium-sized rural producers – "peasants" broadly defined – in the main cities and highways throughout the country (García Aguilera & Mantilla Monsalve, 2018).

The prominence achieved by the PNAP meant that the questions of how to understand, what to do, and where to direct the Colombian countryside will take on renewed validity (Salcedo et al., 2013) and that its answers could not be easily enunciated from the old paradigm of modernization and agricultural development and, even less, without a broad set of rural actors. This was interpreted by some indigenous, peasant, and Afro-descendant organizations that met in Bogotá between March 15 and 17, 2014, to evaluate the experience of the PNAP and qualify its proposals to fully enter into the debate on understanding and ways to address the problem of rurality. As a result of this meeting, the Agrarian, Peasant, Ethnic, and Popular Summit (hereinafter CACEP)[2] emerged and a *Single List of Demands* was built: *Mandates for living well, structural agrarian reform, [land and food] sovereignty, democracy and peace with social justice.*

This list of demands, which reflected the priority concerns of the peasant movement writ large, materialized with diverse permutations and iterations in diverse regional and national contexts (summits, conferences, encounters) across Latin America over the past two decades. In addition, Via Campesina, a global amalgam of some 180 peasant and small producer organizations and movements, has played a major role not just in Latin America but in other countries and regions across the world in articulating the concerns and demands of the peasant movements and translating these demands into strategic actions. In addition to the "single list of demands" elaborated by CACEP, Via Campesina has introduced into the debate the concept of an alternative model of agricultural development based on what has been described as an "agroecological revolution" (Altieri & Toledo, 2011; Rosset & Martínez-Torres, 2012). Through the networking process in the transnational peasant and family farmer movement, La Vía Campesina has been a major factor in the increased emphasis given by diverse popular social movements in the region to both agro-ecology and sovereignty, and in taking agro-ecology to scale.

The critical unsettled question regarding this alternative model is whether it is constructed within or outside the institutional and policy framework of the capitalist system, that is, does it point toward an alternative *form* of development or an alternative *to* development? Is it based on what ECLAC economists (regarding the policy agenda of the pink tide governments) have described as "neodevelopmentalist extractivism"? Or what Svampa (2011) conceives of as an "ecoterritorial turn towards new alternatives?" On this question, there is no consensus, although Via Campesina is clear about its conception of agrarian change and agricultural development as predicated on abandoning capitalism in each and all contemporary manifestations, namely, corporate agribusiness, extractivism, and neoliberalism.

---

[2]The organizations that make up CACEP are: Asociación Campesina Popular (Asocampo), Asociación Nacional Agraria y Campesina (Asonalcam), Asociación Nacional de Zonas de Reserva Campesina (Anzorc), Autoridad Nacional Afrocolombiana (Anafro), Coalición de Movimientos y Organizaciones Sociales de Colombia (Comosoc), Congreso de los Pueblos (CDP), Coordinador Nacional Agrario (CNA), Federación Nacional Sindical Unitaria Agropecuaria (Fensuagro), Mesa de Unidad Agraria (MUA), Movimiento por la Constituyente Popular (MCP), Movimiento Social y Político Colombiano Marcha Patriótica (MAPA), Organización Nacional Indígena de Colombia (ONIC), Proceso de Comunidades Negras (PCN).

Conclusion

In this chapter, we examined the political dynamics associated with three cases of peasant/landless workers movements that in the 1990s – the decade in which the policy agenda of the World Bank and the IMF was implemented by most governments in the region – challenged both state power and the neoliberal policy agenda. These peasant movements were in the vanguard of a class struggle against the advance of capitalism in the development process. In their political activism, these movements replaced the working class as the primary force of resistance against the advances of capitalism – the advance of speculative investments in the financial sector, monopoly capital in the agricultural sector, and extractive capital in the large-scale acquisition of land and the extraction of natural resources in high demand on capitalist markets. By the end of the decade, the political activism of these and other peasant movements had a significant impact on politics, succeeding in generating widespread discontent and in some policy circles rejection of the neoliberal policy agenda, thereby creating conditions that would allow the political left to capture state power in the context of a primary commodities boom. The political dynamics of this "progressive cycle" are explored in the following chapter.

Chapter 4

The Progressive Cycle: A Left Turn in Latin American Politics

At the turn of the new millennium, several forces of change – including the rise of China as a world economic power, primary commodities boom, and the demise of neoliberalism as an economic doctrine and model – created an entirely new context for the capitalist development process in Latin America. Features of this new context included the rapid expansion of "resource-seeking" or extractive capital and a pink tide of regime change, leading to the formation of left-leaning ("progressive") regimes that are oriented toward both neodevelopmentalism (postneoliberal inclusionary state activism) and extractivism (natural resource extraction and primary commodities exports as a strategy of national development). Not that the outcome of these trends and associated developments, such as a pronounced primary commodities boom, were uniform. In fact, it is possible to trace out three different patterns of subsequent political developments.

One was the formation and continuity of regimes aligned with the United States and that continued to follow the neoliberal line in their economic policies. These included Chile, which was nominally socialist but whose policies were no different from traditional neoliberal regimes except for less dogmatism and more pragmatism; Peru, where the government was taken over by a populist who nevertheless stuck with the neoliberal policies of his predecessors; Colombia, the United States' staunchest ally and fully committed to a neoliberal policy regime; and Mexico, another staunch US ally and advocate of free-market capitalism. In 2016, these countries signed the Trans-Pacific Partnership agreement, a massive trade and investment pact promoted by the United States but written in secret by the ideologues of some of the United States' largest corporations. With the text of the trade pact reviewed by over 600 corporate lobbyists, the Alliance for Democracy (2016) justly describes it as "NAFTA on Steroids."

A second pattern was related to the formation in South America of a bloc of postneoliberal progressive regimes oriented toward the new developmentalism (inclusionary state activism) as well as extractivism, that is, the use of resource rents, collected or extracted from the multinational companies given concessions to exploit and export the country's natural resources, to finance their social programs and bring about a more "inclusive" form of development, or poverty reduction (Gaudichaud et al., 2019). This included the two largest countries on the continent, Argentina, and Brazil, which together accounted for over 70 percent of the regional economy and exports and which in the early 1990s joined Uruguay and Paraguay to form a subregional trading bloc (Mercosur) in opposition to various subsequent efforts of the United States to create a continental free trade zone. The governments in both countries pursued this neodevelopmentalist and extractivist policy regime until it was brought to an abrupt end in Argentina by the election on November 22, 2015 of Macri, who represented the forces of right-wing opposition and reaction – and the rejection of the quest for an alternative postneoliberal development model. Behind these political developments, which can also be traced out in Brazil, Venezuela, and Bolivia, was a change in the correlation of forces engaged in the class struggle, a "development" that responded to and reflected the evident end of the commodities boom (around 2012) and with it the end of the capacity of these regimes to sustain their progressive policies. Indeed, in the wake of recent regional developments along this line analysts have begun to write about and debate the "end of the progressive cycle" in Latin American politics. A key proposition in this debate is the point made by Gaudichaud (2016), namely that "reality can't be radically transformed only through institutions" – or, we might add, policy reform.

A third pattern of policy experiments and political developments associated with the demise of neoliberalism and the 10-year primary commodities boom (2003–2012) involved Venezuela, Bolivia, and Ecuador – more radical postneoliberal regimes that were oriented in theory (political rhetoric and development discourse) if not in actual fact toward a postdevelopment model in which, in the cases of Bolivia and Ecuador, it would allow people to "live well"; or, in the case of Venezuela, were engaged in a process of revolutionary transformation (the Bolivarian Revolution) oriented toward the "socialism of the twenty-first century."

At the level of trade, these regimes joined Cuba and several smaller countries in the Caribbean to form the *Alianza Bolivariana para los Pueblos de Nuestra América* (ALBA), a postneoliberal intergovernmental alternative trade regime. In the case of Venezuela, the revolutionary process can be traced back to the regime formed by Hugo Chávez in 1998. Like the other postneoliberal regimes in the region, the Venezuelan government's development strategy was financed by and hinged on an extractivist approach, but unlike the other postneoliberal regimes it was not dependent on foreign direct investment or on the state to strike a deal with global extractive capital. However, as in the case of these two regimes the collapse of the commodities boom and the dramatic fall in the price of oil, the one commodity on which the entire policy regime was dependent, together with the machinations of US imperialism funding of the sabotage of and right-wing opposition to the protosocialist regime, pushed the country toward the brink of a severe economic crisis. Whether the combined effect of this crisis, US intervention, right-wing opposition, and economic sabotage would be enough to overthrow the regime or lead to its collapse was uncertain, but there is no doubt that the revolutionary process in the country – like the progressive cycle in Latin American politics – today is in serious jeopardy.

The election of Macri, together with the recent coup in Brazil, and the referendum in Bolivia – as well as the institution of the Trans-Pacific Free Trade regime – are indications of a new conjuncture in the capitalist development process and another pendulum swing in the correlation of class forces, and with it the likely end of the progressive cycle and the return of the Right. At issue in this development is what has turned out to be a reactionary rather than progressive developmentalist model, which served initially to deradicalize and demobilize the popular movements and ultimately to cultivate the return of the Right. With Macri, the country had entered a new political phase in which the goal was no less than to implant a neoliberal model of capital accumulation.

Three Decades of Class Struggle

As noted in the introduction to this volume, the process of capitalist development set in motion by the architects of the Bretton Woods system and the advocates of "development assistance" – international cooperation with the development agenda of the "economically backwards" countries seeking to escape the yoke of colonialism and imperialist exploitation – advanced in two stages: a phase of state-led development (1948–1980) and the subsequent "neoliberal era" in which the forces of national development were advanced within the institutional and policy framework of the Washington Consensus as to the virtues of free-market capitalism. As for the neoliberal era, the process of development and social change – the development of the forces of production and the corresponding changes in the social relations of production and the resulting dynamics of class struggle – can be traced out decade by decade. The 1980s in Latin America saw the institution of a new economic model, which was used as a template for adjusting the macroeconomic policies of governments in the region to the requirements of the new world order. Because of the manifest dismal failure of this "structural adjustment program" and the Washington Consensus to bring about any advance in the economic development process, the architects of the development idea at the end of the decade revised the neoliberal policy agenda by adding to the basic menu of structural reforms a "new social policy" oriented toward "inclusive development" (i.e., poverty reduction).

The 1990s saw a dramatic growth in the influx of capital in the form of foreign direct investment, a deepening and extension of the "structural reform" agenda (to include Argentina, Brazil, and Peru, which had not participated in the first cycle of neoliberal "structural reforms") and the growth in the countryside of powerful antineoliberal social movements. By the end of the decade, most countries in the region had adopted the "new social policy" (poverty reduction, inclusive development) agenda of the post-Washington Consensus and the associated neodevelopmentalist strategy devised by economists at ECLAC and the policy framework for "comprehensive development" devised by economists at the World Bank. However, this agenda did not sway the leadership of the antineoliberal social movements that dominated the political landscape in many countries.

By the end of the decade, notwithstanding the massive influx of capital and the widespread adoption of a social reformist and assistentialist policy agenda, the ideologues and advocates of the neoliberal policy agenda were very much on the defensive in countries such as Ecuador with a powerful antineoliberal resistance. In Peru, the political cycle played out in much of South America from Venezuela to Argentina and Brazil seemed to have been about 10 years behind.

At the turn into the new millennium, and the third decade of the neoliberal era, widespread discontent and the rejection of neoliberalism across the region gave way to a tidal wave of left-leaning regimes with a progressive agenda based on the search for a more inclusive form of development. Even hardline neoliberals and the proponents of the erstwhile Washington (and now Davos) Consensus had come to the view that the reduction of extreme poverty was an essential part of what was now described as an "inclusive economic growth" policy agenda and strategy based on the agency of the free market. This agenda was – and is – advanced by conservative private foundations and neoliberal policy forums across the world, which are heavily financed by the superrich and the global ruling class and their corporations. However, under conditions in Latin America at the turn of the new millennium it was the post-Washington Consensus on the need for inclusionary state activism and greater income and wealth distribution that prevailed. The resulting progressive cycle in Latin American politics implicated the governments of Argentina and Brazil in what has been described as a pink tide of regime change, and the governments of Venezuela, Bolivia, and Ecuador in what might be viewed as a "red" tide of regimes pushing for more radical change, that is, socialism. In this chapter, we will discuss the dynamics of class struggle associated with this progressive cycle.

Brazil: Corporatism and the Class Struggle from Below[1]

Two types of class struggle have dominated Brazilian social relations in recent decades. For over two decades of military dictatorships (1964–1984) the ruling class waged war on workers and peasants, imposing tripartite agreements between state and capitalists and appointed "union" leaders. The absence of authentic class-based unions and the economic crises of the early 1980s set in motion the emergence of the "new unionism." The CUT (*Central Única dos Trabalhadores*), organized around heavy industry, and the rural landless workers' movement in the rural areas, emerged as leading forces in the class struggle. The deteriorating political control of the military led to opposition from two directions: (i) the agro-mineral and export bourgeoisie, which sought to impose a civilian-electoral regime to pursue a neoliberal economic development strategy and (ii) the new class-based unionism which sought to democratize and expand the public ownership of the means of production.

The CUT allied with the liberal bourgeoisie and defeated the corporatist, military-backed candidates of the Right. In other words, the combined class struggle from below and from above secured electoral democracy and the ascendancy

---

[1] This section draws on the author's research archives as well as earlier work published in Petras and Veltmeyer (2019, pp. 156–167).

of the neoliberal bourgeoisie. Under the neoliberal regimes at the time, three changes that further conditioned the class struggle from below took place:

1. The CUT secured legality and collective bargaining rights and became institutionalized.
2. The CUT and the MST backed the newly formed Workers Party (PT), a party that was dominated by leftist middle-class professionals intent on taking power through electoral processes.
3. The CUT increasingly depended on financing by the Ministry of Labor, while the PT increasingly looked toward private contractors to finance their election campaigns.

From the mid-90s to the election of Lula da Silva in 2002, the CUT and the MST alternated direct action (strikes and land occupations) with electoral politics – backing the candidates of the PT, which increasingly sought to moderate-class disputes. Class struggle from below intensified during the impeachment of neoliberal President Collor de Mello and his resignation from the presidency on December 29, 1992, after two-and-a-half years in power. However, once Collor was ousted, the CUT moderated the workings of the class struggle from below.

With the hyperinflation of the 1990s, the CUT and the MST engaged in defensive class struggles, opening the way for the election of hardline neoliberal Fernando Henrique Cardoso. Under his presidency, a severe "adjustment" that prejudiced workers was implemented to end inflation. Strategic sectors were privatized. Lucrative public oil and mining enterprises were privatized, and banks were denationalized; agribusiness took center stage.

The class struggle from below intensified, while Cardoso supported the class struggle from above for capital. The MST-led land occupations intensified, as did violent repression; and workers strikes, and popular discontent multiplied. The PT responded by harnessing the class struggle to its electoral strategy. The PT also deepened its ties with private contractors and replaced its social democratic program with a clientelist version of neoliberalism.

The rising tide of class struggle from below led to the presidential victory of the PT, whose economic program was based on IMF agreements and ties to the dominant classes. Under the PT, the class struggle from below weakened and dissipated. The MST and the CUT subordinated their struggles to the PT, which promoted negotiated solutions with the capitalist class. The dynamics of this moderate form of class struggle excluded structural changes and revolved on incremental changes of wages and consumption and increases in poverty spending. The electoral success of the PT depended on ever-greater financing by private contractors based on awarding billion-*real* public contracts for multimillion dollar bribes. The lower- and working-class vote was secured by a well-funded antipoverty program and the vote-getting campaigns of CUT and the MST. The high price of export commodities based on the booming Asian market provided a vast increase in state revenues to finance capital loans and social welfare.

The class struggle led by the PT ended with the bust of the mega-commodity boom. After the second election of Dilma Rousseff in 2014, the exposure of massive corruption involving the PT further exacerbated the crisis and mass support for the PT. As the economy stagnated, the PT adapted to the crises by embracing the structural adjustments of the ruling class. As the PT leaders shifted to the class struggle from above, they ignited protest from below among the middle class, workers, and employees – and even within the PT itself. Mass demonstrations protested over the decline of public services.

By 2016, a "moderate" class struggle in Brazil bifurcated into a mass class struggle from above and a much weaker struggle "from below." As the rightwing judicial system exposed corruption in the PT regimes, and the economy spiraled into the worst recession in 50 years, the Right mobilized three million street demonstrators who sought to overthrow the Rousseff regime, whose popularity plunged to single digits. The counter response of sections of the Left drew less than a million. The class struggle from above was advancing and the Left was in retreat, as demonstrated by subsequent events (the success of the forces on the Right to finally depose President Rousseff).

Argentina: High-intensity Class Struggle[2]

Argentina has been the center of high-intensity class struggle over the last half-century. A ruling class-backed military dictatorship from 1966 to 1973 harshly repressed trade unions and their political parties (mostly Left Peronist). In response, industrial workers led major uprisings in the major cities (Cordoba and Rosario included), ultimately forcing the military-capitalist rulers to retreat and convoke elections.

The period between 1973 and 1976 was a tumultuous period of rising class and guerrilla struggle, high inflation, the emergence of death squads, and successful general strikes. A situation of "dual power" between factory committees and a highly militarized state, ostensibly led by Isabel Perón and death squad leader José López Rega, were ended by a bloody US-backed military coup in 1976.

From 1976 to 1983, over 30,000 Argentines were murdered and made to "disappear" by the military-capitalist regime. The vast majority were working-class activists in factories and neighborhood organizations. The military-capitalist class victory led to the imposition of neoliberal policies and the illegalization of all workers' organizations and strikes. The high-intensity class struggle from above ended the class struggle from below.

The loss of authentic factory and community-based workers' leaders was a historic defeat with an impact that persisted for decades. The subsequent military defeat of the Argentine Armed Forces by the British in the battle over the Malvinas led to a negotiated transition in which the neoliberal economic structures and

---

[2]The first part of the following section (1976–2001) is based on field research conducted by James Petras and the author and reported on in Petras and Veltmeyer (2002). The second part (2002–2015) is based on research conducted by James Petras and the author reported on in Petras and Veltmeyer (2018).

military elite remained intact. The electoral parties emerged and competed for office but offered little support to the legalized trade unions.

Between 1984 and 2001 Radical and Peronist presidents privatized and denationalized the economy, while the re-emerging right-wing Peronist trade unions engaged in ritual general strikes to defuse discontent from below and collaborated with the state. The economic crash of 2000–2001 led to an explosion of class struggle, as thousands of factories closed and over one-quarter of the laborforce was unemployed (*los desocupados*, the social base of the class struggle led by the *piqueteros*).

In this conjuncture and situation, members of the middle class lost their savings as banks failed. A major popular demonstration in front of the Presidential Palace was repressed, resulting in three dozen killings. In response, over two million Argentines engaged in general strikes and uprisings, seized the Congress and besieged the banks. Millions of unemployed and impoverished workers and middle-class assemblies, representing nearly 50 percent of the population, took to the streets. But fragmentation and sectarian disputes prevented a serious alternative government from emerging from below.

Intense class struggle from below toppled three presidents in less than two years (2001–2002), but the mass protest remained without leaders or a hegemonic party. In 2003, a center-left Peronist, Néstor Kirchner, was elected and, under pressure from the mass movements, imposed a moratorium on debt and financed an economic recovery based on rising commodity prices and rechanneling debt payments.

In the decade from 2003 to 2013, a low-intensity class struggle emerged as the dominant feature of the political landscape. This struggle, led by the middle classes, led to labor reform and the recovery of capitalism from a systemic crisis. The Kirchner regime channeled the revenues from the mega-commodity boom into increases in wages, salaries, and pensions. It also subsidized and attracted foreign and domestic agro-business and mining capitalists.

By the end of the decade, the capitalist class felt relatively secure and the threats from below were diluted. High growth led to increases in class struggle from above. Agribusiness organized boycotts to lessen taxes; Buenos Aires business and professional groups regrouped and organized mass protests. Leftist parties and trade unions that were either co-opted or fragmented were engaged in economistic struggles. Some factions within the Workers Party even joined the right-wing demonstrations. In 2012, the commodity boom came to an end in conditions that allowed the hard right to assume power. The Kirchner–Fernández regime itself leaned to the right in embracing extractive capitalism as an economic paradigm.

From 2013 to 2015 the Right dominated electoral politics. The trade unions were once again under the leadership of right-wing Peronists. Popular movements were in opposition but without any significant political representation. After a decade and a half, the cycle of the class struggle had come full circle from intense class struggle from below, to middle-class-mediated class struggle and the resurgence of the class struggle from above.

Bolivia: From Popular Uprisings to Andean Capitalism and Communal Socialism[3]

Between 2000 and 2005, major popular rebellions took place in Bolivia (Farthing, 2018; Paige, 2020; Petras & Veltmeyer, 2005; Webber, 2008). They included the "water war" in Cochabamba in 2000; a mass worker–peasant uprising in La Paz in 2003, which ousted neoliberal incumbent President Sánchez de Lozado; and a second uprising in 2005, which drove incumbent President Carlos Mesa from power and led to new elections and the victory of radical coca farmer and peasant leader Evo Morales to the presidency.

Morales and his MAS (Movement to Socialism) party assumed power in 2006, ending a period of intense class struggle and popular uprisings. In this period, the government implemented a series of piecemeal socioeconomic reforms and cultural changes while incorporating and co-opting the indigenous movement and the trade union leadership. The net effect was to demobilize the popular movement. The key to the stability, continuity, and re-election of Morales was his ability to separate socioeconomic and culture reforms from radical structural changes. In the process, Morales secured the electoral support of the masses of peasants and workers, isolated the more radical sectors, and ensured that the class struggle would revolve around short-term wage and salary issues that would not endanger the stability of the government.

The key to the periodic recurrence of revolutionary class struggle in Bolivia has been the fusion of a multiplicity of demands. High-intensity class struggle resulted from the multiple points of socioethnic, national, and cultural oppression and class exploitation. Immediate economic demands were linked to class struggles for long-term, large-scale systemic changes (Webber, 2008).

The major protagonists of the social upheavals demanded an end to deep and pervasive ethno-racial discrimination and indignities. They rejected foreign capitalist pillage of natural resources and wealth that provided no positive returns for the mining and rural communities. They fought for indigenous self-rule and a role in governance if not the government. They resented the denial of symbolic indigenous presence in public or private spaces. Wages that were low relative to profits and hazardous employment with no compensatory payments radicalized the miners. In this context, where the indigenous population was denied governmental access and representation, they relied on direct action – popular upheavals and demands for social revolution were the route to secure social justice (Webber, 2008).

The coming to power of Evo Morales opened the door to a new kind of mass politics based essentially on his ability to fragment demands. He implemented cultural and economic reforms and neutralized demands for a social revolution.

---

[3]The following discussion is informed by a comprehensive review of the literature, in particular, studies by Farthing (2018), Paige (2020), and Webber (2008). The author here has also drawn on the author's research archives related to research conducted over the past decade and materials previously published in Petras and Veltmeyer (2005, 2011, 2019). The author is grateful to Routledge for permission to republish some of these materials.

President Morales convoked a new constituent assembly that included a strong representation of Indian delegates. Bolivia was renamed a "plurinational" state. Formal recognition and approval of the "autonomy" of Indian nations was approved. He frequently met and consulted with Indian leaders. Symbolic representation de-radicalized the indigenous movements (Webber, 2008).

The government took a majority share in several joint ventures with gas and oil corporations and increased the royalties and tax rates on profits of mining companies. Morales rejected outright nationalization under workers' control. Evo Morales denounced imperialist intervention in Bolivia and elsewhere and expelled US Ambassador Goldberg for plotting a coup with the extreme right-wing opposition in Santa Cruz. He expelled the Drug Enforcement Agency and the US military mission for meddling in internal affairs. He increased social spending and salaries and wages incrementally each year by between 5 and 10 percent. These reforms were compatible with long-term contracts with dozens of major foreign multinational mining companies that continued to reap and remit double-digit profits. Although the government claimed to "nationalize" foreign-owned mining companies, in most cases, it meant simply higher tax rates, comparable to the rates in the major capitalist countries. The revolutionary demands to socialize the "commanding heights of the economy" faded and revolutionary mass energies were diverted into collective bargaining agreements (Webber, 2008).

While the Morales regime spoke of respecting *Pachamama* (Mother Earth) he pursued the most blatant exploitation of land reserves of any president to date, opening 8 of 17 bioreserve parks to foreign and domestic extractive capitalist exploitation, arguing that development would provide the revenues to reduce poverty – ignoring the villagers uprooted in the process, losing access to water and land (Petras, 2013a).

While the government celebrated indigenous culture, all its major decisions were made by *mestizo* and European-descended technocrats. MAS bureaucrats overruled local assemblies in the selection and election of candidates. While government legislation proposed "land reform," Santa Cruz's "hundred families" still controlled vast plantations, controlling the agro-export economy. They continued to receive most government credits and subsidies. Poverty, especially extreme poverty, was reduced but still affected most of the population in the indigenous communities. Public lands, offered for Indian settlement were located far from markets and with few support resources. As a result, few families were resettled.

While Evo Morales articulated an anti-imperialist discourse, he constantly traveled abroad to Europe to sign off on lucrative private investment deals. Corruption, Petras (2016, 2020) has argued, crept into the MAS party, and pervaded its officials in Cochabamba, El Alto, and La Paz. The net effect of Evo's domestic reform and cultural inclusive agenda was to neutralize and marginalize radical critiques of his macroeconomic adaptation to foreign capital.

His affirmation of indigenous (*Indio*) culture neutralized the opposition of indigenous peasants and farmworkers to the Euro-Bolivian plantation owners who prospered under his "extractive export strategy."

The class struggle focused on narrow economic issues directed by trade union leaders (COB), who consulted and negotiated agreements in accordance with Evo's economic guidelines. In short, under President Morales the class struggle from below diminished, popular rebellions disappeared, and collective bargaining took center stage. The Morales decade witnessed the lowest intensity of class struggle in a century. The contrast between the 1995–2005 decade and the 2006–2015 period is striking. While the earlier period under Euro-Bolivian rulers witnessed several general strikes and popular uprisings, during the later decade there were none. Even the hostile, racist landed and mining oligarchy of Santa Cruz eventually came to political agreements and ran on joint electoral platforms with the MAS, recognizing the benefits of fiscal conservatism, social stability, capitalist prosperity, and class peace.

Under Morales's conservative fiscal regime, Bolivian foreign reserves increased from under US$4 billion to over US$15 billion – an achievement that pleased the World Bank but still left most peasants below the poverty line. In large part, the success of Evo in defusing the class struggle and channeling "radicalism" into safe channels was due to the incremental changes that were underwritten by a decade-long rise in commodity prices.

With the primary commodities boom the prices of iron ore, oil, tin, gold, lithium, and soya soared, allowing the regime to increase state expenditures and wages without affecting the wealth and profits of the agro-mineral elite. But, as the megaboom ended in 2013–2015 (exports fell by 50 percent in 2015) and nepotism and corruption in official circles flourished, the MAS lost provincial and municipal elections in major cities. The MAS regime, plagued by corruption scandals, attempted to foist unpopular candidates on the mass base and lost. The main opposition to the regime was from the center-right elements of the middle class. The dormant and thoroughly coopted COB and peasant movements continued to back Morales but faced an increasingly rebellious rank and file. The electoral decline was most evident in the defeat of a government-sponsored referendum in February 2016, asking the electorate to vote in favor of Evo's re-election, potentially extending his presidency until 2025. Most of the big cities voted against the MAS initiative, rebelling against corruption and abuses by government officials. As for the progressive policy regime of poverty reduction pursued by the Morales-Linera regime – a progressive regime undercut by the insistence of the government to assuage foreign investors by accumulating one of the biggest reserves of foreign currency in the region, and even lending money from this reserve fund to the World Bank and foreign investors at ridiculously low interest rates rather than investing it productively – the end of the commodities boom has effectively curtailed this regime (Almeyra, 2016).

Ecuador: Middle-class Radicalism within a Citizen's Revolution[4]

The last decade of the 20th century in Ecuador began and ended with an uprising of the indigenous communities that formed the most powerful social movement

---

[4]This section relies heavily on data collected by the author in various annual research trips to Ecuador and fieldwork conducted over the years 2005–2019 as well as material published in Petras (2013b) and Petras and Veltmeyer (2005) with permission from the publishers.

in opposition to the neoliberal agenda of the governments at the time: the Confederation of Indigenous Nationalities of Ecuador (la *Confederación de Nacionalidades Indígenas del Ecuador*), or more commonly, CONAIE. This movement, together with the Zapatista rebellion, in Chiapas (the *Ejército Zapatista de Liberación Nacional*, or EZLN) played a major role in the subsequent demise of neoliberalism as an economic doctrine and development model.[5] But, notwithstanding this important political development, Ecuador has had a long history of palace coups of little socioeconomic consequence, at least up until the first half-decade of the 21st century. The prelude to the popular upheavals of the recent period was a "decade of infamy." Right-wing oligarchical parties alternated in power, pillaging billions from the national treasury. Overseas bankers granted high-risk loans that were transferred to overseas accounts. Major oil companies, namely Texaco, exploited and contaminated large tracts of land, and water, with impunity. Client regimes granted the United States a major military base in Manta, from which it violated Ecuadorean air and maritime sovereignty. Ecuador surrendered its currency to the US dollar, eliminating its capacity to pursue sovereign monetary policy (Petras & Veltmeyer, 2005).

The ethno-class struggle in Ecuador has been deeply contradictory. CONAIE (the Confederation of Indigenous Nationalities of Ecuador), founded in 1986, led major uprisings in the 1990s and was the driving force in toppling oligarch Jamil Mahuad in 2000. Yet it allied with rightist Colonel Lucio Gutiérrez and formed a three-person junta which eventually gave in to US pressures and allowed the vice president and oligarch, Gustavo Noboa, to assume the presidency.

In the run-up to the presidential elections of 2002, CONAIE and the trade union led by the oil and electrical workers' unions intensified the class struggle and mobilized the working class and Indigenous communities. However, in the 2002 presidential elections, CONAIE's political arm (*Pachakutik*) and most of the militant trade unions backed Lucio Gutiérrez. But once elected, Gutiérrez embraced the agenda of the Washington Consensus, privatizing strategic sectors of the economy and backing US policy on Venezuela, Cuba and other progressive governments in the region. Further, Gutiérrez arrested and dismissed militant oil worker leaders and promoted agro-mineral exploitation of indigenous territory.

Despite CONAIE's eventual disaffection from Pachakutik it remained in the government up until Gutiérrez was ousted in 2005 by a movement largely made up of a disaffected middle-class "citizens movement." Subsequently, during the 2005 elections, the trade unions and CONAIE backed Rafael Correa. Less than two years later they denounced him for supporting petroleum company exploitation of regions adjoining Indian nations.

---

[5]The important role of CONAIE as a powerful force for political change is formed by the country's indigenous people – with reference to the insurrections of 1900 and 2000 and the defenestration of several neoliberal presidents – is well understood by the indigenous communities and nationalities mobilized by CONAIE ("Ecuador. The political strength of the indigenous people has an imposing history," *Resumen Latinoamericano,* October 8, 2019. https://www.resumenlatinoamericano.org/2019/10/08/ecuador-la-fuerza-politica-de-los-indigenas-tiene-historia-y-es-imponente/).

CONAIE and the trade unions intensified their opposition in 2008 precisely when Correa declared the national debt illegitimate, defaulted on Ecuador's US$3 billion debt, and reduced bond payments by 60 percent. CONAIE and Pachakutik were marginalized because of their opportunist alliances with Gutiérrez. Their attacks on Correa, as he proceeded to increase social expenditure and infrastructure investment in the interior, further diminished their strength. In the elections for a constituent assembly, Pachakutik received barely two percent of the vote. While the trade unions and CONAIE continued to mobilize in support of ethno-class demands, Correa increased support among indigenous communities via infrastructure programs financed by the mega-commodity boom, large-scale loans from China, and the reduction of debt payments.

Faced with declining support from the popular classes, CONAIE and sections of the trade unions supported a US-backed police coup attempt on September 30, 2010. Pachakutik leader Clever Jimenez called the right-wing coup a "just action," while tens of thousands of people demonstrated their support for Correa and his Country Alliance Party (*Alianza PAIS*).

Correa's "Citizen Revolution" (*Revolución Ciudadana*) is essentially based on the deepening of a capitalist developmental model rooted in mining, oil, and hydroelectric power. Over the past decade of Correa rule, the government has embraced big oil and sought World Bank loans to finance the agro-mineral growth model while harshly repressing the indigenous movement (CONAIE) and dissident urban social movements. This repression is rooted in the government's embrace of an extractivist model of capitalist development and its dependence on foreign direct investment, an embrace – and dependency – that has led the government to take the side of multinational corporations in the extractive sector in their conflict with the communities on the extractive frontier.

During the commodity boom from 2006 to 2012, Correa expanded health, education, and welfare provisions, while limiting the power of the coastal elite in Guayaquil. With the end of the boom and a subsequent decline in prices, Correa attempted to weaken left-wing and trade union opposition by passing restrictive labor legislation and extending petrol exploration into the highlands where the indigenous communities are concentrated.

In November 2013, trade unions, especially those in the public sector, formed a "United Workers Front" to protest Correa's legislation designed to curtail the organization of independent public sector unions. In the 2014 municipal elections, the right-wing oligarchical parties defeated Correa in the major cities including Guayaquil, Quito, and Cuenca. Once again, CONAIE and the trade unions focused their attack on Correa and ignored the fact that the beneficiaries of his decline were the neoliberal hard-Right. In June 2015, the hard-Right, led by the mayor of Guayaquil, Jaime Nebot, and millionaire banker Guillermo Lasso, led a series of massive protests over a progressive inheritance tax. They sought to oust Correa via a coup. Pachakutik supporters participated in the protests. CONAIE attacked Correa and called for an uprising rather than backing his progressive inheritance tax.

In other words, the antiextractive indigenous-labor coalition, the United Workers Front and CONAIE, favored the ousting of Correa and rejected many of his policies but facilitated the ascent to power of the traditional oligarchical Right.

The class struggle in Latin America as elsewhere over the years has unfolded in cycles that reflect changes in the correlation of forces in different conjunctures of the capitalist development process, forces that can be mobilized either toward the right or the left depending on the relative strength of these forces.

We can identify four major cycles in this struggle over the past six decades of capitalist development – three decades under the agency of the state (state-led development) followed by three decades under the sway of the neoliberal model of free-market capitalism. In the first two decades of this development process, the class struggle took the form of a struggle by organized labor for higher wages (a fair share of the fruits of the workers' labor) and improved working conditions, a struggle by proletarianized peasants for land, and to reclaim their right to pursue their rural livelihood based on agriculture. Over the course of these decades, both the labor movement and the land struggle were somewhat successful in bringing about a decided if only relative improvement in the social condition of their members. However, by the end of the 1970s both movements had been either defeated or brought to ground, their capacity to organize and their forces of resistance disarticulated. Under these conditions, with the political left in disarray and the political right on the offensive and in full control of the state apparatus, the movement for revolutionary change gave way to a neoconservative counter-revolution that halted and to some extent reversed the gains made by the peasantry and the working class over the previous decades.

With this change in the correlation of force in the class struggle, the 1980s in Latin America, on the periphery of the world capitalist system, saw the steady advance of capital in both agriculture and industry, a resulting destruction of the forces of production in both sectors reflected in what has been analyzed as "a decade lost to development" (no economic growth, a deterioration in the social condition of people in the popular sector) – and a slow but steady reorganization of the resistance in the countryside. To facilitate the advance of capital, a program of structural reform in macroeconomic policy was imposed on governments in the region, and a new world order was established regarding international relations of trade and the flow of capital. In the 1990s, capital in the form of multinational corporations and foreign direct investment moved into the region big-time, expanding sixfold by volume from 1990 to 1997 – having purchased at bargain basement prices many of the assets of the lucrative state enterprises and banks placed on the auction block. Under these conditions – and within the framework of the Washington Consensus on the virtues of free-market capitalism – the 1990s have been described as the "golden age of US imperialism," with reference to its having facilitated an invasion of capital that by one account resulted in a net outflow of US$100 million over the course of the decade (Saxe-Fernández & Núñez, 2001). The new millennium, however, would see another major change in the correlation of diverse forces in the class struggle – a sea tide change in the politics of this struggle. Conditions of this change included (i) an effective organized resistance against the neoliberal policy agenda mounted by new sociopolitical movements rooted in the peasantry and the rural landless workers, and in some contexts the indigenous communities; (ii) conditions of an economic and political crisis that came to a head in Argentina in 2001; (iii) a resulting disenchantment and widespread rejection across the region of neoliberalism as an economic model; and, at a different level, (iv) a number of changes in the world economy including the ascension of China as an economic power and the demand for natural resources to fuel the rapid growth of the Chinese economy.

Under these conditions, the new millennium opened with the formation of a series of left-leaning regimes that responded to the challenge that the peasant and indigenous social movements provided to the existing neoliberal regimes and the political forces ranged in their support. Taking advantage of the political opening provided by the social movements, and in response to the growing demand in some circles for a more inclusive form of development, center-left postneoliberal regimes with a progressive policy agenda were established in Venezuela (1998), in Argentina and Brazil (2003), and then in Bolivia (2006) and Ecuador (2007). Milestones in the dynamics of sea tide regime change – and resulting utopias and dystopias – include (i) a popular rebellion in Venezuela in 1998 that brought Hugo Chávez to power and with him the Bolivarian Revolution; (ii) an uprising, in 1990 and then again in 2000, of the indigenous nationalities and communities of Ecuador organized in the form of CONAIE; it placed the neoliberal policy agenda on the defensive not only in Ecuador but throughout the region, creating conditions that would bring to power a series of "progressive" postneoliberal policy regime and Correa's "citizens" revolution; (iii) in Bolivia, a period of revolutionary ferment (2000–2005) marked by the gas and water wars, the rise of Evo Morales to power, the creation of the Movement for Socialism (MAS) as an instrument for the sovereignty of the people, and the formation in 2006 of a new multiethnic and plurinational political regime backed by the social movements and oriented toward "socialism" and a postdevelopment model of "living well" in solidarity and harmony; (iv) in Argentina, the transmutation of an economic crisis – with its low point in 2001 – into a political crisis, giving rise to a historic movement of unemployed workers (*los piqueteros*) and in 2003 a "progressive" political regime headed by the Kirchners; (v) the emergence of "local initiatives of organization for taking and exercising popular power," "virulent street protests of rejection of decisions made by the national and transnational power" and widespread resistance albeit in "subterranean" forms and localized arenas (Gaudichaud, 2016; Zibechi, 2012); (vi) a turnaround in the fortunes and the capacity of the US imperial state to dictate or influence policy marked by the emergence of anti-imperial regimes in Argentina, Brazil, Bolivia, and Ecuador as well as Venezuela; and (vii) the rejection, in 2005, of the proposed Free Trade Area of the Americas (FTAA/ALCA).

Even though the United States lost access to military bases in Ecuador and Bolivia, it has refigured its military alliances in the region – expanding its bases in Peru and Paraguay as well as Honduras – and succeeded in the project of rejigging a free trade regime in the form of the Trans-Pacific Free Trade Alliance. The capacity of the United States to exercise its imperial power – both the hard power of military force and the soft power of development assistance and cooptation – has drastically diminished in the region. In this context of diminished imperial power, the United States continues its policy of supporting various attempted coups (in Honduras and Venezuela) and right-wing economic destabilization efforts (Venezuela), and strategic support of US-based capital in its Latin

American operations, it has had to rely more and more on trickle-down economics in the form of assistentialist neodevelopmentalism – tacit support for the new economic model of inclusionary state activism.

The End of the Progressive Cycle?

The class-ethnic alliances in Bolivia and Ecuador have had divergent outcomes. In the former, they brought to power the center-left government headed by Evo Morales. In the latter, they led to opportunist alliances, political defeats, and ideological chaos. The class struggle from below has led to a variety of political outcomes, some more progressive than others. But, despite the claims of some popularly elected presidents like Evo Morales, none resulted in a worker–peasant–indigenous regime.

The class struggle over the past two decades took a cyclical pattern, rising in opposition to right-wing neoliberal regimes (De la Rua in Argentina, Cardoso in Brazil, Sánchez de Lozado in Bolivia, Mahuad in Ecuador), but then ebbing with the coming to power of a new cycle of center-left regimes. The exception here was Ecuador, where the main protagonists of the class struggle backed the rightist regime of Lucio Gutiérrez before falling into disarray.

The key to the success of the center-left regimes was the decade-long boom in commodity prices, which allowed them to dampen the class struggle by piecemeal assistentialist welfare reforms as well as an increase in wages and salaries. However, the incremental reforms weakened the revolutionary impulses from below. The decompression of the class struggle and the channeling of the struggle into institutional channels led to the co-option of sectors of the popular leadership and the separation of economic demands from struggles for popular political power.

From a historical perspective, the class struggle for a time succeeded in securing significant reductions in unemployment and poverty increases in social spending and the securing of legal recognition. At the same time, the leaders of the class-based movements abided by the extractive capitalist model and its devastating impact on the environment, the economy, and communities of indigenous people. Minority sectors of the popular movements in Brazil struggled against the Workers' Party regime's devastation of the Amazon rainforest and the displacement of indigenous communities. In Bolivia, President Evo Morales spoke at international forums in defense of *Pachamama* and in Bolivia opened the TIPNIS national reserve to oil and mining exploitation, committing matricide! Likewise, in Argentina President Cristina Fernández faced limited trade union opposition when she signed a major agreement with Monsanto to further deepen genetic altered grain production and a major oil agreement with Chevron-Exxon to exploit oil and gas exploitation by fracking in the *Vaca Muerta* (Dead Cow) complex. In Ecuador, the CONAIE-Gutierrez agreement and subsequent support of Correa led to a deepening of ecological degradation and diminished opposition to Correa's extractive capitalism.

The biggest blow to the extractive capitalist model did not come from the class struggle but from the world market. The decline of commodity prices led to the large-scale reduction of the flow of overseas extractive capital. However, that decline also weakened the center-left and led to a resurgence of the class struggle from above. In Argentina, Bolivia, Ecuador, and Brazil, the upper classes organized large-scale street protests and were victorious in municipal and state elections. In contrast, the class struggle organizations remain wedded to defensive economic struggles over wages and welfare cuts by their former allies on the center-left.

In this situation we can observe the rise of the class struggle from above under conditions that included the demise of several center-left regimes, the economic crises of a commodity-based extractive capitalist development model, and the cooptation and or demobilization of the class struggle organizations.

In Brazil, Argentina, Ecuador, and Bolivia, the class struggle advanced from above in seeking to oust the center-left from the administration and the legislature and reimpose neoliberal free trade policies. They sought to reverse social spending and progressive taxation, dismantle regional integration, and reinstate repressive legislation. The election in Argentina was the clearest signal of this change in the correlation of force in the class struggle. Over the subsequent five-year period 2015–2019, we saw the return of the hard neoliberal right in the presidency of Macri, the break-up of tripartite (labor, capital, government) cooperation, and the return of bipartite capital–state rule.

Cut loose from easy negotiations involving steady incremental gains, the popular movements combined the struggle for short-term gains with demands for long-term structural changes. Revolutionary class consciousness is likely to emerge in some situations.

The return of the Right resulted in regressive socioeconomic measures across the board, intensifying the class struggle as a result. For example, almost immediately on assuming power the new Macri government embarked on a rapid-fire series of conservative economic reforms, threatening public-sector employment and social programs. By March 2016, with Macri barely three months in office, 200,000 state workers had been fired and 54,000 workers were laid off just in the construction industry. These and other such policy measures can be expected not only to spark a working-class revolt but to bring together disparate sectors of the urban and rural working population. The stage was set to put in motion the dynamics of another revolutionary class struggle (Katz, 2023).

The demise of the neoliberal era was signaled by the rise to power of Hugo Chávez in Venezuela and the emergence of postneoliberal regimes in South America. The clearest expression of this "reflux in the post-neoliberal decade" – to use Gaudichaud's expression – was Macri's elevation to the presidency in the 2015 elections, which not only led to a regime that was ideologically committed to a return of the neoliberal policy agenda and friendly relations with the United States, but according to some Latin American pundits (see, e.g., James Petras), reflected a clear change in the correlation of force in the regional context of the class struggle.

Chapter 6 elaborates on the significance of this electoral contest, but its meaning is clear enough: the end of the progressive cycle. A return of the Right also took place in Brazil where President Dilma Rousseff appointed a neoliberal "Chicago Boy" economist, Joaquin Levy, as finance minister and launched an IMF-style regressive structural adjustment policy designed to reduce social expenditures and attract financial speculators. His failure led to his early retirement from office. The Right also gained momentum in Ecuador because of the government's rhetoric regarding *buen vivir* and extractivism. In Peru, the daughter of Fujimori, the author of one of the most drastic neoliberal programs, representing diverse interests on Peru's neoliberal middle class and the Far Right, led the polls for the next presidential election. As it turned out, another right-wing hardliner (Pedro Pablo Kuczynski) won the elections. Even in Venezuela, where President Maduro attempted to assiduously stay the course of a socialist-oriented Bolivarian revolution under pressures from both within and without, under pressure from a violent capitalist class offensive launched in February 2014, the government was forced to turn toward a production pact with capital. Washington had channeled millions of dollars to parties on the Far Right and violent extra-parliamentary and paramilitary groups as a means of destabilizing the center-left Maduro government. This aided the right-wing Democratic Unity Movement (MUD) in its victory in the legislative elections in December 2015 by a better than a two to one margin over the Chavista Venezuelan United Socialist Party (PSUV).

In support of this diagnosis and prognosis, progressive social legislation in the region had come to a virtual halt, even before the recent political advances of the US-backed right-wing parties with their neoliberal economic agenda. However, paralysis and even retreat – and several electoral defeats of center-left regimes – did not mean a return to the neoliberal 1990s, the heyday of US imperialism in the region, a period of privatizations, pillage, and plunder that plunged millions into poverty, unemployment, and marginality.

Whatever the recent voting results and the situation on the front of electoral politics, the collective memory of hardship resulting from "free-market" neoliberal policies were seared in the memory of the working population. Evidence of this was the immediate and subsequent responses of the social and political left both in Argentina and elsewhere to Macri's ascension to political power. In less than three months after taking office and after firing nearly 200,000 public employees, Macri faced a general strike convoked by all the trade union confederations.

In this context any attempt by the newly elected officials to "unmake and reverse" the social advances of the past decade met with militant resistance, if not open class warfare, as well as a range of institutional and political constraints. Also, a careful analysis of the policies proposed by the neoliberal right suggests that their implementation and impact demonstrated their failure and the rapid demise of any new right-wing offensive, aborting the reflux of the neoliberal policy agenda.

Conclusion

The victory of Macri in Argentina and the right-wing coup in Brazil did not, as many had predicted, augur a new conservative cycle in Latin American politics. For one thing, Macri's economic team soon faced mass opposition and lacked any political support outside the upper-class neighborhoods. Their policies polarized the country and undermined the stability that investors seek. Brutal devaluations and the end of capital controls was a recipe for inciting general strikes. Conflict, stagnation, and hyperinflation put an end to the enthusiasm of local and foreign investors. Moreover, Macri could embrace Washington because Argentina's natural trading partner is China. The Macri regime was the beginning and the end of a reversion to neoliberal disaster, like what took place at the end of the 1990s.

As for the PT, its fall from grace was more a product of judicial prosecution than the action of trade unions and social movements that opened political space for new working-class struggles free from the constraints of corrupt leaders and bureaucrats. The Right's return to power in Brazil was tainted with the same corruption; its capitalist partners were in jail or faced prosecution. In other words, the fall of the PT was only part of the decline and decay of all the capitalist parties.

Over time, the crisis of the "New Right" might yet stimulate the formation of a new authentic Left that is free from corruption and links to big business. Under these conditions an authentic working-class party may emerge that pursues socioeconomic policies that will put an end to the exploitation of labor and the pillaging of the country's natural resources and the public treasury. In other words, a Left that in word and deed sustains the environment and respects nature and the rights of Afro-Brazilians, indigenous people, and women.

Chapter 5

The Class Struggle in Peru, 2021–2023

Jan Lust

Introduction

The election in 2021 of Pedro Castillo as Peru's first leftist president came as a surprise. However, a closer look at the development of the left-wing forces over the first two decades of the new millennium, and a series of corruption scandals as well as a political crisis of the Right (2017–2020) and the socioeconomic impact of the coronavirus (2019–2021), help us to understand the victory of the Left in the presidential elections. The electoral triumph of the political Left also demonstrates that the negative political impact of the armed struggle in the 1980s and 1990s has lost its influence on the electorate.

It is important to underline that since progressive military dictatorship of Juan Velasco (1968–1975), Peru's political history, and certainly the history of the Left in general terms, did not follow the same path as in other South American countries. For instance, the military dictatorship of the years between 1968 and 1980 was totally different from the dictatorships in Uruguay, Argentina, and Bolivia. While in most of the South American countries in the 1980s the strategy of armed struggle was a something of the past (the "armies of national liberation" and revolutionary movements of the 1960s and 1970), in Peru it restarted after the failed guerrilla struggles of the 1960s. In addition, the battles that were organized by the *Partido Comunista del Peru, Por el Luminoso Sendero de José Carlos Mariátegui*, commonly known as the Shining Path, in the period 1980–1992, had no precedents in Latin America at the level of ideology and brutality.

In the 1980s, various South American countries adhered to the neoliberal policy agenda of structural reform designed by economists at the World Bank and the IMF. Peru, on the other hand, pursued a more heterodox liberal policy agenda during the first regime of Alan García (1985–1990), who represented the political party *Alianza Popular Revolucionaria Americana* (APRA). It was the election in 1990 of Alberto Fujimori as president of the country that introduced Peru to a harsh neoliberal policy regime of austerity measures and structural reforms (on this policy regime see Chossudovsky, 1997). The "fall" of Fujimori in 2000, and the liberalization of political life after a decade of political repression of the progressive forces under the umbrella of parliamentary democracy, opened the possibilities for increased political activities of the Left.

The augmented open and public participation of the Left in political life almost resulted in the victory of the nationalist candidate Ollanta Humala in the presidential elections of 2006. García, who by that time had succumbed to the neoliberal policy virus, beat Humala in the second round, and so the neoliberal extractivist development model, which was implemented by Fujimori in the 1990s, continued to be in force in Peru as virtually all the other countries in the Andes and the Southern Cone succumbed to the pink tide of progressive policy reform. The electoral victory of Humala in 2011 demonstrated an increased acceptance by the citizenry of the proposals of the Left, although the nationalist government continued to pursue the dominant neoliberal model. It was the election of Castillo in 2021 that brought Peru "into line" with the other countries in the region.

In this chapter, we delve into the class struggle in the period 2020–2023, as manifest in the battles between the Left and the Right just before, during, and after the leftist government of Pedro Castillo. We begin with a characterization of the economic development process in Peru over the past twenty years. We then turn to the victory of the Left in the presidential elections of 2021. At issue in these elections is the class struggle that preceded Castillo's assumption of state power and the effect of the change in the Left's political strategy implemented in the 1980s. The following two sections study Castillo's cabinets, the class position of the political Right, the politics of economic sabotage, and the reasons for Castillo's fall. In the last two sections we examine the mass mobilizations at the end of 2022, and in 2023 the rise of a new social movement and the return of the Right to governmental power. In the last section, we present our conclusions.

The Economics of Exploitation and Inequality

The Peruvian economy depends on its growth on the export of its natural resources, principally mining products, and foreign direct investments (FDI) in the country's extractive sectors. The increase or decrease in the price of Peru's commodities in the international markets, and the evolution of China's demand for the country's mineral resources, are decisive factors in the evolution of Peru's economy – in the pattern of economic growth, economic slowdown, and even degrowth (Dancourt, 2016; Gonzales de Olarte, 1986). They are also critical factors in the evolution of the government's fiscal revenues and its ability to finance its development and social programs (Lust, 2019a). In Fig. 5.1, real gross domestic product (GDP) growth rates are presented for the years between 2000 and 2022. The data illustrate the dependent character of the Peruvian economy.

The surprisingly robust growth rates in the period 2004–2011 were the result of the commodities boom. As for the reduction in the rate of economic growth

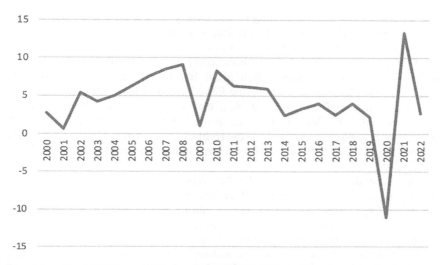

Fig. 5.1. Real GDP growth rates: 2000–2022. *Source*: "Producto bruto interno por tipo de gasto (variaciones porcentuales reales) – PBI", Banco Central de Reserva del Perú. Available at <https://estadisticas.bcrp.gob.pe/estadisticas/series/anuales/resultados/PM04923AA/html/2000/2022/>

in 2009, it was caused by the international financial crisis. The reduction in the GDP growth rates as of 2011 was a direct consequence of the slowdown in the economic growth rate of the Chinese economy, whereas the data on degrowth in 2020 can be traced back to the impact of the coronavirus. Overall, in the period 2000–2022, mining contributed from 46 to 63 percent of total export value.

The Peruvian economy is a dependent economy. Its dependency is founded on an international division of labor that in general terms leads to uneven development – the industrial development of countries at the center of the world system – while limiting the same development for others on the periphery. The dependent economies within the international division of labor are subjugated by conditions induced by the development process in the metropolitical centers of the world capitalist system (Dos Santos, 1986, p. 305). However, Peru's economic extractive development model is not the direct consequence of the country's position and role in the world economy, that is, its endowment of abundant mineral resources, but rather is the result of the power and the class hegemony of extractive capital in the economy as well as the government's alliance with neoliberal policymakers since the 1990s (Lust, 2019b, pp. 119–226).

Peru's role in the globalized capitalist world as a provider of mineral resources for capitalist development abroad is only one part of the country's insertion in the world economy. It is also a provider of cheap labor, that is, the Peruvian labor-force participates in global processes of outsourcing, what are called "global value chains." While the primary function of Peru's economy is fulfilled by the transnational companies operating in the country, a secondary role was assumed by a complex of micro, small, and medium-sized business enterprises.

The insertion of the country's workforce in global processes of outsourcing implies that it is participating in cutthroat competition to "pimp their cheap labor to Northern lead firms" (Smith, 2016, p. 84). But it should be underlined that the relatively low educational levels of the Peruvian workforce – around 80 percent of the population of 25 years and older have only a secondary level of education (Lust, 2023, p. 170) – is expressed in the fact that in the period 2000–2019 manufacturing exports were mainly low-technology intensive manufactures.[1] FDI inflows are mainly in the extractive sector, finance, and communication (Lust, 2023, p. 85).

The dependent character of the Peruvian economy is reproduced in the internal structure of the economy. It has enormous nontradable sectors with an overwhelming number of microenterprises and a relatively small manufacturing sector. Hence, economic dynamism can only come from the extractive sectors, mainly mining. FDI fortifies the national internal economic structure.

The question of the nontradable sectors brings us to the overall business structure of the Peruvian economy. It is important to point out that most of the country's laborforce is employed in microenterprises in the informal sector. These enterprises are characterized by low productivity, a lack of investments in technology, a workforce based on manual labor, and remuneration just above or below the official minimum wage level (Lust, 2019c, p. 782). In Table 5.1, we present the number of private formal companies according to sales for the years 2012 and 2020.

Table 5.1. Private Formal Companies According to Sales, 2012, 2020.

	Micro Companies	Small Companies	Medium-sized and Big Companies
2012	1,557,700	61,322	9,582
2020	2,651,740	101,926	15,534

Sources: INEI (2014, 2015, 2016, 2017, 2018, 2019, 2020, 2021).

A microcompany is valued at a maximum rate of 150 Taxation Units. The annual sales of a small company lie between 150 and 1,700 Taxation Units. The sales of medium-sized and large companies are higher than 1,700 Taxation Units. The value of 1 (one) Taxation Unit varies year by year. For instance, in 2012, it was around US$1,363 and in 2015 US$1,206 (although the Taxation Unit in *sales* increased, the reduction is caused by the depreciation of the Peruvian currency).

---

[1]*Source:* See for these data the United Nations Comtrade Database, which can be found here: https://comtrade.un.org/data/. We also used the statistics provided by the Department of Economic and Social Affairs of the United Nations. These data can be found here: https://unstats.un.org/wiki/download/attachments/79008899/Trade%20grouped%20by%20technology-intensiveness.pdf?api=v2 (consulted 19/03/2022).

Remuneration just above or below the official minimum wage level is an indication of superexploitation. However, the problem of superexploitation can be generalized.

In 2022, the poverty line (the basket of basic food and non-foodstuffs) for a family of four stood around US$437 (US$109 for every individual). According to data from the Peruvian Bureau of Statistics and Informatics (INEI for its acronym in Spanish), in the period April 2022–March 2023, the average labor income was US$412.[2] The nominal minimum wage was set at US$270.

Although it seems that the nominal minimum wage level would be sufficient to finance the monthly basket of basic food and non-foodstuffs for one person, it is not sufficient to sustain a family of four. Also, the average labor income is insufficient. This situation obliges more than one family member to labor for income. In addition, since in 2022 more than 70 percent of the Peruvian working population was informal[3] and supposedly earned a remuneration around the nominal minimum wage level, it might be concluded that most of the country's Economically Active Population is superexploited.

In Peru, superexploitation is institutionalized. This means that the state accepts that individuals receive payments that are not sufficient to reproduce their labor power. Data for the period 2004–2019 show that in companies that employ between one and ten individuals (excluding the independent worker), around 80–90 percent of these workers earned a wage below the officially established minimum wage level.[4] In addition, labor regimes have been implemented in accordance, among others, with the size of the company in which one is employed. In general terms, workers in microenterprises have lesser rights than individuals employed in big or transnational companies (Lust, 2023, pp. 156–157).

The role of Peru in the international division of labor and the key function of the export of mineral resources and FDI in the extractive sectors for economic development, a state dominated by extractive capital and a superexploited working-class, are determinant factors in the overall economic and social panorama of the last 20 years. Within different sectors of the Left, Castillo's presidency was considered a possibility for structural and radical social transformation. But it did not turn out that way. The next sections are about what happened since the electoral victory of Castillo.

---

[2]*Source:* An article published on the governmental website www.gob.pe. This article was titled: "Población ocupada del país alcanzó 17 millones 27 mil 200 personas en el primer trimestre del presente año." See for this article: https://www.gob.pe/institucion/inei/noticias/818665-poblacion-ocupada-del-pais-alcanzo-17-millones-27-mil-200-personas-en-el-primer-trimestre-del-presente-ano (consulted 10/11/2023).

[3]*Source:* An article published on the website of ComexPerú, a business association. The article was titled: "Informalidad laboral peruana continúa al alza: ¿cómo nos posicionamos en la región?" See for this article: https://www.comexperu.org.pe/articulo/informalidad-laboral-peruana-continua-al-alza-como-nos-posicionamos-en-la-region (consulted 10/11/2023).

[4]*Source:* National Institute of Statistics and Informatics, Household Surveys of Peru, 2004–2019.

The Victory of the Left in the Presidential Elections of 2021

The electoral victory of Pedro Castillo cannot be considered a surprise. However, the victory of a political party that openly declared itself Marxist definitively caused a shock on the political Right. This party, *Perú Libre*, had the stated intention to contribute to a process that would convert Peru into a socialist country.[5] Since the decade of left-wing oriented armed struggle of the 1980s, any reference to socialism had been stigmatized by the Right and transmitted to the population through its mass communication channels.

The triumph of the Left is in part the result of the slow increase of its popular support. Already in 2006, the nationalist candidate Ollanta Humala succeeded with the help of the progressive forces to participate in the second round of the presidential elections. Alan García, the candidate of the former social-democratic organization APRA, won the elections. Five years later, Humala accomplished his plan to become president. Backed by the Left, he succeeded in beating the right-wing candidate, Keiko Fujimori, the daughter of the president who turned Peru toward neoliberalism. Without any real political organizational insertion in the population as expressed in the presence of party committees in popular districts, in the 2016 presidential elections the Left obtained about 20 percent of the valid vote. In 2021, in the first round of the presidential elections, the Left obtained 26 percent of the vote; 18.9 percent corresponded to the candidacy of Castillo.

The victory of the Left was an electoral rather than a social victory. This means that it was not a product of a sustained qualitative increase in the dynamics of class struggle. The Left won the elections, but not the minds of the population. The small electoral progress of the self-declared progressive forces since 2016 indicates the weak social support for Castillo's political proposals and intentions. In Table 5.2, data are presented on the number of strikes, the number of workers involved in these strikes, and the man-hours lost due to these strikes in the period 2001–2020.

Table 5.2. Strikes, Workers Involved, and Man-hours Lost, 2001–2020.

Year	Strikes	Workers Involved	Man-hours Lost
2001	40	11.050	488.930
2002	64	22.925	912.648
2003	68	37.323	881.362
2004	107	29.273	582.328
2005	65	19.022	478.738
2006	67	19.565	446.584

---

[5]This information has been taken from a document that presents the ideology and program of the political party *Perú Libre*. For this document see: http://perulibre.pe/wp-content/uploads/2020/03/ideario-peru-libre.pdf (consulted 13/09/2023).

Table 5.2. (*Continued*)

Year	Strikes	Workers Involved	Man-hours Lost
2007	73	48.096	2,216.520
2008	63	34.011	1,520.960
2009	99	36.114	1,452.466
2010	83	30.606	1,279.380
2011	84	26.770	1,799.416
2012	89	25.845	1,878.696
2013	94	26.736	1,573.202
2014	95	40.681	3,153.018
2015	47	32.066	1,925.632
2016	41	20.463	3,084.056
2017	45	56.610	3,006.494
2018	54	21.496	738.864
2019	67	110.154	2,085.856
2020	23	126.868	3,653.184

Source: Ministerio de Trabajo y Promoción de Empleo (2020).

The data in Table 5.2 show that in the five years before the electoral win of Castillo, the number of strikes did not increase. However, the number of individuals involved in these strikes in 2019 and 2020 did grow substantially. The man-hours lost in these years are the same as in 2014, 2016, and 2017. In Fig. 5.2, the data are presented on the registered number of monthly social conflicts in the period January 2018–July 2021. A structural increase of social conflicts before the election of Pedro Castillo cannot be determined.

The fact that the Left achieved state power because of an electoral rather than social victory is the consequence of a change in the strategic conceptions of what might be called the socialist Left. These changes can be brought back to the beginning of the 1980s with the return of parliamentary democracy after 12 years of military dictatorship.

The participation of the Left in the presidential and municipal elections of 1980 helped to bring about changes in the conceptions of how to advance the struggle for a socialist society. While in the years before the Left had worked underground, some of its representatives now had been elected to form part of the Senate and the Chamber of Deputies. So, instead of fighting against the bourgeois political system, the Left began forming part of it. Roberts (1996, p. 84) writes that the electoral success of the left-wing electoral alliance *Izquierda Unida* (IU) forced the organization to consider the possibility of assuming governmental responsibility nationally within the institutional confines of the "bourgeois" state. This prospect proved to be highly divisive. Success also required leftist parties that had specialized in conspiratorial organization, social protest, and demands to

90 Latin American Politics in the Neoliberal Era

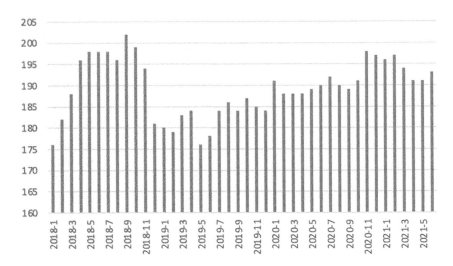

Fig. 5.2. Number of monthly social conflicts: January 2018–June 2021.
Sources: Reporte De Conflictos Sociales N.° 209, Julio 2021. Available at <https://www.defensoria.gob.pe/wp-content/uploads/2021/08/Reporte-Mensual-de-Conflictos-Sociales-N°-209-julio-2021.pdf>; Reporte De Conflictos Sociales N.° 197, Julio 2020. Available at <www.defensoria.gob.pe/wp-content/uploads/2020/08/Reporte-Mensual-de-Conflictos-Sociales-N°-197-julio-2020.pdf>; Reporte De Conflictos Sociales N.° 185, Julio 2019. Available at <https://www.defensoria.gob.pe/documentos/reporte-mensual-de-conflictos-sociales-n-185/>; Reporte De Conflictos Sociales N.° 185, Julio 2019. Available at <www.defensoria.gob.pe/wp-content/uploads/2018/08/Reporte-Mensual-de-Conflictos-Sociales-N°-173-Julio-2018.pdf>

assume positions of authority and implement public policies under severe fiscal and administrative constraints.

During the 1980s, it became clear that the Left was not fully capable of combining parliamentary work with the class struggle outside the buildings of democracy. Although it participated in the struggle of the trade unions and the popular movement in general, it was not able to adequately unite both terrains of class struggle. Responsibilities in the municipalities and issues related to electoral campaigns absorbed all energy, leaving no time for articulating the struggle in and outside the parliamentary institutions, national, regionally, and locally (Lust, 2019b, p. 173).

The return of democracy made political work in the municipalities more important than trade-union work. The party cells or units were no longer really concerned with working in trade unions but started to be more interested in municipal life (Lust, 2019b, p. 173). According to Roberts (1998, p. 247):

> parliamentary politics reinforced party hierarchies and shifted the focus of organizational work from the social terrain to the

electoral sphere. [...] Because their leaders and cadres were preoccupied with congressional tasks and electoral campaigns, the parties became increasingly disengaged from popular struggles in the social sphere.

In conditions of organizational weakness, the political Left embarked on actions that led to the spread and deepening of the neoliberal ideology in society and the cult of entrepreneurship. As we have explained elsewhere, this ideology, disseminated through the means of mass communication, helped create the idea within the proletariat, the peasantry, and the proletarian fraction of the independent intermediate class that the solution to their economic problems was capitalism based on the free and unregulated functioning of the markets (Lust, 2019b, p. 258). Self-employed workers, for instance, began to see themselves as entrepreneurs.

The neoliberal ideology of deregulated markets, privatization of state-owned companies, and the reduced presence of the state in the economy succeeded in entrenching itself in the popular districts. The fact that these policies were introduced by a government (the Fujimori regime of the 1990s) that also turned clientelism into a social policy, contributed to the initial support of the oppressed, and exploited the masses for policies that increased their own oppression and exploitation. In this context, it should be noted that class consciousness contributes to class formation, but the lack of class consciousness contributes to the "declassing" of class.

The electoral Left battled for votes with a political Right that was "fractured, represented by oligarchs, the new rich, opportunists and religious fanatics" (author's translation) (Durand, 2022). The decomposition of the Right, expressed in its fragmentation, made it possible that with a minimum of valid votes, Pedro Castillo and Keiko Fujimori succeeded to pass to the second round of the presidential elections. As already mentioned above, Castillo obtained 18.9 percent of the valid vote. Fujimori had received 13.4 percent of the vote.

The corruption scandals during the presidencies of Pedro-Pablo Kuzcynski (2016–2018) and Martín Vizcarra (2018–2020) also contributed to the fragmentation of the political Right. However, it was, and still is, unified at the level of political ideology, that is, neoliberalism. The political Right is a bloc in power.

Clear evidence of the unity of the political Right can also be demonstrated by their struggle against Pedro Castillo. During the election campaign and when in government, the right-wing organizations joined forces to impeach Castillo and his ministers. Differences between their organizations are caused by personal disputes between the leading individuals. Also, religious points of view or liberal political, social, and economic paradigms can cause differences (Lust, 2023, p. 195). We should point out that currently most of the political Right in the Peruvian Congress is extremely conservative.

The Castillo Government, the Class Position of the Political Right, and Economic Sabotage

The policies that have been developed and implemented during the Castillo presidency lacked a vision of what Castillo and *Perú Libre* really wanted to do with the governmental power they had obtained. The *Perú Libre* program and the governmental program were not really documents that contained a clear political vision. The *Perú Libre* program hinged on different contradicting ideas. On the one hand, it looked for increased state intervention in the economy, and on the other hand, it wanted to maintain the market functioning without state involvement. It might be argued that it wanted to combine the concept of *buen vivir* (living well in social solidarity and harmony with nature) with the principles of a market economy.

The fact that no political proposals were developed or debates initiated that could have started processes that might have led to certain political, economic, and social transformations has first of all to do with the impossibility to govern due to the continuous impeachment procedures against Castillo's ministers initiated by the political Right (70 ministers were replaced in the 500 days that Castillo's presidency endured), the processes that were going on to find enough votes in Congress to impeach Castillo himself (on November 2021 the right-wing opposition presented its first impeachment motion against Castillo), and to gather national and international political and social support for the impeachment of Castillo (Caballero, 2023, pp. 80, 141–146). As a matter of fact, from the outset of his presidency, Castillo faced a ferocious opposition from the majority in Congress to proposals that would harm the political and economic status quo. At the beginning of August 2021 (one week after the beginning of Castillo's presidency), congressmen were talking about the possibility and necessity to impeach him (Caballero, 2023, p. 77).

The first victim of the offensive of the Right was the Minister of Foreign Affairs, Héctor Béjar (within one month after Castillo assumed the presidency of Peru), who had dared to initiate a process that would lead to an autonomous and noninterventionist foreign policy. Further, Béjar proposed that Peru would leave the right-wing American multilateral alliance "Lima Group."

The main reason for the ferociousness of the class struggle prosecuted by the political Right was that extractive capital, especially foreign investments in mining operations, might lose the possibility to continue obtaining super-profits on the investments in the mining sector. The end of what are called fiscal stability pacts that impede the government to change the tax system would mean the end of the incredible profitability of the Peruvian mining sector. The Right considered President Castillo a permanent threat to the interests of the major businesses in the country.

Other factors that impeded the development and possible implementation of proposals were the political and professional weakness of Castillo's ministers. Furthermore, it might be argued that the political and ideological weakness of the Castillo presidency and the lasting attacks by the political Right contributed to Castillo's slow turn toward policies that had no relation with radical processes of political, economic, and social transformation, with the sole objective of securing political oxygen.

Notwithstanding the radical character of the Castillo proposals in his first presidential discourse, especially regarding the Constituent Assembly, on the economic terrain Castillo wanted class peace. For this reason, he not only chose the social democrat Pedro Francke as his Minister of Economics and Finance, but he also ratified the neoliberal Julio Velarde as President of the country's central bank. Velarde is a leading figure of the political Right. Not only he is the chief of the central bank since the start of the Third Millennium, but he was also its director in the years 1990–1992. Both are against a constitutional change. According to Francke, the implementation of the Castillo proposals does not require a change of the constitution.[6]

Apart from the search for class peace, Castillo himself favored national and foreign private investments. He continuously tried to convince the corporations that his government was very open to private capital. Almost at the end of Castillo's governmental period, the president of the central bank assured that the companies "were not afraid anymore of the government," but even so mistrust persisted.[7]

In contrast to the efforts to convince capital of the good intentions of the Castillo cabinets, proposals related to labor questions had a more radical character. At the Ministry of Labor and the Promotion of Employment, intentions emerged that proposed to eliminate special and temporary labor contracts, and to reinstall collective negotiations in the public sector.[8]

The principal measure elaborated during the government of Castillo was related to the question of outsourcing. The government considered it an attack on labor rights. Hence, it proposed that the principal activities of a company were not allowed to be outsourced.[9] This proposal was in line with the requirements to form part of the organization of advanced capitalist countries, the Organisation for Economic Co-operation and Development.[10]

Perú Libre considered mining to be very important for the country's progress. In line with some of the policies implemented by the former president Rafael Correa of Ecuador and Evo Morales of Bolivia, it wanted to use the financial resources that could be obtained from the extraction of mineral resources to increase social welfare. In other words, it sought to change neoliberal extractivism

---

[6]*Source:* An article that was published in the Peruvian newspaper *La República*. This article was titled: "Medidas económicas no requieren cambiar la constitución." See for this article: https://larepublica.pe/economia/2021/08/12/pedro-francke-medidas-economicas-no-requieren-cambiar-la-constitucion (consulted 19/07/23).

[7]*Source:* An article that was published in the Peruvian newspaper *La República*. This article was titled: "Julio Velarde: 'Empresarios ya no le temen al gobierno.'" See for this article: https://larepublica.pe/economia/2022/11/03/julio-velarde-empresarios-ya-no-le-temen-al-gobierno-pedro-castillo-bcrp-fitch-ratings (consulted 09/07/23).

[8]*Source:* An article that was published in the Peruvian newspaper *La República*. This article was titled: "Negociación colectiva y fin del CAS son bien vistos por Ejecutivo." See for this article: https://larepublica.pe/economia/2021/09/30/negociacion-colectiva-y-fin-del-cas-son-bien-vistos-por-ejecutivo-tribunal-constitucional (consulted 11/07/23).

[9]*Source:* An article in the Peruvian magazine *Semana Económica*. This article was titled: "Empresas no podrán tercerizar trabajadores en su núcleo de negocio." See for this article: https://semanaeconomica.com/que-esta-pasando/articulos/empresas-no-podran-tercerizar-actividades-de-su-nucleo-de-negocio (consulted 11/07/23).

[10]*Source:* An article in the official Peruvian state newspaper *El Peruano*. This article was titled: "5 claves de la nueva norma que prohíbe la tercerización laboral en actividades del núcleo de negocios." See for this article: https://elperuano.pe/noticia/140048-5-claves-de-la-nueva-norma-que-prohibe-la-tercerizacion-laboral-en-actividades-del-nucleo-del-negocio (consulted 29/07/2023).

for progressive extractivism. The party's points of view regarding extractivism were in accordance with what is considered "productivist neoextractivism" (Svampa, 2013, pp. 34–35, 2019). For this reason, the Castillo cabinets did not modify the mining policies in the sense that it changed the relationship between the mining corporations and the peasant communities or that it started a public discussion on the economic and social planning of the Peruvian territory. It only intended to increase mining taxes.

The idea of augmenting the tax payments for mining businesses formed part of the comprehensive tax reform that was presented, in 2021, by the Minister of Economics and Finance. The objective was to increase fiscal pressure and tax income. Not only would the mining companies see their taxes raised, but also individuals. Who earned more would have to pay more.[11] The proposals, elaborated in cooperation with the World Bank, did not prosper in Congress.[12]

At the start of his governmental period, Castillo announced a Second Agrarian Reform.[13] This plan proposed to improve productivity and income through technical assistance, the creation of cooperatives and a bank for agricultural development, and industrialization, among others.[14] We should remember that the agricultural sector is characterized by a massive number of subsistence farmers and the concentration of the land in a few hands (Lust, 2019b, p. 141). No Second Agrarian Reform was implemented, nor were concrete measures developed that would provide the conditions for the reform.

When it turned out that Castillo would be Peru's new president, the value of the US dollar increased immediately. The rise of the dollar was expected because of economic insecurity that caused his election. Furthermore, the election program

---

[11] *Source:* An article that was published in the Peruvian newspaper *La República*. This article was titled: "Reforma tributaria apunta hacia los que más ganan." See for this article: https://larepublica.pe/economia/2021/10/28/reforma-tributaria-apunta-hacia-los-que-mas-ganan-pedro-francke-sunat (consulted 09/07/23).

[12] *Source:* Two articles that were published in the Peruvian newspaper *La República*. These articles were titled: "El MEF alista reforma tributaria para el sector minero y mypes" and "Comisión de Constitución bloquea reforma tributaria." See for these articles: https://larepublica.pe/economia/2021/10/19/el-ministerio-de-economia-y-finanzas-alista-reforma-tributaria-para-el-sector-minero-y-mypes-pedro-francke (consulted 09/07/23) and https://larepublica.pe/economia/2021/12/16/comision-de-constitucion-bloquea-reforma-tributaria-mef-congreso (consulted 09/07/23).

[13] The Second Agrarian Reform supposes a First Agrarian Reform. It is considered that the First Agrarian Reform was implemented during the military government of General Juan Velasco (1968–1975). During this government big landowners were expropriated, and agricultural state companies and cooperatives promoted.

[14] *Sources*: Information taken from the website of the Peruvian Ministry of Agrarian Development and Irrigation. This website can be found here: https://www.gob.pe/institucion/midagri/campa%C3%B1as/6052-segunda-reforma-agraria (consulted 10/07/23) and from an article that was published in the Peruvian newspaper *La República*. This article was titled: "Banca de fomento se enfocaría en el 91% de agricultores sin créditos." See for this article: htttps://larepublica.pe/economia/2021/10/18/banca-de-fomento-se-enfocaria-en-el-91-de-agricultores-sin-creditos-agricultura (consulted 10/07/23).

of *Perú Libre* referred to tax increases for mining businesses, the review of free trade agreements, and a new constitution, among others. Because of the increase of the dollar's value, inflation was starting to rise.

Castillo's election led to economic sabotage in the sense that capital fled the country. According to the President of the Peruvian Central Bank, capital flight in 2021 was the largest experienced in 50 years. Around US$15 billion left the country. However, if we include the "Net Errors and Omissions" account of the Balance of Payments, capital flight in the first three-quarters of 2021 was more than US$20 billion.

Capital flight in combination with a worldwide increase of the US dollar led to a depreciation of the Peruvian currency. The attack on the Peruvian currency was an instrument in the class struggle, that is, in the battle against the possibility of a structural and radical political, economic, and social change (Lust & Cypher, 2021, p. 26).

In 2022, the exchange rate started to stabilize itself at the levels seen before Castillo's rise to governmental power. An increasing trust in the individuals in charge of the economy, such as the Minister of Economics and Finance and the President of the Central Bank, and an increasing conviction that Castillo and *Perú Libre* would not change the political and economic course of Peruvian society, explains the stabilization of the exchange rate of the Peruvian currency.

The Fall of Castillo and the Weakness of the Left

After about 18 months of being harassed by the political Right through continuous impeachment procedures against his ministers and processes of impeachment against himself, the permanent accusations of corruption, and attacks on his family members, Castillo took the decision to take the initiative in the class struggle. Although his government did not form any real threat against the interests of capital, it was the possibility to become a threat that made the political Right fear Castillo in power. Governmental power can become political, economic, and social power when it is able to mobilize the masses. Political state power provides increased possibilities to attain this objective because the political organizations with state power can determine the political and social agenda and have enormous and multiple possibilities to communicate with the population. For this reason, it is of no surprise that large companies helped to organize and finance the social protests against the Castillo regime (Caballero, 2023, pp. 170–171).

The permanent political crisis prevented Castillo from fulfilling the minimum electoral promises outlined in his governmental program. On December 7, 2022, he announced that he would dissolve Congress and call for new congressional elections. This new Congress would have the task of elaborating a new constitution. However, Congress considered the action of Castillo an auto-coup. After he was impeached by right- and left-wing congress members, including members of *Perú Libre*, he was subsequently arrested.

Although one might attribute the fall of Castillo to the political work of sabotage and destruction of the political Right, it was Castillo and the entire Left who were not able to adequately confront the political Right. From his first day in the governmental palace, Castillo was economically and politically self-castrated. This self-castration impeded the implementation of the governmental program. He was economically castrated when he maintained a neoliberal economist as president of the Central Bank and a rightwing Keynesian economist as Minister of Economics and Finance. Castillo was politically castrated when he did not establish a durable political alliance with political forces outside *Perú Libre* and did not create nation-wide political committees to construct popular support for his presidency. In relation to the question of political autocastration, it must be reminded that *Perú Libre*, or its presidential candidate Pedro Castillo, only accumulated 18.9 percent of the valid vote and the left-wing political alliance *Juntos por el Perú*, 7.9 percent. This meant that around 75 percent of the valid vote was not in favor of a left-wing candidate. These results should have formed the basis for a discussion within governmental circles about how to increase the political and social bases of the government.

It can be argued that it was the right choice to maintain mainstream economists in charge of the economy to gain time to develop the political and social forces in order to combat the political Right and capital. However, Castillo failed to avoid political castration because not only *Perú Libre* did not want to share the governmental power with other left-wing organizations, also his advisors and people around him did not have the political power, contacts, and vision to broaden the political base of Castillo. This brings us to the weakness of the Left.

The fact that *Perú Libre* and individuals around Castillo were not really interested in developing a left-wing political front to defend the Castillo presidency and did not create popular base committees cannot only blamed on them. It is the whole of the Left that is guilty of the political and social weakness of the Castillo cabinets. As argued above, as of the 1980s most of the Peruvian Left converted itself into an electoral force. So, having lost the elections when the Left was forced to leave the municipalities, they also lost its political work with the masses.

The results of the regional and municipal elections of 2022 have demonstrated the lack of political and social bases of the Left and of *Perú Libre* in particular. It confirms the simple electoral character of the Peruvian progressive forces. They completely disappeared one year into the Castillo presidency. These results are principally the product of Castillo's economic self-castration or the lack of clear left-wing-oriented governmental policies, expressed in the incapacity of the different Castillo cabinets to implement the governmental program, and the former president's political autocastration or the fact that the Left did not develop and implement a strategy to win most of the population for its proposals after the electoral victory.

When we compare the results of the regional and municipal elections with the presidential elections, it might be concluded that Castillo lost almost 2.2 million votes (presidential elections: 2,724,752 votes), while Verónica Mendoza of *Juntos por el Perú* lost 132,577 votes. In the case of the elections for congress, *Juntos por el Perú* did not lose much. However, *Perú Libre* lost 1.2 million votes (congressional elections: 1,724,303 votes).

Social Protests and a New Social Movement

The impeachment and imprisonment of Castillo gave rise to massive protests against the government of the first female president in Peruvian history, Dina Boluarte. Boluarte had been his vice-president and just like Castillo, she was a former member of *Peru Libre*. While Castillo had *resigned* from the party, Boluarte had been *expelled* from the party, and this was before the events of December 2022.

The population demanded new general elections and a Constituent Assembly. A part of the protests also demanded the release and restitution of Castillo. The protests were a struggle for power instead for economic and social demands.

The demands for new elections and a Constituent Assembly are not surprising if – with reference to the economic model used by the government to make economic policy and the neoliberal constitution of 1993 – one considers the workings of capitalism on the distribution of wealth and income. Data on wealth and income distribution from 2000 to 2020 show that the share of the top one percent of income earners increased from 20.3 to 28.1 percent while the share of the bottom 50 percent over the same period fell from 7.8 to 5.7 percent.[15] Evidently, the economic model used by the government to shape economic and social policy within the framework of the overtly neoliberal constitution of 1993 favored the well-to-do and did not meet the socioeconomic expectations of the mass of the population. The social conditions lived by this population, much of it composed of the working class and the rural poor, gave rise to mass demonstrations and protest actions that over time were increasingly organized, mobilized primarily not by the unions or the political Left but the peasant and indigenous communities from the regions who had assumed the leadership of the growing protest and resistance movement.

The protests were initiated and led by the population from the southern regions of the country (Puno, Ayacucho, Andahuaylas, and Cusco). The principal electoral bases of the Left and Castillo were located in these regions.[16] The leadership of those regions in the protests against the Boluarte government appears to be caused by the identification of these populations with Castillo, a rural schoolteacher, and the overt racist attitude of leading individuals in Congress during Castillo's 18 months in government (Béjar, 2023, pp. 46–47; Quiroz & Beraun, 2023, pp. 176–177).[17]

From December 2022 until March 2023, massive protests were organized, week after week. The protests were primarily located in the regions and included roadblocks and strikes. On one day, there were even 146 roadblocks (Motta Villegas, 2023, p. 78). The repression against the protests caused the death of more than sixty citizens, some of whom did not even participate in the protests. However, the repression could not stop the protests.

---

[15]*Source:* Data taken from the website of the World Inequality Database. See for this data: https://wid.world/world/#sptinc_p99p100_z/PE/last/eu/k/p/yearly/s/false/19.159000000000002/35/curve/false/country (consulted 21/09/2023).

[16]*Source:* Data taken from the website of the Peruvian National Office of Electoral Processes (ONPE for its acronym in Spanish). See for this data: https://resultadoshistorico.onpe.gob.pe/SEP2021/EleccionesPresidenciales/RePres/P/200000 (consulted 21/09/2023).

[17]*Source:* Information taken from an article that was published by the Peruvian News agency PrensaPeru.pe. This article was titled: "María del Carmen Alva, discrimina al presidente del Perú, Pedro Castillo, saluda a unos y a otros no, por ser andinos." See for this information: https://prensaperu.pe/2021/08/12/maria-del-carmen-alva-discrimina-al-presidente-del-peru-pedro-castillo-saluda-a-unos-y-a-otros-no-por-ser-andinos/ (consulted 21/09/2023).

The epicenter of the mass demonstrations was Peru's capital city Lima. At the end of March, the protests started to diminish. Not only in Lima, but also in the regions. The government did not flinch, and the protesters needed to go to work again.

The decentralized organization of the protests, and the fact that no specific or clear leadership could be identified, favored the organization of the protests and the participation of the people from all regions. It obliged the periodical organization of centralized meetings of the regional movements. One of the biggest meetings took place in July 2023, with 700 representatives from all over the country.[18]

Notwithstanding the activities of coordination, the decentralized organization of the protests made it relatively difficult for individuals who were not involved in the organization to exactly know when and where the demonstrations started. Social media was the principal means of diffusion.

The continuing protests against the government, a consequence of the unwillingness of the government and Congress to move the general elections to the first half of 2023 and their refusal to organize a referendum on the question of a new constitution, contributed negatively to economic development. In the first half of 2023, the economy contracted by 0.4 percent and 0.5 percent in the second half.

It should be underlined that it was not the left-wing-oriented political parties who were the main organizers of the protests, but the peasant and indigenous communities from the regions. The social movement against Boluarte and Congress politically saved the electoral Left – the communist, socialist, and social-democratic parties.

For about three decades, the electoral Left showed itself to be incapable of organizing the masses. For this reason, it might be argued that if the communities in the regions would not have started to protest, there would not have been any protest at all. According to former Minister of International Relations of the Castillo government, Béjar, "it is a popular, grassroots movement, much broader than the political left." However, "it is also true that most militants of the different existing left-wing organizations are fully committed to supporting this popular movement."[19]

The protests organized by the social movements from the regions did not recognize the leadership of any one organization but rather that of a multitude (Quiroz & Beraun, 2023, p. 136). It seems as if we are at the beginning of a process that might lead to a second independence, that is, the independence of the regions from Lima, the end of internal colonialism and the creation of a plurinational people's state (Béjar, 2023, p. 47).

---

[18] *Source:* Comisión Organizadora del I Encuentro de las 26 Regiones, "Conclusiones del I Encuentro Nacional de los Pueblos y Organizaciones del Perú." See for these conclusions: https://es.scribd.com/document/663231908/Conclusiones-del-Primer-Encuentro-Nacional-de-los-Pueblos-y-Organizaciones-Sociales-del-Peru/ (consulted 03/04/2024).

[19] *Source:* Reference taken from the Argentinian website www.resumenlatinoamericano.org. See for this reference: https://www.resumenlatinoamericano.org/2023/01/18/peru-hector-bejar-peru-vive-momento-constituyente-de-un-nuevo-sistema/ (consulted 27/09/2023).

The Return of the Right

The Boluarte regime is an authoritarian right-wing government. The massive repression and dozens of deaths among the protesting population led the current president to be labeled as a murderer.[20]

Apart from brutally repressing social protests, the regime also introduced preventive repressive mechanisms. The arrests of members of the Popular Defense Front of Ayacucho based on the accusation of terrorism, the detention of individuals from the regions who were housed in the National University of San Marcos to participate in the national demonstrations that were held in Lima, and the prohibition of demonstrations in the historical center of Lima are some examples of these mechanisms. Furthermore, the politicization of the national police by organizing what are called "Demonstrations for Peace" in Lima, and the public show of force of the repressive forces just before national demonstrations against the regime in Lima,[21] demonstrate the intentions of the regime, in cooperation with Congress to solve sociopolitical problems using repression.

The Boluarte cabinets are made up of individuals that form part of the whole of the political Right. At the time of this writing (October 2023), the regime is governing with the full support of the right-wing-dominated Congress. However, polls at the beginning of January 2023, one month after Boluarte replaced Castillo, show that the vast majority of the population wanted the president and Congress to resign and that new elections should be held as soon as possible.[22] Worldwide, Peruvians are manifesting themselves against the regime.[23]

---

[20] *Sources:* Human Rights Watch: "Deterioro letal. Abusos por las fuerzas de seguridad y crisis democrática en el Perú." See for this article: https://www.hrw.org/es/report/2023/04/26/deterioro-letal/abusos-por-las-fuerzas-de-seguridad-y-crisis-democratica-en-el (consulted 26/09/2023) and CIDH & OAE: "Situación de Derechos Humanos en Perú en el contexto de las protestas sociales." See for this article: https://www.oas.org/es/cidh/informes/pdfs/2023/informe-situacionddhh-peru.pdf (consulted 26/09/2023).

[21] *Source:* An article that was published in the Peruvian newspaper *La República*. This article was titled: "Gobierno busca intimidar a quienes protesten el 19 de julio." See for this article: https://larepublica.pe/politica/gobierno/2023/07/15/dina-boluarte-gobierno-busca-intimidar-a-quienes-protesten-el-19-de-julio-toma-de-lima-protestas-alberto-otarola-fuerzas-armadas-pnp-280005.

[22] *Sources:* Information taken from the website of the Institute for Peruvian Studies (IEP for its acronym in Spanish). The article was titled: "IEP Informe de Opinión – Enero 2023 (Informe Completo)" and can be found here: https://iep.org.pe/noticias/iep-informe-de-opinion-enero-ii-2023/ (consulted 26/09/2023). Another article was titled: "IEP Informe de Opinión – Mayo 2023 (Informe Completo)." This article was published here: https://iep.org.pe/wp-content/uploads/2023/05/Informe-IEP-OP-Mayo-2023-Informe-completo.pdf (consulted 26/09/2023). The last source that was used was titled: "IEP Informe de Opinión – Agosto 2023 (Informe Parcial)." This report was published here: https://iep.org.pe/wp-content/uploads/2023/08/IEP-Informe-de-Opinion-Agosto-2023.-Informe-parcial-280823.pdf (consulted 03/04/2024).

[23] *Source:* Data regarding the public opinion on the Boluarte regime. This data was published on the website of the Peruvian newspaper *La República*. This data can be

The impeachment of Castillo and the reduction of the former governmental party *Peru Libre* to the role of a small opposition party in Congress was definitively in the interests of the principal business groups. Of course, capital really did not have anything to fear from Castillo's presidency, yet some insecurity persisted. Insecurity regarding the economic course of the government immediately vanished when Boluarte replaced Castillo. At the start of her presidency business expressed their trust in the new president.[24] Furthermore, the proposal to prohibit outsourcing of the core activities of the companies was swept off the table.

Notwithstanding the support of the companies and policies in favor of capital, short-term (three months) company expectations in the economy were still much lower than before Castillo's presidency. This has to do with the protest movement and the fragmentation of the political Right. The country's political course is still not clearly defined. The Boluarte regime is governing on a strong authoritarian automatic pilot. In addition, it is interesting to observe that company trust was relatively rapidly restored after the outcome of the first round of the presidential elections. It became clear that Castillo was not a threat to company interests.

The police and military repression of the social protests, the massive detention of protesters, the arbitrary detention of supposed leaders of the protests, the attacks on the independent press, and the massive deployment of police forces only seen in police states had also worked to isolate the regime internationally. Also, criticisms of the handling of the crisis and the violation of human rights denounced by the presidents of Colombia,[25] Mexico,[26] and Chile[27] created

---

found here: https://data.larepublica.pe/encuesta-iep-peru-aprobacion-desaprobacion-presidencia-congreso-de-la-republica-ejecutivo-legislativo/ (consulted 26/09/2023). Another source was an article published on the news website Hispantv.com. The article that was reviewed was titled: "Al grito de 'asesina', interrumpen discurso de Boluarte en Nueva York." See for this article: https://www.hispantv.com/noticias/peru/572285/interrumpen-discurso-boluarte-grito-asesina (consulted 26/09/2023).

[24]*Source:* Information taken from the website *Infobae*. The article that was reviewed was titled: "Gremios empresariales expresan disposición a trabajar con Dina Boluarte para reactivar la economía del Perú." See for this article: https://www.infobae.com/america/peru/2022/12/08/gremios-empresariales-expresan-disposicion-a-trabajar-con-dina-boluarte-para-reactivar-la-economia-del-peru/ (consulted 21/09/2023).

[25]*Source:* An article that was published in the Mexican edition of the Spanish newspaper *El País*. This article was titled: "Perú declara persona 'non grata' al embajador mexicano y lo expulsa el país." See for this article: https://elpais.com/mexico/2022-12-21/peru-declara-persona-non-grata-al-embajador-mexicano-y-lo-expulsa-del-pais.html (consulted 21/09/2023).

[26]*Source:* An article that was published in the Peruvian newspaper *Gestión*. This article was titled: "AMLO vuelve a referirse al Perú y a defender a Pedro Castillo." See for this article: https://gestion.pe/peru/politica/amlo-vuelve-a-referirse-al-peru-y-a-defender-a-pedro-castillo-mexico-celac-noticia/ (consulted 21/09/2023).

[27]*Source:* An article that was published in the Chilean edition of the Spanish newspaper *El País*. This article was titled: "Tensión entre Perú y Chile por las críticas de Gabriel Boric a 'los atropellos' contra las manifestantes." See for this article: https://elpais.com/chile/2023-01-26/tension-entre-peru-y-chile-por-las-criticas-de-gabriel-boric-a-los-atropellos-contra-los-manifestantes.html (consulted 21/09/2023).

diplomatic tensions. Apart from the Latin American presidents, the United Nations also worried about what was going on in Peru and demanded a report on the question of human rights violations.[28] In addition, although the United States expressed its support for the Boluarte regime, the Department of State declared that human rights abuses cannot be committed with impunity. The executive summary of its country report on human rights practices in Peru included the following declaration:

> Significant human rights issues included credible reports of unlawful or arbitrary killings; restrictions on free expression and media, including the existence of criminal libel laws and violence or threats of violence against journalists; serious government corruption; and lack of investigation of and accountability for gender-based violence.[29]

Conclusion

The first left-wing presidency in Peru was a disaster. Not only did it fail to put its program into practice but it also contributed to the return of the Right to governmental power. The current Boluarte regime forms part of the authoritarian trend in Latin American politics as described in this book. It seems that Peru is returning to the darkest episodes of the 1990s, with the police and the armed forces on a permanent state of alert.

Although the presidency of Castillo had never been a threat to the economic interests of Capital, his "fall" ended the possibility of a movement toward a process of political, economic, social, and cultural transformation. Castillo might have become a threat in the case the revolutionary Left would have been able to determine the political course of the different Castillo cabinets or if it would have had an important influence on Castillo.

But the revolutionary Left did not have access to Castillo or his cabinets. Nor did the social-democratic Left have the political capacity to initiate social reforms such as the Second Agrarian Reform. It had no intention of mobilizing the population for these reforms.

The Left's change of political strategy to attain state power, developed in the 1980s, may be considered as the subjective basis of the failure of the progressive

---

[28] *Source:* An article that was published in the Peruvian newspaper *La República*. This article was titled: "ONU pide al gobierno informe por violaciones de derechos humanos en protestas." See for this article: https://larepublica.pe/politica/actualidad/2023/03/01/protestas-en-peru-onu-pide-al-gobierno-informe-por-violaciones-de-derechos-humanos-en-protestas-dina-boluarte-paro-nacional-fuerzas-armadas-amnistia-internacional-47093 (consulted 24/09/2023).

[29] *Source:* A human rights report on Peru for 2022, published by the US Department of State. See for this report: https://www.state.gov/wp-content/uploads/2023/02/415610_PERU-2022-HUMAN-RIGHTS-REPORT.pdf (consulted 26/09/2023).

forces to have a decisive influence on the Castillo government. Consequently, Castillo did not look for popular support but for congressional support.

When Castillo began his presidency, around 75 percent of the electorate was not in favor of a left-wing government. However, instead of implementing policies and actions that would have helped to obtain the support of most of the population, he continuously tried to get along with Congress or to appease the right-wing majority and capital to secure the political oxygen needed to govern. The political Right did not let him govern.

The call for a Constituent Assembly, Castillo's most radical proposal, also did not prosper. This was to be expected because, first, the change of political strategy by the Left in the 1980s implied that it did not put its trust in the mobilization of the masses for social reform. Second, it did not have the majority in Congress.

The return to governmental power by the Right was just a matter of time. Castillo's decision to take the initiative in the class struggle was doomed to fail as he had not created the political and social bases for this decision. This was also impossible because of his political strategy of class peace instead of class struggle.

In the short term, Peru's democratic and social future is bleak. The authoritarian government of Boluarte embodies the attack on the democratic institutions. The massacre of protesters has been the sole tactic used by the government, accompanied by the right-wing dominated Congress, to maintain itself in power. Most of the population are demanding new elections.

Although the political situation is definitively not in favor of the progressive forces, the new emerging social movement can change this in the medium term. As a matter of fact, the "fall" of Castillo has given rise to a new social movement, that is, a movement led by the regions.

The movement is still weak because of its decentralized character but has the potential to grow and even to become hegemonic. Whether the second independence becomes a reality depends on the dynamism of the social movements and the political revolutionary parties with a solid political and social base in the regions.

Chapter 6

The Politics of Social Change in Mexico

The wave of democratization that swept across Latin America in the 1980s revived a waning interest in the study of social movements in the region.[1] By all accounts, this interest has not been dampened by an apparent difficulty in locating and defining, let alone explaining, these movements. There are several dimensions to this difficulty – to what some see as a state of confusion, others a "theoretical impasse," and others again, including the author, a conscious retreat by many intellectuals from the class realities that these movements exhibit.

First, in certain academic circles, there can be found a refusal or failure to confront as a theoretical object the social movements that have formed in the region under conditions generated by the neoliberal economic policies implemented within the institutional framework of the new world order of free market capitalism and globalization. This is evidenced in certain academic circles by a tendency to analyze social movements in purely descriptive terms and to do so without any reference to the institutionalized structures of the operative capitalist system and usually with an analytical focus on a single movement in a particular country and no attempt at comparative analysis. Munck and O'Hearn (1999) describe this tendency as a characteristic feature of most academic studies at the time. In part, this reflects the emergence in the 1980s of a theoretical impasse associated with a postdevelopment rejection of structuralism in all its diverse expressions, including modernization theory, Latin American dependency theory, and Marxist political economy (Munck & O'Hearn, 1999; Schuurman, 1993). The postmodernist/structuralist/Marxist emphasis on subjectivity, heterogeneity, and cultural difference, together with a concern to move beyond the centrality of class in the study of social movements, reinforced a tendency to particularize and describe rather than generalize and theorize the dynamics of the social movements.

---

[1]Burgwal (1990) identified over 500 titles of studies in this area dating back to the early 1980s. Since then, the number of studies has grown dramatically as evident in diverse efforts to catalog and characterize these movements (inter alia, Munck & O'Hearn, 1999).

One outcome of this postmodernist/development perspective has been a trend toward decontextualizing social movements regarding the objectively given or structural conditions generated by the workings of the world capitalist system. Another has been discouragement of a comparative analysis which presupposes shared, that is, structural, conditions. A second characteristic of studies of Latin American social movements is a focus on specific conditions that gave rise to the social movements formed in the 1980s that preceded the advent of the neoliberal world order, and in the 1990s, with reference to the Zapatista insurrection. For the most part, these studies also have not theorized these conditions or made intra- or international comparisons as to the structures that underlie or produce them. In these studies, the cause of social movements is generally found in the institutionalized practices and policies of neoliberal capitalism, but they are generally viewed in culturally specific rather than systemic or structural terms, and in such terms, the social basis of these movements is portrayed or conceived as radically heterogeneous – specific to diverse and distinct social groupings and categories of individuals – while their struggle dynamics are generally reduced to a search for some form of socially constructed collective identity.

The Formation of a New Social Movement – The Zapatista Rebellion

Mexico is a very complex country, with a broad range of class situations and political responses in the form of popular uprisings and diverse social movements to the advance of capitalism in the development process. Although similar movements, mounted by the indigenous communities on the extractive frontier and what remains of the peasantry in Latin America, namely a semiproletariat of landless workers, were formed across the region, particularly in Bolivia, Ecuador but also in Paraguay, none have had the momentous impact of the Zapatista uprising on January 1, 1994, in the form of an "army of national liberation" (Pinheiro Barbosa & Rosset, 2023).

The conditions that gave rise to the EZLN insurrection have an economic and a political dimension, both the subject of extensive study both before and after the point when the Zapatistas changed the political landscape in Mexico. In economic terms, the statistics are staggering, particularly as relates to the distribution of wealth and the extent and depth of poverty, which – based on official statistics – affects over 70 percent of the population (vs 44 percent nationwide). In a state that accounts for 21 and 47 percent of the country's oil and natural gas reserves, 35 percent of the country's coffee production, 55 percent of its supply of electricity, and is the country's second largest producer of beef and corn, 47 percent of the largely rural and indigenous populace has no access to potable water; one-third of all households are without electricity; as many as 59 percent have no basic sanitary facilities such as drainage; and three-quarters of all individuals consume less than 1,500 calories a day (vs the minimum level of 2,155 prescribed by the WHO). Whereas 13 percent of Mexico's population is illiterate, in Chiapas 31 percent is. Most households have no access to public services of all sorts, located as they are in an officially defined "marginal zone" (*a bolsillo de olvido* in Marcos' evocative description), characterized by an exceedingly high rate of impoverishment and exclusion, deprivation of basic human needs and public services, not to speak of the denial of fundamental human rights and the lack of democracy, and social justice.

As for the structural source of these conditions, there is no mystery. Some have been in place for hundreds of years. Others have been formed in a process that can be traced back to the advent of neoliberalism and the advance of extractive capital in the development process. One feature of this process in the context of Chiapas is the transformation of the dominant class, hitherto mostly coffee producers, and cattle ranchers, into agro-exporters with diversified holdings and operations in agro-industry, commerce, transportation, and services concentrated in San Cristobal, Tuxtla, Comitán, and the Soconusco region ("the other Chiapas"). In this process, large numbers of indigenous peasant producers in Los Altos were forcibly separated from their means of production and proletarianized, leading to the formation of a semiproletariat of rural landless workers and *jornaleros* that make up an estimated 65 percent of all peasant producers in the region, what the World Bank terms the "rural poor." In addition to these and other conditions of class exploitation, the indigenous population in the state, as elsewhere in the south-east of the country, were subjected to the negative socioenvironmental and health impacts of the extractive operations the multinational companies in the sector, and conditions of extreme oppression by the political *caciques*, members of *la familia Chiapaneca*, a small number of dominant class landowning families that have maintained a stranglehold over the instruments of political power from at least the days of Porfiro Diaz – the seven-term Mexican president, whose cumulative 31 years in power ended in May 1911 – denying the largely indigenous population their most elementary rights (Tejera Gaona, 1996, pp. 299–301).

In addition to the exploitation and oppression experienced by the local population, mostly of Mayan descent, as a result of their relations of production and relations to political power under the control of the "Chiapas family" ever since the Spanish colonial administration, the Lacandon jungle and lowlands, described by Lourdes Arizpe as "the last social frontier," have been subject as of the 1940s but particularly in the 1960s and 1970s to a process of massive migration involving many thousands of largely indigenous peasants from Los Altos pushed off their lands by the more powerful agro-export farmers and cattle ranchers; Tlzeltales from Ocosingo, Choles from the North, Tzotziles from Los Altos, Tojolabales from the Llanos, Zoques from the Central Valleys of Chiapas in response to the government's efforts to colonize the *Lacandona* so as to create a laborforce for the construction of a series of hydroelectric and oil exploration megaprojects; and an estimated 100,000 Guatemalans fleeing from the bloody counter-insurgency operations of the armed forces.

On these conditions and the migratory process that by 1994, the year of the Zapatista insurrection, brought large numbers of dispossessed peasant farmers and rural landless workers into the Lacandona, see Benjamin (1989) and Wager and Schultz (1995). With a rural population of barely 12,000 in 1960, the Lacandona by 1994 had to absorb up to an estimated 300,000 rural migrants, placing severe pressure on the social and economic systems in place, not to speak of a fragile ecosystem already rendered extremely fragile by illegal logging and oil drilling. Tejera Gaona (1996, pp. 299–332), in this situation, argued that the Zapatista rebellion cannot be reduced to the ethnic factor in the same way as so many earlier peasant and indigenous rebellions could be. Although the ethnic or indigenous factor was clearly present in the uprising, the overriding factor was class, the objective conditions of which, Terjera Gaona argued, had a greater role to play in the Zapatista rebellion – in unifying diverse ethnic groups – than did a shared ethnic cultural identity.

In addition to these conditions of socioeconomic, ecological, and demographic change that characterized the Lacandon region in the 1970s and 1980s, and that resulted in a particularly volatile and complex multiethnic society and the rapid growth of a number of very new and highly marginalized communities, the population in the state were subjected like no others in Mexico to legal and paramilitary support for the violent landgrabs and expropriations perpetrated by the dominant class, which by electoral fraud and other means secured their control over the Institutional Revolutionary Party (PRI) party-state apparatus. One clear indication of this control was the Presidential election of 1988, when the PRI captured 94 percent of the vote in San Cristobal, 98 percent in Comitán, and 96 percent in Ocosingo. It was such electoral fraud that closed off all roads to change except for armed rebellion, leading Marcos to declare the day after the EZLN's capture of four cities, "This is a warning to the government that we are fed up with the lack of democracy ..." (quoted in Ross, 1994, p. 19).

Marcos and the Zapatistas might have been fed up with the lack of democracy, but what spawned the rebellion and uprising were the workings and advance of capitalism and imperialism in the Mexican countryside. As far as Marcos and the EZLN were concerned, the enemy was imperialism in the form of neoliberal globalization. This was made clear by Marcos himself as early as 1992, a year-and-a-half before the 1994 uprising, and soon after the Zapatistas' first skirmish with the government's armed forces. And the point was made not as eloquently but as clearly with the EZLN's unexpected irruption and capture of four cities, and subsequently in the convocation of a series of national and tricontinental (intergalactic) encounters and forums "against neoliberalism and for humanity."

There is some question about the precise mix of objective (socioeconomic) and conjunctural and political conditions involved in the Zapatista rebellion, as well as the structural and the conjunctural aspects of the situation in which the Zapatistas launched their armed struggle for "liberty, democracy and social justice."[2] But the objective or structural conditions confronted by the Zapatistas were not that different from those faced by the indigenous peoples and peasant farmers throughout the region and across the country. In the period of the Salinas presidency, 1988–1994, these conditions were unleashed by means of a dogmatic and

---

[2] By some accounts the government, the army, and the United States' CIA were all aware of the existence of an insurgent force in the area, but they grossly underestimated any possible impact it might have. They certainly did not anticipate a capacity to take over any urban centers or cities as the EZLN did.

radical implementation of a neoliberal reform agenda. It is estimated (Zermeño, 1997, p. 322) that these reforms brought about the destruction of one out of every two small and medium-sized enterprises in the country, adding to the widespread impoverishing conditions of un- and underemployment. The peasant economy, and thus the indigenous community, was a prime target of these reforms and bore the brunt of the adjustment process.

With the deregulation of prices and the market, coffee prices plunged 50 percent in a single year, with similar developments in the production and marketing of corn and beans, the two staple commodities and consumption goods of the peasant sector of agricultural production. In these and other cases, with the government abandoning both protective measures (subsidized credit and technical services and support), the small noncapitalist producers in Chiapas and elsewhere, together with the thousands of small and medium-sized firms and enterprises that make up the petty bourgeois sector of the economy, were suddenly confronted with the naked forces of the world market, and – to use Marcos' evocative language – with "the bloody jaws of the wild beast."

Under the impact of these forces, productivity and total output from 1989 to 1993 fell by 35 percent; thousands of direct producers were forcibly separated from their means of social production, adding to the dynamics of land struggle that are reflected in the fact that at least 30 percent of Mexico's unresolved land petitions at the time came from Chiapas, and incomes in the depressed rural sector fell even more precipitously than elsewhere in Mexico – from 65 to 70 percent by some estimates (Hernandez Navarro, 1994, p. 44).[3] NAFTA, taking effect on the very day that the Zapatistas emerged from their jungle redoubt, in this context, as Marcos observed, constituted "a death sentence" for the Zapatistas and other small producers.

The objectively given conditions of the Zapatista uprising are clear enough. The critical question, however, as well as the key issue of debate, relates to the subjective conditions of political organization and ideology, and the mobilization of the social forces of opposition generated under these conditions. In these terms, two striking features can be noted. One is the stepped-up level of organization achieved within indigenous society in the years preceding and beyond the uprising, the formation of a mass movement based on direct actions taken to recover the land seized over the previous 30 years and more by means of violent expropriation by the more powerful agro-export farmers and cattle ranchers. This struggle by land-hungry peasants was combined to some extent in diverse contexts with a mass line strategy pursued by a number of left organizations such as *Pueblo Unido*, the *Central Independiente de Obreros Agricolas y Campesinos* (CIOAC), the *Partido Comunista Mexicana* (PCM), and the *Fuerzas de Liberación Nacional* (FLN), and a strategy pursued by several mass-line or

---

[3]The purchasing power of wages in 1994, according to Tejara Gaona (1996, p. 349), was only 44 percent of that in 1981; and this was before the worst wage compression of the past decade in 1995. In addition, the jornaleros of Los Altos continue to experience the most severe conditions of superexploitation in the country.

Maoist organizations formed in the late 1960s and 1970s, in a context of migration to the countryside of a significant number of urban left intellectuals, mostly UNAM students, after the 1968 massacre at Tlatelolco. In the early 1970s, the FLN established a rural front in three areas, encountering the organizational work of the San Cristobal dioceses and indigenous organizations and communities, but with other mass-line class-based organizations. By the late 1980s, the rural front of the FLN had established an effective base of operations and training camps in a number of base communities of indigenous peoples in the area, as well as liaison with a number of organizations such as the *Partido Revolucionario Clandestino Union del Pueblo* (Procup), formed in the 1960s by the legendary Lucio Cabañas and still maintaining a presence in Guerrero and elsewhere in Mexico (Wager & Schultz, 1995).

A second striking characteristic of the movement that spawned the Zapatista uprising was the capacity of the FLN rural front, under the command of Marcos, to mix with the population and gain the active support and trust of thousands of indigenous *Tzeltales, Tzotziles, Zoques, Choles,* and *Tojozales* of Los Altos and La Selva. Here, the EZLN achieved in 10 years of ideological and political struggle what no other Marxist-oriented political or guerrilla organization had managed to achieve in decades.

It was in the conjuncture of these conditions that the Zapatistas burst onto the center stage of history to "make a revolution against capitalism" and in search of a solution to "the great pillars of the right to land and other questions (freedom, democracy and social justice)." In so doing, they provided a direct challenge to both the theory and the practice of revolutionary change, helping to exorcise the specter of subjective idealism and irrationalism that in the 1980s had resurfaced in the form of postmodernism and poststructuralism.

The Struggle for Social Change in the Neoliberal Era

The forces of opposition and resistance in Mexico today are diverse and fragmented, although not heterogeneous in the form celebrated by postmodernist analysts of the "new social movements" (Veltmeyer, 2000). From the perspective of this postmodern/structuralist/Marxist analysis, the salient feature of these movements is the social construction by diverse social groups of their collective identity based on their subjective interpretation of their experiences, this with scant or no reference to the objective conditions of capitalist development. However, the reality constituted by these movements in their own actions would appear to be quite otherwise. In terms of this reality, these movements can be placed into three categories, according to their social base, the political forces and types of agencies involved, as well as the form and direction of struggle.

On the one hand, some forces of opposition are brewing within the corporatist structure assembled by the PRI party-state. Within this structure, diverse groups of unions, campesino organizations, and urban popular organizations, as well as reactionary and progressive factions of PRI, are waging a struggle for survival and to extend their rights, benefits, and state protection (NACLA, 30, 4, 1997, p. 13). Beyond the arena of this struggle, opposition forces have been (and are) being mobilized by the PRD within the institutional framework of the liberal democratic electoral apparatus in the context of a deep economic and political crisis which had led it to split from the PRI. These opposition forces were first mobilized in 1988 in the context of impending Presidential elections. Since then, they have waxed and waned. As a national democratic movement, with a recent upsurge marked by the capture of the Mexico City government by Cuauhtemoc Cardenas and considerable electoral gains in the legislative assembly of both the PRD and the right-wing opposition of the PAN. However, the experience of other countries in the region as well as Mexico itself suggests that the limit of this electoral response in mobilizing forces of opposition will soon reach its limits if it has not already done so.

The most dynamic forces of opposition and resistance in Mexico and elsewhere in the region have been mobilized by the peasant-based and led social movements (Vergara-Camus, 2023). And, in this context the EZLN has played an important role in mobilizing the forces of opposition within the indigenous peasant sector and in stimulating a "constellation of small transitions toward democracy," opening a broader road that is blocked by the forces of reaction (Garcia de Leon, 1995, p. 17).

Arguably, the indigenous peasant sector has been the most seriously affected by the neoliberal policies, excluded as it is from the government's economic model and project for productive transformation. However, the government's program of neoliberal policies has also devastated the economic operations of the small and medium independent producers that constitute a middle class in the rural society. In this context, as well the conditions of a severe economic crisis, these producers have organized in the form of *El Barzón*, constituting a social movement of opposition to neoliberal policies that has amassed within the space and time of but a few years a membership in the many hundreds of thousands.

From the outset, the leadership of El Barzón, representing as it does a very different social base, has sought an alliance and the concertation of actions with the Zapatistas, being both supportive of the EZLN as a political organization and disposed to concert actions with its political apparatus, the *Frente Zapatista de Liberación Nacional*. It is too early to tell how effective such a political alliance and concertation of forces of resistance might be in political terms, but El Barzón demonstrated considerable mobilizing capacity and is very representative of one of the three major sectors of the rural society, the EZLN having demonstrated equal effectiveness in representing the interests of the small and semiproletarianized indigenous producers (Veltmeyer, 2000). As for the rural proletariat, the third element, it is the least organized sector of rural society with little mobilizing capacity.

As noted above, the most dynamic sector of opposition and resistance to the neoliberal agenda of globalization and modernization can be found in certain sectors of rural society. However, Mexico today is primarily urban, with a large proletariat divided between individuals employed by a large variety of capitalist and small business enterprises in the so-called formal sector and a larger number working for themselves in the streets and backyard marginal operations of the so-called informal sector. It has been estimated that despite the loss of up to an estimated million jobs as a direct and indirect consequence of the December 1884 economic crisis, and an official unemployment rate that fluctuates between 4.5 and 6.8 percent, well over 50 percent of the working class is either un- or underemployed.[4] Further, the vast majority of workers are paid or remunerated at or below a level (a federally mandated minimum wage of 24.50 pesos or three dollars a day) that places them under officially drawn poverty lines. In this context, which includes the production of social wealth, and the exposure of a large and growing part of the urban proletariat to conditions of extreme poverty, a movement has been formed to the purpose of organizing workers in opposition to the neoliberal agenda and to mobilize these forces.

As it happens, this movement of independent workers was formed before the Zapatista rebellion in an effort of some unions to break free from the corporatist structure of the powerful but thoroughly accommodated Confederation of Mexican Workers. But the Zapatista rebellion was a powerful catalyst for this movement, a stimulus toward insurgency and mobilizing actions. Within days of the uprising (January 7, 1994), several independent unions carried out a large-scale mobilization in opposition to the government's siege and military operations against the EZLN and, at the same time, to demand implementation of its minimum wage protection as well as the end of summary dismissals and layoffs without compensation.

Subsequent actions of the independent workers movement were similarly concerted with the Zapatista struggle for social change, raising questions about and diverse interpretations of the political dynamics of struggle against neoliberalism. On January 12, a column of workers and students marched to the *Zócalo*, demanding that the government stop its bloody offensive against the indigenous communities at the base of the EZLN. Four days later, thousands of workers took to the streets in Juchitán, Guadalajara, Torreón, and elsewhere to demand a political solution to the conflict in Chiapas. In these actions, however, the independent unions were part of a broad but unorchestrated urban-based national movement for democracy formed within the popular sector of a reconstituted "civil society." On the one hand, the EZLN tactic of armed struggle, pursued under particularly unfavorable conditions for any other form of struggle, provided this movement, formed in the context of the 1985 earthquake and a subsequent political crisis in the PRI regime, a much-needed stimulus. On the other hand, the mobilizations of this movement generated sufficient political pressure to force the government into a unilateral cease-fire, to negotiate the demands of the Zapatistas. and subsequently to abandon its attempt to suspend the ceasefire and confront the EZLN with armed force. In this context, several massive demonstrations, each bringing over 100,000 protestors into the streets (in one day alone, over 100 recorded acts of protest), were sufficient to pressure the government to abandon its strategy of direct confrontation and make a show of returning to the negotiation process. Subsequent mobilizations have not been so successful, despite the time brilliant tactical strokes of the EZLN. Nevertheless, the government has been constrained to limit its actions against the Zapatistas and to treat it as a serious political force.

---

[4]INEGI estimated that in 1996, 47 percent of all workers were encompassed in its most inclusive unemployment category, the underemployed, and that only 25 percent of all individuals were adequately remunerated or employed under conditions of economic security.

It is difficult if not impossible to assign the independent workers movement the importance and centrality in the class struggle that Roman and Velasco Arreguí do. The central dynamic of class struggle from January 1994 to the present to a considerable degree has been constituted by an orchestration of forces mobilized by the Zapatistas in Chiapas and stimulated by them across the country both among indigenous organizations and communities, and within the popular sector of civil society, including assemblies of unionized workers that in some cases have decided collectively to unite with the EZLN in their struggle. In the context of these mobilizations, in the first six months of 1995 over 250,000 protesters of government policies took to the streets in 1,327 recorded demonstrations. Over this entire period, the average number of protest actions increased from 2.1 a day in January to 4.6 in February, 9.8 in March, and 11.4 in April (cited by Ballina & Alonso Urrutia in *La Jornada*, July 3, 1995).

Regarding this process of mounting protests, in the months following the uprising, from August 1994 to February 1995, the EZLN convoked three national democratic conventions to mobilize the social forces of resistance and opposition – to create a "force of forces" in the struggle for social transformation and democracy or, as Garcia de Leon (1995, p. 17) sees it, a "constellation of small transitions towards democracy."

The inclusion of thousands of union committees in this process, Roman and Velasco Aregui (1997, p. 105) argue (this time with more reason), sowed the seeds of a potentially powerful tie between an explosive indigenous movement and a critical element of the union movement which exhibited its mobilizing potential on May Day 1996. In July 1996, in response to a year-long public plebiscite held on its political future, that is, on the political form that it should take, the EZLN formed the *Frente Zapatista de Liberación Nacional* (FZLN). One of its first actions was to enter into an agreement with the interunion coordinating committee (the First of May) constituted by the independent workers movement to jointly promote a National Consultation on Labor and Union Freedom (*Trabajo y Libertad Sindical*) and to take steps to form a worker-peasant-indigenous peoples alliance.

In the context of this alliance, and of similar political alliances formed and pursued within other popular sectors of "civil society" such as the independent (and heavily indebted) small and medium-sized producers represented by El Barzon, the Zapatistas established what amounts to a critical political pressure point, an essential reference through which popular organizations in rural society and the urban centers could orchestrate their on-going struggle against the operating capitalist system. Indications are that it was precisely the threat of an increasingly organized and unified civil society that provoked the Zedillo government in 1995 into breaking the cease-fire with the EZLN just four days before the third National Democratic Convention (CND) and the constitution of a national Liberation Movement. And it is the same concern that lay behind the government's subsequent and on-going strategy to prolong the negotiation process with the EZLN while at the same time undermining its mobilizing and organizational efforts at the local as well as national level.

The problem for the Zapatistas, and for the possible formation of a nationwide broad interclass social movement of resistance and opposition, was what road to take or how to build it. The EZLN appears to be traveling the same road that so many class-based organizations took in the 1970s and 1980s, namely a shift from various forms of direct action for social transformation and radical change toward a struggle for democracy – for the expansion of space within which civil society can organize and mobilize their social forces.

This involution of the objectives and direction of struggle, and an associated transformation in the agency involved, is taking place in Mexico within the context of the opening of a broad new road of community-based mobilizations for a participatory form of democracy and a possible side-road of electoral politics. One of many examples of such developments can be found in the Popular Defense Committee of Durango (*Comité de Defensa Popular de Durango*-CDP) born in a wave of Maoist organizations in the 1970s and once active in at least 20 *colonias*, with an estimated membership of 70,000. From its original radicalism it entered the electoral arena in the 1980s, in search of middle-class support, without, it was hoped, abandoning its popular base. By 1992, it had become incorporated (via Pronasol, the government's National Solidarity Program) into the government's "new social policy" of poverty reduction, a policy replicated by other governments over the course of the 1990s (Lomeli, 2013).

The danger of this road taken by the CDP of Durango and by so many other left organizations over the years was acknowledged by Marcos and the EZLN. It is one reason for their insistence in their Fourth Declaration from the Lacandon jungle on a new form of politics – that the exercise of any power achieved would not take the form of a political party or acceptance of any positions that might be offered in the government or available in the national or state legislatures. As for the conversion of the EZLN from a political arm of the movement into a political force able to operate effectively at the national level, and its strategy to challenge the state through a series of political alliances designed to mobilize and unify the forces of opposition rather than continued armed rebellion, Marcos and the Zapatistas were guardedly cautious if not ambivalent. The challenge for the Zapatistas in this process has been to avoid the pitfalls into which so many political organizations over the years have fallen and still litter the political landscape. It remains to be seen whether the EZLN and the broad coalition of forces that it is working to generate can do so. The future of Mexico largely depends on it, as does the fate and the form of resistance and opposition to neoliberalism throughout Latin America, not to speak of the Left and the possibility of it finding a role to play beyond an electronic interface.

The Development Dynamics of Extractive Capitalism in Mexico

The plunder of Mexico's mineral resources via the operations of foreign mining capital has been facilitated by legislation that gives mining companies free reign to operate in the country, but also because in cases where the government imposes some conditions and restrictions they are easily circumvented. This is evident from a report submitted in February 2012 by Mexico's Auditor General. This is not the first such report by the AG. In a report on an audit of government spending in 2008, the AG had noted that the General Directorate of Mines had ceded the right to explore for and extract minerals to companies that failed to provide documentary evidence of their nationality as required by law, and that the officials provided licenses to mine without the required studies to ensure protection of the environment and livelihoods.

According to the investigative journalist Francisco Bárcenas (2012, p. 31), the AG put his finger on the ulcer that has caused – and continues to cause – Mexico to bleed minerals so profusely over the years. The AG established that the fees paid for the concessions to mine are below the costs of the administrative procedures involved. The Auditor's report literally reads:

> The amount of the fees currently paid is symbolic and contrasts with the volumes extracted from the nonrenewable mineral resources, since their value is well above the concession fees charged by the State over, as observed in the period 2005 to 2010, when the value of production amounted to 552 billion pesos [USD 46 billion] and the fees charged were only 6.5 billion pesos [USD 543.4 million], some 1.2 percent of the first.

Furthermore, there is no evidence provided that the fees charged were actually paid. Further still, the report reveals the utter laxity of the application of the law and the "omissions of the authorities in monitoring compliance with the law" (Bárcenas, 2012). In this manner, the wealth obtained by the extraction of mineral resources in Mexico is accumulated by private capital – in particular, Canadian capital. What the report shows then is that regarding the plunder of Mexico's mineral wealth, the conquest continues, or in the words of Eduardo Galeano (1973), the "open veins of Latin America" continue to bleed.

As Bárcenas notes, this has repercussions. Each day social protests erupt over the environmental devastation caused by mining in various parts of the Mexico, or the unfair contracts signed with the owners of the land under which the coveted ore lies, or the damage to people's health caused by the use of chemicals by mining companies, or the lack of safety for the mine workers.[5] Examples abound, both in Mexico and elsewhere in the region, particularly in the form of protests by indigenous communities over the introduction of mining operations in their territories without their consent, destroying their social environment and livelihoods, and jeopardizing their very existence as a people.

As Bárcenas editorializes this situation in which the nation's resources ("minerals that belong to all Mexicans") are extracted – plundered to be more precise – without any or very few benefits to its citizens, it "should be reason enough to undertake

---

[5] Of all economic activities, mining causes more negative health effects and diseases that can reduce life expectancy by up to 15 years, according to the Pan American Health Organization. Scientific evidence from across the world support the fact that the mining industry pollutes surface and groundwater, the air, soil, vegetation, and fauna, with incalculable costs to the health of the affected population and thus the economy.

a thorough review of mining legislation and policies." Needless to add, the problem goes well beyond a review of mining legislation and policies and even beyond the issues of corporate social responsibility and politics of the new extractivism, which attempt to regulate capital in the extraction of minerals. At its core, the "politics of resource extraction" involves a class struggle over the imperialist exploitation of these resources.

The Policy Dynamics of Neoextractivism in Mexico Under López Obrador

The Latin American experience of neoliberalism can be dated from the presidency of Miguel de la Madrid (1982–1988). De la Marid's *sexenio* coincided with the installation of a new world order based on the belief in the virtues of free market capitalism. The price of admission into the world system, and in the case of Mexico a condition for negotiating a program of debt relief (Mexico, together with Argentina and Brazil, accounted for 75 percent of accumulated Third World debt), was a neoliberal program of "structural reform" (*privatization* of enterprise, *deregulation* of markets, *liberalization* of commerce and the flow of capital, *decentralization* of governance and administration, *globalization* of economic activity). The linchpin of these structural reforms was the privatization (and de facto denationalization) of state-owned enterprises in the strategic sectors of the economy, and the elimination of barriers to the free movement of capital – a reform that unleashed a massive inflow of foreign direct investment, particularly, as noted in previous chapters, in the extractive sector – investments in the extraction of natural resources and their exportation in primary commodity form to capitalist markets.

Under the presidency of Salinas de Gortari (1988–1994) all of Mexico's major banks except for Banorte, and key firms in the industrial sector, were auctioned off, resulting in the privatization – and de facto denationalization – of the commanding heights of Mexico's national economy. The two enterprises exempt from this privatization program, Pemex, the state-owned producer, transporter, refiner, and marketer of Mexican oil and natural gas that was nationalized as early as 1938 and CFE, the state-owned electric utility of Mexico. However, even these two state-owned enterprises were opened to foreign direct investment in the energy reform law of 2013, pushed through the senate by a center-Far-Right coalition of PRI and PAN, and its most productive operations effectively denationalized.

As Saxe-Fernandez argued, the law signified the privatization and dismantling of both Pemex and CFE. Nevertheless, in 2022 AMLO rallied to the defense of state ownership in announcing that before his six-year presidency was over he would put in place a legal mechanism to prevent the effective privatization and denationalization of CFE. However, notwithstanding this announcement, and the promise to challenge the neoliberal privatization agenda ("energy reform") of his predecessor and thereby to restore Mexico's energy sovereignty, by postponing the scheduled renewable energy auctions he effectively imposed an indefinite moratorium on new wind and solar projects, a major concern of progressives. Critics argue that notwithstanding AMLO's antiprivatization and energy sovereignty discourse, the government has effectively accepted the participation of foreign investors in the market for energy, oil, and gas and thus the de facto privatization of both Pemex and CFE. Further, the government thus far has made no effective move to protect the environment and the workers employed in these enterprises, or to regulate the operations and extractive projects of the multinational corporations that have invested in the extraction of Mexico's natural resource wealth.

In fact, according to Tornel (2023a), AMLO's government has not made any substantial changes to the regulatory framework. The country, he notes, still operates under the neoliberal framework consolidated over the last three decades, most notably the 2013 Constitutional Reform, which AMLO has heavily criticized for opening private investment into the energy sector. Despite enjoying one of the most comfortable majorities in Mexican democratic history from 2019 to 2022, AMLO's government has not made significant changes to either the taxation structure, the energy, or extractive policies deployed by previous governments, in the latter case only temporarily halting new contracts and mining contracts (Tornel, 2023a). Instead, Tornel notes, the government has chosen to defund environmental and regulatory entities under a "republican austerity" program to fund a nationalistic development project which entails substantially increasing funding for dirty energy sources and the military.

From the perspective of the indigenous leaders and communities on the extractive frontier, despite AMLO's progressive discourse and his rather grandiose National Development Plan as well as his project of a "fourth revolution," his policies and actions differ very little from the old modernist and colonial politics. For example, the government's plan for an Intra-oceanic Corridor and his infrastructure project of what the government describes as the "Maya Train" have the hallmarks of a traditional modernist development plan, and – given the lack of consultation with and opposition of the indigenous communities that will be impacted by the Maya Train project – the project smacks of (neo)colonialism.

Both López Obrador's mega-project, the Mayan Train, and the interoceanic corridor have generated the fierce resistance of the Mayan communities that will be directly impacted by the associated infrastructure projects. In the case of the Mayan Train project, which, according to the government, will generate over 100,000 jobs and through tourism boost the development of a historically forgotten region of Mexico. The project, initiated in 2018, when completed will extend 500 kilometers and cross five Mexican states and 41 municipalities. It has unleashed controversy and forces of resistance not only from the indigenous communities but from various environmentalists, academics, and NGOs. But one of the most ignored groups in this fight against the megaproject, which is only one part of López Obrador's National Development Plan, are the Mayan people who have called Yucatán home for more than a thousand years. As Angel Sulub, a Mayan activist and member of the National Indigenous Congress (a national indigenous movement founded in 1996 following the Zapatista uprising in the southern state of Chiapas) sees it, the Mayan Train is neither a train nor Mayan (Estebanez Garcia, 2023).

From the perspective of the indigenous communities along the Mayan Train route, the project is an extension of the modernist development strategy pursued by the government for much of the 20th century; as such it will promote hyper tourism as well as agribusiness, which has devastated much of the forest and has polluted water and soil with the use of agro-chemicals that are present in water, including in breast milk and in the urine of children, according to recent studies.

Another litmus test of López Obrador's progressive credentials is his stance on the advance of extractivism in the mining sector, and the government's stance on the politics of conflict between the companies and the communities on the extractive frontier. Tetreault (2020) views the government's policies and actions in this sphere as akin to "neoextractivism," that is, the use of the additional revenues derived from the exportation in primary commodity form of the minerals and metals extracted by the multinational companies to finance the government's development investment and social spending programs. Indeed, the government's social spending priorities and several actions taken by the government to regulate the companies gives some credence to this characterization of AMLO's policies. Even so, critics have pointed out that in general the government has allowed the companies to regulate themselves with the vaunted "corporate social responsibility" program advanced within the social pact engineered by UN economists to incorporate the multinational companies in the private sector into the development process.

In his analysis of the economic and political dynamics of extractivism in the mining and petroleum sectors in the first months of López Obrador's presidency, Tetreault (2020) points to the ways in which the policies implemented by him are designed to finance rent-distribution social programs as well as development infrastructure – what we have defined as neoextractivism. His conclusion is that the government's policies and programs in the extractive sector are designed to open the petroleum and mining sectors to foreign investment to accelerate extraction rates, as well as manage the resistance and opposition of negatively affected communities and to garner their support for extractive projects. Another conclusion drawn by Tetreault is that AMLO's policies do not address the fundamental concerns and demands of most community-based resistance movements, which is for these communities to effectively exercise the right to decide whether to accept these projects. In lieu of this, the government appears to be more concerned to encourage the communities to come to terms with the companies – to have the communities in resistance to accept the promise of "corporate social responsibility" (as well as local community development projects and other bribes) – and to demobilize the resistance.

Conclusion

The advent of López Obrador on the political stage raised hopes on the political Left that Latin America might be headed toward another Left turn, heralding another progressive cycle in Latin American politics. However, analysis of AMLO's actual policies, as opposed to his populist rhetoric, suggests skepticism on this score. Like Evo Morales in his 14 years as President of Bolivia, and Rafael Correa's 10-year stint as President of Ecuador, López Obrador was unable or unwilling to directly confront the contradictions inherent in extractive capitalism and thus escape the development trap of an extractivist model of development. His credentials as a leftist (actually, as a center-left populist), together with the hopes raised by his progressive stance and policies, have been compromised by this failure. More promising perhaps have been President López Obrador's efforts in the direction of bringing about a coalition of progressive forces and a regional alliance of progressive-minded countries.

As for MORENA, it is a coalition of progressive forces that López Obrador initially cobbled together as a democratic sociopolitical populist movement to protest political corruption, electoral fraud, and the policies of the "power mafia" – a typical populist agenda. But in 2014, after failing to reach the presidency in the 2012 elections, it was restructured as an antineoliberal and populist party serving as a means of contesting subsequent presidential elections. It was this coalition that propelled López Obrador to capture the presidency in 2018. One lesson that we can draw from López's Obrador's presidency, as well as the presidency of Brazil's Lula and recently the presidency of Gustavo Petro (Colombia), is the importance of forming as broad as possible a coalition of progressive forces.

Chapter 7

The Turn Back to the Right

In addition to Argentina and Brazil, in 2018–2019, no fewer than 14 governments replaced an existing regime with a new regime by means of democratic electoral politics.[1] The elections evidenced a strong trend toward the restoration of conservatism and neoliberalism (Macri, Duque, Peña Nieto, Bolsonaro, Piñera). The exception was Mexico, where the presidential elections brought to power a coalition of political forces on the center-left (MORENA – a Movement of National Regeneration) led by López Obrador or AMLO. Mexico was not part of the pink tide and progressive cycle in Latin American politics. But even so, the election of AMLO after a long succession of center-right neoliberal regimes (Salinas de Gortari, Zedillo, Fox, Calderón, Peña Nieto) led to a renewal of the hope for progressive change that was dashed with the latest swing of the electoral politics pendulum to the right and the emergence of even more steadfast neoliberal regimes.

Electoral politics is one of the four arenas and major fronts of the class struggle (others being the struggle of workers for higher wages, the peasant movement resistance to the neoliberal policy agenda, and the territorial struggle of the communities on the extractive frontier). The social base of this struggle is the capital-labor relation – that is, the relation between the working class, or labor, and the capitalist class, or Capital. However, in the last cycle of development and resistance, the class struggle or popular movement (resistance against the neoliberal policy agenda) was led by the peasantry, or, more accurately, the semiproletariat of landless or near-landless rural workers generated by the advance of capitalism in the countryside. Developments in Argentina – over 500,000 workers in December 2018 took to the streets to protest Macri's neoliberal policies – suggested that in the next cycle of electoral politics, the major front in the class struggle, whatever the outcome at the level of the presidency, the working class would pay a leading or at least a more important role.

---

[1]These struggle dynamics on the front of electoral politics, and the information and details on these dynamics discussed in this chapter as well as Chapter 2 viz. the end of the progressive cycle and the pendulum swing of electoral politics to the right, can be traced out in the weekly news reports provided by Resumen Latinoamericano, Tercer Mundo, and Diario de urgencia/*The Dawn News*, Buenos Aires. www.resumenlatinoamericano.org.

Latin American Politics in the Neoliberal Era:
The Changing Dynamics of Class Struggle, 119–127
Copyright © 2025 by Henry Veltmeyer
Published under exclusive licence by Emerald Publishing Limited
doi:10.1108/978-1-83797-841-020241008

As previously noted, electoral politics is but one of four major fronts in the class struggle. There are two other fronts that warrant a closer look. First, there is the extractive frontier, where the indigenous communities are locked in a protracted struggle to defend their territorial rights and their way of life against the extractive operations of Capital and the struggle to restore their territorial rights and their access to the commons (on this front, see chapters nine). And then we have the front of the anti-imperialist struggle based on political resistance against the interference of the United States in national politics and the efforts of the US government to project state power and impose its will and policies in the region against this resistance. We will come back to this critical issue in Chapters 9 and 10. Needless to add, this front of the class struggle primarily concerns Venezuela, which, since the election of Hugo Chávez as President, like Cuba, finds itself in the crosshairs of US imperialism.

The Changing Dynamics of the Class Struggle

The dynamics of the class struggle and the forces of social change formed on the left and the right of the pendulum of Latin American politics can be traced out as a dialectical process formed in the emergence of a progressive cycle of regimes seeking to move beyond neoliberalism, if not capitalism and extractivism. No sooner than the emergence of a progressive cycle the forces of capitalist development formed and organized on the Far Right engaged a struggle to advance the forces of capitalist development and restore the neoliberal policy agenda. This struggle, which coincided with the end of a primary commodities boom, in some countries resulted in the capture of the State apparatus by means of democratic electoral politics in some instances, and in others by means of a "soft coup" orchestrated by the Far Right. However, the right-wing authoritarian regimes in this context have been rather short-lived, giving way to the emergence of another left turn in Latin American politics. In any case, to determine the possible or likely outcome of this latest change in the pendulum of electoral politics it is important to gauge the strength and endurance of the forces mobilized against what appears to be another pink wave. The question is: what is the current correlation of force in the class struggle – does it favor the Left or the Right? In this chapter, we provide some brief glimpses into the forces and circumstances that led to a turning of the political tide and the emergence of authoritarian neoliberalism as well as a brand of populist conservativism introduced by Jair Bolsonaro.

A Conservative Lollapalooza[2]

The role of Bolsonaro in rebranding populism – which has a long history in Latin America (in the form of presidents who campaign on an antielite populist program but then once in power invariably turn to the right – and bringing it into the mainstream of South American politics is highlighted by a "rightwing huddle," the third edition of an event held in August 2023 (in Campinas, São Paulo

---

[2]This section draws on material published in Petras and Veltmeyer (2019).

state) by *CPAC Brasil* – a spinoff of the US Conservative Political Action Conference (CPAC). The event, which brought together right-wing personalities and politicians from Brazil and other parts of South America, could be viewed as evidence that Bolsonaro's brand of conservatism is becoming more mainstream elsewhere in South America (Osborn, 2022). As argued by Osborn, Brazil's CPAC spinoff shows how Bolsonarism has spread, and notwithstanding his defeat in the 2022 general election is still echoing in Brazil and across South America. In fact, around 50 percent of the Brazilian electorate favored his far-right program, leaving the victorious social democrat, the PT leader Lula da Silva, hanging onto somewhat precarious political power (Minga, editorial No. 10, 2024).[3]

Other guests at the CPAC event (see Osborn, 2022) included Brazilian congressman Eduardo Bolsonaro (son of Brazilian President Jair Bolsonaro), who welcomed former Chilean presidential candidate José Antonio Kast (who lost to now-Chilean President Gabriel Boric last December) and Argentine congressman Javier Milei, who won the presidential primaries and the general election in 2023 (Osborn, 2022). Also in attendance was one-time aide to former US President Donald Trump, Jason Miller, whose messaging app *Gettr* was a co-sponsor of the event.

While Bolsonaro lost the presidential election to the PT leader Lula da Silva, Kast's and Milei's upbeat appearances at CPAC Brasil are evident that Bolsonaro's brand of conservatism CPAC – inspired in part by Trump – has reverberated across the region. As in Brazil, in both Chile and Argentina, far-right politicians have been endorsed by voters at levels not seen in decades. Milei, for his part, rose from being a relatively obscure economics professor to the figurehead of a libertarian coalition that contested the 2023 primaries of the presidential election (which Milei later won). A self-described anarcho-capitalist, Milei proposes to dramatically shrink the size of the Argentine state. Now as President of the country, he has free rein to implement his far-right policy agenda in the form of classic neoliberal and conservative programs.

Against this political backdrop, former Argentine President Macri in April 2023, paid a visit to Mar-a-Lago to meet personally with Trump. Macri understood that the meeting would spark a controversy inside his coalition, *Clarín*'s Ignacio Miri[4] wrote, but he went forward in an effort "to send a message to people who voted for him in the past and today [who] looked favorably at Javier Milei," another rightwing populist in the mold of Bolsonaro who won the presidency of Argentina in November.

In Chile, Kast remains prominent on the political Right despite his election defeat, promoting the campaign for voters to reject the country's draft constitution when put to a public referendum by the government in September 2022. As it turns out, the government's proposal for progressive reform of the constitution

---

[3] *Minga*, a peer-reviewed, open access journal in social sciences, arts, Latin America, development studies, activism and social transformation is published in Cochabamba, Bolivia.
[4] https://foreignpolicy.com/2022/06/17/cpac-brazil-far-right-south-america-bolsonaro-kast-milei-trump/

was overwhelmingly rejected, forcing the leftist president Boris and his government to go back to the drawing board and come up with another draft of a proposed "progressive" constitution.

At the regional level, one might very well conclude that the electorate is turning to the Far Right in response to deteriorating economic conditions as well as seemingly endless corruption scandals. On the other hand, the Far Right has not overtaken the moderate right in all countries. Center-right politicians have seized power in Uruguay and Ecuador (in Uruguay, a far-right former army commander won eleven percent of the vote in the 2019 election after founding a political party that year). Even so, in Argentina, Chile, and Brazil, the relatively new prominence of far-right politicians is noteworthy because these countries experienced bloody right-wing dictatorships during the Cold War, leading much of the public to spurn far-right politicians in the following decades.

These dictatorships are now distant realities for a new generation of voters, and Latin American scholars point to factors such as a lack of economic opportunity, corruption scandals, and online social forums as fueling the popularity of political figures who were previously on the fringe. That is certainly the case in Argentina, where a long-running economic crisis – with no apparent end in sight – helps explain voters' openness to Milei and other politicians on the far-right.

Ecuador: Another Swing of the Electoral Pendulum to the Right

The assassination of presidential candidate Fernando Villavicencio (*El Tiempo*, August 9, 2023)[5] was the latest episode in the degradation of public life in a country marked by serious unaddressed structural problems and a major increase in violence related to organized crime and the incursion of narco-capitalists (Human Rights Watch, 2023). A journalist, former trade unionist, and politician, Villavicencio built his identity as an anticorruption activist radically opposed to the government of Rafael Correa. His reporting led to the conviction of Correa, and an eight-year sentence for corruption, which led him to seek exile in Belgium. Toward the end of the Correa government, Villavicencio himself went into exile in Peru. He then returned during the government of Lenin Moreno, who, on succeeding Correa as president took a sharp turn to the right.

Villavicencio's murder, allegedly at the hands of organized crime operatives, shocked the country and altered the campaign leading up to the general elections on August 20, 2023. In a special electoral cycle marred by political violence, voters had to choose from eight candidates. The snap elections were triggered after President Guillermo Lasso invoked the *muerte cruzada* (impeachment) clause to avoid further impeachment proceedings against him in parliament.

---

[5] On August 9, 2023, 11 days before the 2023 Ecuadorian general election, presidential candidate Fernando Villavicencio was assassinated after leaving a campaign rally in Quito, the capital of Ecuador.

In an interview conducted by *Nueva Sociedad*, Pablo Ospina and Franklin Ramírez Gallegos (2023), both university-based researchers, analyzed the causes behind the country's decline in the run-up to the elections in the following terms: It is difficult to understand such a rapid change and such a radical degradation of the security situation in Ecuador since the country turned to the US dollar as its currency, a development that enormously facilitated money laundering from drug trafficking, and as a result, the progressive installation or development of different criminal groups linked to transnational crime. But, as Ospina saw it, two events triggered this rapid deterioration.

First was the 2016 peace agreement in Colombia, which, Ospina argued, removed from the scene a group that offered order and a certain state rationality at the border. Above all, this group generally refrained from attacking Ecuadorian targets because it wanted to avoid closer collaboration between the Ecuadorian and Colombian militaries in counterinsurgency operations. But once FARC demobilized, the border soon would be dominated by a dozen smaller dissident and irregular groups, which dispute territory and trafficking routes and do not have the same policy toward Ecuador. In the context of what Paley and Granovosky-Larsen (2019) describe as the expansion of drug war capitalism, these drug traffickers do not hesitate to kill journalists (as happened in March 2018) or to penetrate that country's rather weak and lax defenses to assassinate members of rival groups in this drug war. The second factor, he argued, was the pandemic, which seems to have disrupted drug trafficking, creating a kind of drug distribution crisis, along with disputes between Mexican and Colombian cartels and the associated "organized violence" and "capitalist warfare" (Paley & Granovosky-Larsen, 2019). But it also increased the potential for recruiting criminal groups in Ecuador, given the desperation among a notable part of the population. Not only crime but also immigration reached levels comparable to those during the 1999 crisis.

Ramírez had a similar albeit different take on the deterioration of conditions in Ecuador, which presumably helped bring about political conditions for a switch to the right in electoral politics. First, he agrees with Ospina regarding the role of the Colombian peace accords, but he pointed out that there was also illegal mining, smuggling, human trafficking, and arms trafficking. And all of this against the backdrop of the weakening of the state in recent years has left the border particularly vulnerable and porous for gangs and drug traffickers to enter and leave the country. That is why *Esmeraldas*, a province with a large Afro-Ecuadorian population and one of the most "forgotten" in Ecuador, is one of the areas with greatest violence and increases in crime, linked in many cases with Mexican cartels. "We have lived" he argued "through a cycle of a weakening state."

As for this issue of a weakened state, Ramírez in his interview with *Nueva Sociedad* noted that a program of institutional reforms that began with Lenin Moreno and his agreement with the IMF, and continued under Lasso, weakened the capacity for state intervention in the economy (Ospina & Gallegos, 2023). These reforms, he noted, lacked a strategic vision as to how these reforms would affect different sectors and policies and reduced state capacity of the government to regulate economic activity and cope with the expansion and incursions of drug capitalism. The increase in cocaine production in Colombia, coupled with the fact that Ecuador has a dollarized economy with a deregulated financial system, has made Ecuador not only a drug transit country but also a place for collection and processing. Ecuadorian drugs leave from the ports of Guayaquil and Manta, which has exponentially multiplied disputes between gangs seeking to control those export circuits and microtrafficking.

Ramírez on this point argues that prisons play an important role in the expansion of an illicit economy run by drug capitalists and organized crime because that is from where business is directed. Prisons are, he adds – here echoing the arguments advanced on this point by Paley and Granovsky-Larsen (2019) and Gutierrez (2021) – places where the state has completely lost its monopoly on violence. "The police and the Armed Forces have gained autonomy at the same time they are penetrated by organized crime, with very little civilian oversight." Further, he added: "we cannot understand the criminal control over the prisons without understanding the complicity of the police. We are in the state of exception number 17, but it isn't linked to any institutional strategy or state presence" (Ospina & Ramírez, 2023).

Peru: The Weakness of the Political Left, The Lack of Class Consciousness, and the Failure of Leadership

The Peruvian presidential elections of 2021 were surprisingly won by a candidate of a Marxist-oriented political party (Perú Libre, 2020, p. 8). Not only was the victory of Pedro Castillo a surprise, but equally surprising was the fact that neither the political Right (including not only the different right-wing political organizations in Congress but also the conservative organizations and directors of the major corporations intervened to avoid Castillo to be officially declared as the winner of the second round of the presidential elections). In these circumstances, it would have been relatively easy to stage an electoral coup.

At the time, it was widely considered in political circles that the candidacy of Castillo and his party *Perú Libre* were a threat to economic growth as they would attack the interests of Capital. However, as detailed in Chapter 5, the organizations that represent the economic interests of Capital had no reason for concern. For one thing and importantly, Castillo did not control Congress. Second, the program of *Perú Libre* presented by Castillo's team in the second round of the presidential elections did not foresee revolutionary changes or the beginnings of socialism, but rather "realistic" structural social democratic reforms in the style of the changes implemented during the administrations of Rafael Correa in Ecuador and Evo Morales in Bolivia. For example, the State was to strengthen its regulatory role within a mixed economy approach, while monopolies and oligopolies would be more actively regulated and, in the strategic mining sector, would be allowed to implement a self-regulatory regime ("corporate social responsibility"). Private companies would be stimulated, and national and foreign businessmen who invested in Peru, paid their taxes, and respected the rights of workers and the environment, would have their rights respected and investments protected. Foreign investors would be the government's allies to move the country forward (Perú Libre, 2021, pp. 7–8). Peru, in this context, would maintain its attractiveness for transnational capital. In addition, the free trade agreements that Peru had signed with a variety of countries, and membership in the World Trade Organization, would have softened the government's nationalistic orientation.

As of the 1980s, much of the Peruvian Left had been converted into an electoral force. This meant that instead of developing political work in direct relationship with urban and rural social base organizations, social movements, and other kinds of citizen organizations, the Left began to develop its relationship with workers, the rural and urban poor, and the middle class, through participation in democratic elections and the parliament. In this context, it could be argued (Lust, 2019b, pp. 172–173) that the return of parliamentary democracy in the 1980s contributed to the weakening of the Peruvian Left.

Although in the 1980s the Peruvian left-wing coalition *Izquierda Unida* was considered the strongest Marxist electoral organization in South America (McClintock & Vallas, 2005, p. 71) a process was slowly started that eliminated the political and social bases of the Left, dramatically weakening the power of unions and organized labor in the class struggle. The key factors in the weakening of the political left were the reduction in the power of the unions in the 1980s and a deepening of the economic crisis at the time.

Based on data on the evolution of the number of unions, strikes, workers involved, and man hours lost, Lust (2023), a Marxist scholar with a research specialization in Peru, concluded that in the years between 2000 and 2020 there was no qualitative leap in the class struggle. Hence, he argues (on this see Chapter 5) that the electoral results of the presidential elections and elections for congress, especially in the case of *Perú Libre*, were not the product of an increase in the class consciousness. *Perú Libre's* electoral win, he concluded, "was nothing more than an inflationary result or a balloon full of air." There did not exist a political and social sustainability of these results. Capital, he added – capital in the form of the multinational companies, invited by the government over the years to provide the investment and technology needed by Peru – was well aware of this and hence did not fear the victory of the Left.

In any case, on December 7, 2022, Castillo himself put an end to his presidency. In a message to the nation, the President announced that he would dissolve Congress and would call for new congressional elections. This new Congress would have the task to elaborate a new constitution. As the current Congress considered the action of Castillo an auto-coup, the political Right, accompanied by members of *Perú Libre*, impeached Castillo and then arrested him. He was subsequently replaced by his former vice-president Dina Boluarte, with the permission and immediate alliance of the extreme right in congress.

Castillo's fall from power was not orchestrated by the political Right, although the permanent political crisis caused by the impeachment process leveled against a range of ministers, and the enduring| accusations of corruption against the President, might tell us otherwise. The decision of President Castillo to dissolve Congress was a direct product of his failure to change the political, economic, and social course of society. Although Castillo did not have a left-wing political history, his combative union past pointed toward his evident social concern and leftist credentials.

The entire weight of the right-wing opposition and other reactionary forces mobilized by the dominant and ruling classes and both local and foreign capital had been working toward the castration of Castillo's presidency and the subsequent right turn in Peruvian politics. Castillo's inability to mobilize his political base, and his serious misjudgment and fatal mistake in seeking to dissolve Congress and rule by decree, gave a golden opportunity for the opposition to remove him from power and thereby deprive the political left from an equally golden opportunity to capture the state as an instrument of progressive social change.

Argentina: A Political Earthquake in the General Elections

Primary elections in Argentina on August 10, 2023, sent a shockwave and seismic shift across the political landscape, with extreme right-wing libertarian (right-wing populist) candidate Javier Milei coming in first with 30 percent of the votes and liberal-conservative opposition candidate, former security minister Patricia Bullrich, coming in second with 28 percent. Peronismo's center-left ultrapragmatic "unity" candidate, Sergio Massa, came in third – for the first time in history.[6] Milei's success in the "open, simultaneous, and mandatory primaries" shattered the two-party polarization that has long defined Argentine politics (as in Colombia until the most recent presidential elections).[7] Voters across age groups, former political loyalties, and socioeconomic demographics – who have felt disenfranchised by the Kirchnerist government and are seeking solutions to the country's constant economic crises – rallied behind the antiestablishment candidate. "Never before has the Far Right obtained so many votes in Argentina," wrote Schuster and Stefanoni for *Nueva Sociedad* (NACLA, 2023). Between Milei and Bullrich, they accounted for almost half of the electorate.

Argentina's primary elections came at a time of economic crisis punctuated by an annual inflation rate of over 100 percent. The government devalued the peso by some 18 percent the day after the election, allegedly to fulfill IMF requirements and limit inflation. Milei has promised to dollarize the economy and do away with the Central Bank and halt if not reverse the progressive reforms introduced with the pink tide of progressive reforms. In addition, Milei's ascension to the presidency is likely to deal a devastating blow to Argentina's social programs and hopes for some action and progress on the environmental front (Milei is a climate change denier).

Bullrich, once a militant revolutionary Peronist who later turned to the right, holds some liberal positions – she supported the decriminalization of abortion and marriage equality – but wields an iron fist against insecurity and social

---

[6]Milei achieved surprisingly good results in popular neighborhoods, including in traditional Peronist areas such as La Matanza and even more in the provinces. In fact, he came first in 16 of the 24 provinces and swept two, including Salta, in Argentina's Andean North (*Resumen Lartinamericano*, March 2, 2024).
[7]Unlike Massa, Milei and Bullrich embody a strongly antiprogressive, refoundational discourse – the ideological inverse of the discourses of the Pink Tide of the 2000s.

protest. Together, Milei and Bullrich, Schuster and Stefanoni write, represent a refoundational discontent that is "similar to but the ideological inverse of the discourse on the pink tide of the 2000s." "A weapon in the hands of the voters to blow up the system," they add.

Conclusion

The election of López Obrador in December 2018 raised the hopes of many on the Left for another cycle of progressive change, signaling the beginning of another left turn. However, the recent irruption of Milei on the political stage could be seen as signaling instead a possible rightward trend in Latin American politics. Coincidentally, it was the presidential election of Macri that signaled an ebbing of the pink tide and the end of the progressive cycle. Also, political developments in Ecuador and Peru also suggest that the pink tide has begun to recede, which does not augur well for the fate or future of the political and social Left and other "progressive forces" (unions, peasants, rural landless workers, indigenous communities). Unfortunately, it is impossible to determine the probability let alone any degree of certainty whether the Left or the Right will benefit the most from the forces of change mobilized in the class struggle. However, the following chapters will shine some light on the dynamics of these forces.

As for what is at stake in these dynamics, according to the President Elect of Argentina Javier Milei, it is nothing less than the "survival of the West." In his speech delivered to the assembly of political leaders and corporate CEOs at this year's World Economic Forum meeting in Davos, Switzerland, Milei in his dangerously appealing populist style argued that the root cause of the world's problems (including widespread impoverishment) is "collectivism," that is, social welfarism and taxes, that is, a vision of the world that inexorably leads to socialism and thus poverty (Milei, 2024). The only way forward, Milei declared, is "free enterprise, capitalism, and economic freedom."

Milei's "special address" (Milei, 2024) marked a return to the orthodoxy of Milton Friedman and the Chicago Boys, who pushed forward an ideology of social cannibalism as the basis for their neoliberal agenda. Since the 1970s, this scorched earth policy has devastated much of the Global South through the IMF's structural adjustment programs, but it also created factory deserts in the West (what Donald Trump, in his inauguration address in 2017, called the "American carnage"). Therein lies the confounding logic of the far-right. On the one side, it calls for the billionaire class to dominate society in their interest (which produces the social carnage). On the other side, it inflames the victims of said carnage to fight against policies that would benefit them.

Chapter 8

Populist Authoritarianism: The Bolsonaro Factor

Much of the critical discourse on the phenomenon of Bolsonarism views it exclusively from the perspective of electoral politics as the expression of right-wing populism, consonant with the emergence across the world of a trend toward right-wing authoritarian populism (see Berberoglu, 2020; Borras, 2018). In this reading of Bolsonarism, it is reduced to a passing phenomenon of political irrationality, something like a nightmare from which the country is expected to wake up with the electoral victory of Luiz Inácio [Lula] da Silva, the leader of the left-of-center Workers Party (PT), in the October 2022 elections. Having subsequently defeated the incumbent Bolsonaro, Lula can be expected to restore the normality of social pacts regarding an equitable distribution of the social product within the policy framework of neodevelopmentalism and neoextractivism, an economic model designed by economists at ECLAC (on this see Bresser-Pereira, 2007; Leiva, 2008). As noted by the sociologist De Farias (2022), this puts an end to the view of Bolsonarism as an aberration and a passing phenomenon. Rather, De Farias argues – and I concur – that it is the expression of deeper transformations in the structure of class society in Brazil, concealing the challenges ahead in an ongoing class struggle and the process of productive and social transformation that Brazil, together with other countries in the region, is undergoing.

The purpose of this chapter is to look behind this issue of Bolsonarism and the broader movement of right-wing populism to expose the forces of structural transformation associated with the advance and development dynamics of resource-seeking "extractive" capital (foreign investments in the extraction of natural resources in primary commodity form for export to capitalist markets). These forces are at work across the region (and elsewhere to be sure) but, apart from passing reference to other such experiences in the region, the central focus of the chapter will be on Brazil. The argument advanced in this context is constructed as follows: First, I reconstruct in the Latin American context the three development-resistance cycles that have unfolded over the past three decades in the neoliberal era. Second, we reconstruct some major structural transformations in Brazil's economy and society associated with the installation of a new world order of neoliberal globalization in the early 1980s. I argue that these transformations express the workings of forces unleashed by the advent of the new world order, particularly as regards the neoliberal model and policy agenda of structural reform[1] and the advance of resource-seeking "extractive" capital (neoliberal extractivism) in the development process (Andrade, 2022). Third, I reconstruct the political dynamics associated with these developments (neoliberalism, extractivism), with reference to the emergence of the so-called "left turn" or "pink wave" of progressive policy regimes – what Edwards (2010) among others view as left-wing populism (Levitsky & Roberts, 2011).[2]

This argument includes reference to the form taken by neoliberalism in Latin America, the region that has experienced the most comprehensive neoliberal transformation in the world but at the same time constitutes its "weakest link" (Sader, 2008). There are several questions about this transformation of note. One relates to a development process that has unfolded across the world in different historical and regional contexts, namely, the transformation of the peasantry into an industrial proletariat; or, in the Latin American context, a semiproletariat of rural landless workers.[3] This proletarianization process can be traced back to what Marx described as a process of "primitive [original] accumulation," namely the dispossession of the direct producers from their means of production, converting them into a reserve army of surplus labor, a laborforce composed of workers forced to exchange their labor power for a living wage, an industrial proletariat. The current cycle of capitalist development and resistance, like the initial phase of capitalist development in the era of European colonialism and extractive imperialism,[4] implicates predominantly the resistance of indigenous commu-

---

[1] Neoliberalism, as David Harvey (2003) understands it, is "a theory of political economic practices that proposes that human well-being can best be advanced by liberating individual entrepreneurial freedoms and skills within an institutional framework characterized by strong private property rights, free markets, and free trade."

[2] Others, including myself, view the so-called "left turn" or the "pink wave" as a return to traditional center-left politics informed by "neodevelopmentalism," namely, a more socially inclusive form of development based on the post-Washington Consensus on the need to bring the state back into the development process and a new social policy of income redistribution aimed at poverty reduction (Leiva, 2008; Levitsky & Roberts, 2014).

[3] The most visible and extensively studied form of this rural semiproletariat in Latin America is the Rural Landless Workers' Movement (the MST) in Brazil, which, together with CONAIE, the Federation of Indigenous Nationalities of Ecuador, led the resistance against capitalism in the form of the neoliberal policy agenda, creating conditions that in the new millennium led to widespread disenchantment and the rejection of neoliberalism, allowing the political class on the Left to capture the state apparatus by means of electoral politics. On these dynamics, see, inter alia, Petras and Veltmeyer (2011).

[4] In this initial phase of capitalist development in the era of European colonialism, this was a system based on the accumulation of state-chartered merchant's capital (mercantilism), slave labor and the pillage of natural resource wealth, agro-extractivism, and the dispossession of the small-scale direct producers, not to mention the appropriation of the global commons – and the resistance of the communities on the extractive frontier – see inter alia, Girvan (2014).

nities on the extractive frontier against the advance and destructive impacts of extractive capitalism, and the appropriation of the global commons. On these resistance dynamics of these indigenous communities on the extractive frontier see, inter alia, Barkin and Sanchez (2019) and Zibechi (2005).

In response to both the demands of the Washington Consensus and the demand on capitalist markets for natural resources, the governments in the region in the 1980s were led to abandon the policy of import substitution industrialization, which in the three biggest economies in the region (Argentina, Brazil, and Mexico) bore fruit in the form of an industrialization process and the growth of a powerful union movement. However, in the 1980s and 1990s, the forces of production that had been built up over decades in the industrial sector were effectively destroyed. In Brazil, for example, while the industrialization of the world economy increased between 1980 and 2020, the share of manufacturing industry in Brazil's GDP steadily declined – from 21.1 percent in 1980 to 11.9 percent in 2020 (De Farias, 2022). This process, which implicated the virtual disappearance of an incipient industrial proletariat, can be traced out in part in a tangible weakening of the labor movement and a dispersal of its forces of resistance.

What was unique about this process was how it intersected with a similar development process in the agricultural sector, which resulted in the formation of a working class with some decidedly unique features. With the closure of the formal labor market in the urban centers in the 1980s and 1990s, the mass of dispossessed "peasants" forced to migrate to the cities in search of an alternate source of livelihood was transformed into a semiproletariat of landless rural workers and an urban precariat of self-employed informal workers (Standing, 2011). These two segments of what could be described as the new Latin American working class – "the dangerous class," in the words of Standing – constituted the social basis of the class struggle for higher wages and land in the neoliberal era. However, in the 1990s, the most powerful forces of resistance mounted against the advance of capitalism and the neoliberal policy agenda of so many governments in the region were mobilized by the peasant movements of rural landless workers and indigenous communities. The working class in the industrial sector, which had been in the vanguard of the class struggle in earlier decades of capitalist development, was notably absent, its powerful forces of resistance weakened or dissipated. By the end of the 1990s, the political activism of these peasant movements had managed to halt the advance of capital and derail the neoliberal policy agenda, creating conditions for a progressive cycle in Latin American politics – a pink wave of postneoliberal regimes oriented toward a more inclusive form of development.

The chapter ends with a discussion of the forces of resistance mobilized in opposition to the advance of resource-seeking "extractive" capital – extractivism – in the development process. In the Brazilian context, the politics of this resistance has been manifest most clearly in the movement of rural landless workers (the MST) and the Workers' Party regime led by Inácio [Lula] da Silva, Brazilian politician and former union leader who served as the 35th president of Brazil from 2003 to 2011 (returning to office in 2023). The argument advanced in this context is that the current conjuncture of the capitalist development process, with reference to the systemic crisis associated with the advance of extractive capital and its assault on both the environment and livelihoods, as well as the correlation of class forces and the phenomenon of Bolsonarism (right-wing populism) is favorable to the Left.

As noted by the sociologist Emir Sader (2011), notwithstanding Lula's electoral success in bridging the notorious divisions within the Left and mobilizing what amounted to a united front, the Brazilian Left under Bolsonaro was more united than ever before, united in response to his reactionary policies that privileged free market capitalism and extractivism. But Lula's successful bid to regain the presidency is also expected to create a favorable environment for uniting the Left in support of a left turn against right-wing populism.

The New Brazil: From Neoliberalism to Neodevelopmentalism

The expansion of the extractive industries is now affecting many more dimensions of social life than was the case with the mining projects in the first cycle of capitalist development in the mercantile era of extractive imperialism (Girvan, 2014). For this reason, in Latin America, some analysts have begun to write about "neoextractivism" with reference to this much more intense process involving faster depletion of the soil, greater use of chemicals in agriculture and mineral processing, export orientation, with little to no value added locally (Gudynas, 2013; Svampa, 2015). With the knowledge gained by these analysts about the dynamics of extractivism in the mining industries and socioenvironmental impacts, we can examine with more clarity the ways in which communities on the extractive frontier have been and are uprooted from their communities and territories by the forces of capitalist development and extractivism, and the encroachment of illegal economies in the private sector related to the cultivation and farming of drug crops (coca, opium, etc.) and large-scaling logging, which, together with the expansion of the soy economy and cattle-ranching, has resulted in a disastrous level of deforestation (Kroger, 2022). Brazil has proven to be an important laboratory of scientific study into these development dynamics and the associated forces of indigenous resistance. For example, recent studies have documented an unprecedented degree of deforestation associated with both the expansion of extractive capitalism in the sectors of cattle ranching and the soybean plantations, and illegal private-sector logging operations,[5] and the weakening of environmental protection by the Bolsonaro regime (Bolsonaro himself has argued that more farming and mining in the Amazon would reduce poverty). Under these conditions, and with the opening of the Amazon as a frontier of capital accumulation by Bolsonaro, deforestation in the Amazon surged to record

---

[5]On the growth of illicit economies related not only to the cultivation of cops destined for the drug trade but also logging and fishing, not only in Latin America but across the world, see Gutierrez (2021).

levels, and in 2021 hit the highest level in decades (Milhorance, 2021).[6] The rate of deforestation, illegal invasions, and attacks on indigenous peoples and exploitation of indigenous lands in Brazil by 2021 had tripled since Bolsonaro took office in 2019 (Indigenous Missionary Center, 2021).

The Amazon has been the focal point of studies into these development dynamics in the context of Bolsonaro's presidency and its systematic dismantling of environmental protections and regulations, which opened the Amazon (the largest rainforest and repository of biodiversity in the world) as a frontier of capital accumulation and globalization, giving license to the burning and clearing of vast expanses of forests by ruthless lumber companies and cattle ranchers. The significance of this large-scale deforestation lies in its devastating local and global environmental impact, which in addition to global warming includes a loss of productivity and biodiversity, and reduced water cycling. And this is before any consideration of the equally devastating local impact of deforestation on communities and the livelihoods and even the lives of the indigenous custodians of this biodiversity.

Reflecting the gravitational pull of extractive capital and extractivism, Brazil's position in the international division of labor in the 1990s changed rapidly, and with this change came a new correlation of forces between fractions of the ruling classes that make up the power bloc that governs the country. A new political, economic, and cultural structure was then consolidated in the turn into the 21st century. As noted by De Farias (2022), it included the consolidation of fractions of the ruling classes linked to the production and commercialization of mineral, agricultural, and agro-processed raw materials. These economic sectors share some common characteristics: (i) production chains that are not very dense and have limited capacity to promote increasingly complex, diversified and dynamic social relations; (ii) a low capacity for generating decent jobs in the formal sector and narrow horizons for the extension of salaried citizenship to the working class; (iii) a voracious process of landgrabs, with degrading developments in the territories under its influence or control; and (iv) direct or indirect mobilization of paramilitary violence as a form of capitalist warfare (and genocidal appropriation of the global commons) – a tool of social control (De Farias, 2022; Paley & Granovsky-Larsen, 2019).

In this context, new power centers were formed in medium-sized urban areas in the interior of Brazil, especially those linked to the soybean complex that has shown an impressive capacity to reorganize much of the national territory. According to the Brazilian Institute of Geography and Statistics (IBGE), between 2000 – at the threshold of a global commodity boom – and 2018, six years past the end of the boom (which saw the GDP fall from an

---

[6]The role of Bolsonaro in the deforestation debacle in the Amazon can be clearly illustrated by the dramatic decrease in deforestation under Lula's subsequent regime. After four years of rising destruction in Brazil's Amazon, deforestation dropped by 33.6 percent during the first six months of Lula's term in office (*The Guardian Weekly*, July 14, 2023, p. 9).

average of 3.5–5.0 percent to zero), soybean production in Brazil increased from 32.8 million tons to 117.9 million tons, while the acreage of soybean production increased from 13.7 million hectares to 34.8 million hectares (De Farias, 2022). In the context of this "development" the agrarian elite component of the ruling class consolidated its position within the soybean complex, which now spans the southern cone (Argentina, Bolivia, Paraguay, Uruguay) as well as Brazil, and demanded new channels of political representation, allowing the ruling class in these areas to exercise hegemony on a regional if not a national scale, increasing its decision-making power and influence.

In its location on the periphery of the world capitalist system, which was formed at the turn into the 20th century in the context of what Lenin had described as "imperialism," Latin America was drawn into the international division of labor as exporters of primary commodities in exchange for the importation of goods manufactured in the center of the system, a role that was reinforced in the post-Second World War period of capitalist development. However, notwithstanding the pronounced feature of this development (namely, the primarization of exports) several countries – most notably Brazil, Argentina, and Mexico – had begun to industrialize as the result of a policy of import substitution industrialization. But with the turn toward neoliberalism in the 1980s governments in the region were constrained to abandon this industrial policy and return to their traditional role as supplier of natural resources in primary commodity form, a development that can be traced out in a process of export reprimarization.

The social pact between Capital and Labor established by the 1988 Constitution expressed the powers and limits of social forces that played a relatively prominent role in the process that led to the end of the civilian-military dictatorship in Brazil. Structured in such a way as to preserve the power structure consolidated during the dictatorship, the formally democratic institutional framework established by the constitution nevertheless allowed for the expansion of the channels of popular pressure on public power and the creation of tools for a relative reduction of social inequalities, Brazil having one of the most unequal social distributions of wealth, land, and income in the world (De Farias, 2022).

During the last four decades of the "New Republic," the structural transformation of Brazilian society has intensified, giving rise to the emergence of new forces with concerns and horizons that overflow from the social pact established in 1988. Among the transformations in the structure of class society in Brazil brought about in the context of these reforms, what stands out is the process of deindustrialization and the consequent weakening and virtual disappearance of an incipient industrial proletariat. De Farias (2022) argues that the development dynamics associated with the advance of the neoliberal policy agenda can also be traced out in the ideological apparatus (the mass media, public universities, industrial federations, and party apparatuses) that in previous decades had allowed the organic intelligentsia and fractions of the ruling classes in the Southeast, particularly in Sao Paulo, to consolidate on a national scale a relative consensus in civil society regarding industrialization as a national development strategy (De Farias, 2022).

This consensus was forged under the presidency of Getúlio Vargas (1930–1945), who sought a political pact with industrialists from the South while maintaining strong ties with the agrarian elites to transition toward an industrialized economy. Subsequently, this strategy was consolidated in the postwar period under the policy advice given by ECLA economists to the government to pursue a strategy of import substitution industrialization. However, developments in the 1980s, and the subsequent liberalization and internationalization of the Brazilian economy, undermined the project of modernization and industrialization that was taken up by the Brazilian Social Democracy Party (PSDB), and reinforced the power and privileges of oligarchic elites within what was a patrimonial state (García & Borba de Sá, 2022). Contrary to the illusion that Brazil's integration into the neoliberal world order would foment an economic growth dynamic, Brazil's insertion into the so-called globalization process eroded the very foundations of the country's capitalist modernity.

In this context, the failure of the São Paulo intelligentsia to rally around the PSDB in contesting the national elections over the last two decades is striking. Another aspect of this failure is the opportunity and political space that it created for both the electoral success of the PT under the leadership of Da Silva [Lula] and the subsequent emergence of Bolsonarism.

The Workers' Party (PT) at the end of the 1990s and into the 2000s was evidently still capable of mobilizing the working class within the policy framework of neodevelopmentalism. But this had nothing to do with advancing a modernist industrialization agenda; it was a matter of reaching both the urban and rural poor through the implementation of direct cash transfer programs such as *Bolsa Familia* (Valencia, 2013). At the same time, the PT has been unable to offer its social base a strategic horizon for creating new values for an alternative form of more inclusive postdevelopment based on social and environmental justice. According to De Farias (2022), this is due to the exhaustion of the government's (neo)developmentalist discourse, which bet on the Brazilian reindustrialization led by the public authorities and by the businessmen elevated to the status of "global players" as a condition for achieving greater national autonomy and the extension of wage citizenship to the masses.

If in the 1950s and 1960s the developmentalist strategy and the commitment to a national bourgeoisie culminated in tragedy, in the 2000s and 2010s – as De Farias sees it – the return to the traditional rhetoric of the Brazilian Left has been a farce.

From Leftist Progressivism to Rightist Populism

Lula's presidency from 2003 to 2010 corresponded almost precisely to a progressive cycle in Latin American politics as well as a boom-bust cycle of primary commodity exports. The downturn in commodity prices in 2012, which coincided with the end of the progressive cycle at the level of politics, saw a drastic reduction of Brazil's rate of economic growth from a decade-long average of around five percent to zero growth. The end of the commodities boom was by no means the only factor responsible for the ending of the PT government headed by Lula and then Dilma Rouseff, Lula's former Chief of Staff. There were undoubtedly other contingent contributing factors, but the collapse of the commodities boom on capitalist markets was a major contributing factor. In any case, Bolsonaro, who headed a coalition of forces on the political Right and campaigned on a populist program, was elected president (October 2018) with 55.1 percent of the popular vote. Over the subsequent three and a half years, Bolsonaro presided over a regime dedicated to the exploitation of the advantages that Brazil's wealth of natural resources gave the country in the global capitalist market. In the process, the neodevelopmentalist modernization program of progressive extractivism, or neoextractivism, pioneered by Lula was abandoned in favor of a neoliberal populist program of agroextractivist policies that accentuated and brought to a head the contradictions endemic to capitalism and extractivism. The difference between the PT government's extractivist regime and that of the Bolsonaro government could be metaphorically described as the dialectic of the carrot and stick, or extractivism with humane capitalism (inclusive development, or neodevelopmentalism, plus corporate social responsibility) versus war waged against both nature and the indigenous and non-indigenous communities of the "rural poor" on the expanding extractive frontier.

The reactionary policies of the Bolsonaro regime included support of foreign investment in the extractive industries in both the industrial and agricultural sectors, particularly regarding expansion of soy/soybean production and resource-based industrialization that increased the opportunities for resource producers to maximize gains from resource endowments. However, notwithstanding the importance to the Bolsonaro government of the extractive industries in these sectors, the major impact of Bolsonaro's policy regime and populist politics was on what was described by the regime as the "development" of the Amazon, but by others (e.g., Fearnside, 2005) as an "onslaught" on the region's natural resource wealth and biodiversity, which assumed the form of a war on the indigenous peoples that inhabit the interior of the Amazon and provided an obstacle to the government's plan to exploit the region's natural resource wealth more fully.

Bolsonaro's War on the Amazon

A striking feature of Bolsonaro's policy regime over the past three years is its strategic concern with developing the economic potential of the enormous reservoir of natural resources in the Amazon region, one of the largest pockets of common resources not yet reduced to the condition of private property in the world today. At issue here for the many critics of the Bolsonaro regime's frontal assault on the ecology of the Amazon, as well the war waged against the indigenous population, is how to make sense of the forces that are driving the chains of mineral and agro-processed products that link the Amazonian region to the global market and to explain the ferocious assault on the indigenous population that inhabit the interior of the state. By some accounts (Estes, 2021) the president effectively gave new license to the killing of these people, viewing them as obstacles to the plans of the government to take full advantage of the enormous reservoir and wealth of natural resources. While previous administrations, which by all accounts also coveted access to and exploitation of these resources, were prepared to rely on the forces and normal workings of capitalism (accumulation by dispossession, agroextractivism) and resist the impulse to eradicate or dislodge the indigenous communities from their territories and habitat, even to provide them a measure of protection to the indigenous peoples' territorial rights and protection from the equally destructive forces of illicit private enterprise, not so Bolsonaro. On assuming the office of the presidency, Bolsonaro almost immediately launched a vicious war against the indigenous population that inhabit the interior of the Amazonian region, this without regard or concern for either the environment or the people protecting it. In the words of Célia Xakriabá, an Amazonian Indigenous leader interviewed by Nick Estes, an indigenous scholar and activist associated with Red Nation (an indigenous-led leftist organization committed to decolonialization and indigenous liberation), "Bolsonaro attacked a woman first, the land, our mother ... We have no choice but to fight back."

The sociologist De Farias, together with other researchers and activist scholars (e.g., García & Borba de Sá), focused their concern with the development and resistance dynamics unleashed by the assault of the Bolsonaro regime on the environment and the indigenous peoples of the Amazon in terms of the idea that the Bolsonaro regime deepened and extended a process of "permanent primitive accumulation" in the Amazonian region – or "accumulation by dispossession," as Harvey (2003) would have it. Historically, De Farias points out that the ultra-concentrated appropriation of public lands in the interior of Brazil was a fundamental pillar for the formation of industrial urban capital throughout the 20th century. Thus, he notes, periods of stagnation in the process of capital accumulation during dictatorial cycles were inevitably followed by an accelerated advance of capitalism or the forces of capitalist development (the expropriation and expulsion of the local population, mostly indigenous) on the Amazon frontier, with an emphasis on the March to the West during the Estado Novo Vargas regime in the 1940s, and on the fiscal and credit incentives provided by the Superintendence for the Development of the Amazon during the dictatorship between 1964 and 1985.

To fast-forward the current conjuncture of capitalist development, the significance of the Bolsonaro regime's assault on the Amazon and the war waged against the indigenous population, as well as his current flirtation with opening the Amazon to a new dynamic of capitalist development was not, therefore, merely an intensification of a regime of plundering the natural resources of the Amazon region. Of greater significance, it could be argued that this ostensible process of primitive accumulation today no longer seems to serve as a lever for driving forward the country's industrialization processes. That is, the dispossession of the communities on the extractive frontier and their forced displacement has not unleashed an accumulation dynamic. Rather, the process seems to have become a strategic horizon, capable of unifying fractions of the ruling classes that supported and were associated with the Bolsonaro regime. They made up a power bloc in the parliament,[7] in a context of aborting the pretensions of a

---

[7]The power bloc behind Bolsonaro's apparent project of the destruction of the Amazon and its people consisted of a coalition of right-wing forces that range from agribusiness, the gun lobby and evangelicals; in the parliament it was collectively known as the "bull, bullet, and bible" bloc.

modern industrialized Brazil and regression to a primary-export model of capitalist development. A driving force behind the Bolsonaro regime's recourse to this model was the advance of extractive capital and its investment in the expansion of soybean plantations in Amazonia, which poses the greatest threat to the environment with its stimulus for massive government investment in infrastructure such as waterways, railways, and highways. "Infrastructure development," Fearnside (2001) notes, "unleashes an insidious chain of investment and profiteering that can be expected to destroy more forest than the plantations as such."

According to a map published by the newspaper Nexo (www.nexojornal.com.br) in April 2017, about 47 percent of Brazil's territory was still made up of public lands concentrated mainly in the North, including military areas, indigenous lands, conservation areas, and public lands not yet allocated (De Farias, 2022). According to this publication, indigenous lands already represent 13 percent of the country's surface, highlighting three parts of the federation with the highest percentages of indigenous areas in their territories: Roraima (46 percent), Amazonas (28 percent), and Pará (22 percent). In turn, the environmental conservation units correspond to 12 percent of the country's area, where again three states stand out for the proportion of these units on their lands: Amapá (63 percent), Acre (32 percent), and Pará (26 percent).

Public lands, especially those vulnerable to disputes, landgrabs, and illegal deforestation, that include unallocated or "unprotected" public lands (to which the federal government has not yet given any destination) correspond to 10 percent of the national territory (more than the areas of São Paulo and Minas Gerais combined), are concentrated in the states of Amazonas (35 percent), Acre (19 percent), and Roraima (17 percent).

The strategic unity of the sectors that are linked to agribusiness and neoextractivism derives from the common objective of transforming these reserves of public resources into land rent. The report *Cartographies of Violence in the Amazon Region*, published in 2021 and prepared by the Brazilian Forum on Public Security in collaboration with the Climate and Society Institute and the Terra Research Group of Emerging Territories and Resistance Networks in the Amazon (*TERRA*) at the University of the State of Pará, records the extent of the violence mobilized by the capitalist development of the interior and the rapidly growing illegal economy formed on the margins and underside of this development, especially crops that supply the lucrative but illegal drug trade and logging, both of which has helped fuel and accelerate a process of deforestation with devastating consequences for both the environment and the rural livelihoods of the indigenous communities.

According to the above-mentioned report (De Farias, 2022)) from 2011 to 2020 there was a 47.3 percent jump in intentional violent deaths (IVMs) in the Amazon region, with an emphasis on the growth of homicides in rural and intermediate municipalities of the Amazon, in the contexts of intensification of environmental crimes and land conflicts. Comparing the rates of IVMs by occupation zones in 2020, the report notes that the municipalities with the highest rates were those under deforestation pressure (37.1 per 100,000 inhabitants), followed by deforested municipalities (34.6) and nondeforested municipalities (29.7), while forested municipalities had the lowest case fatality rate in the region (24.9).

The report also notes that violence stemming from landgrabs, deforestation, the illegal timber market, and illegal mining has been fueled by the presence of organized crime factions and disputes between them over national and transnational drug routes that traverse the region. This growing prominence of an illicit economy and its complex articulation with power networks related to socioenvironmental crimes have meant that between 1980 and 2019 the homicide mortality rate grew by 260.3 percent in the North region, while in the Southeast region it fell by 19.2 percent over the same period.

The indigenous peoples of the Amazon region are a primary target of this escalation of violence, but they are also an important source of resistance to the advance of extractive capitalism and the expansion of an illicit economy. The report *Violence against Indigenous Peoples in Brazil*, with data from 2020, published by the Indigenous Missionary Council (CIMI) identified in that year 263 cases of property invasions, illegal exploitation of resources, and damage to heritage in at least 201 indigenous lands, of 145 peoples, in 19 states (De Farias, 2022).

The report also highlights the growing presence of military and police in the institution: 27 of FUNAI's 39 Regional Coordinations had chiefs appointed outside the agency's ranks, seventeen of whom were military, three military police, one federal police and six people with no prior ties to the public administration. Despite the efforts of the "New FUNAI" to prevent the pending demarcation processes from reaching the homologation stage, to weaken the mechanisms of protection and action in the unapproved Indigenous Lands and to regularize veiled forms of lease on Indigenous Lands for agricultural, mining, and logging exploitation, the report highlights that the ruralist anti-indigenism of the Bolsonaro regime did not achieve any effective legislative change. In particular, the paradigmatic judgment as to the fate of indigenous peoples and communities, and the status of their lands and territories, is still on the agenda of an unfinished battle, a sign of the capacity of resistance of the original peoples in the face of a double offensive of primitive accumulation and extractive imperialism.

Conclusion

This chapter sets out with the idea that Bolsonarism should not be viewed as a temporary or passing expression of political irrationality or exceptionalism. Rather, it was argued that it should be seen as the expression of a profound structural transformation of the class structure and in the development and resistance dynamics of capital accumulation in sectors linked to the productive chains of mineral and agricultural raw materials that were galvanized around the strategic horizon of intensifying a process of primitive accumulation in the in the Amazon region. In effect, as argued by De Farias among others, Bolsonarism can be seen, at least in part, as the outcome of a process of uneven development and deindustrialization fomented and fueled by the advance of extractive capital in Brazil. This process led to an abortion of the social modernization projects advanced by the ideologues of the "New Republic" in the 1980s. Marked by the centrifugal force of centers of power formed in the interior of the country with the reprimarization of Brazil's exports, Bolsonarism does not seem capable of consolidating a new social pact that establishes a minimum consensus among the different classes within civil society. On the other hand, the Brazilian Left seem to be equally incapable of offering a strategic horizon that recognizes the impasse and crisis in which the country is enmeshed. Prisoners of pragmatic calculations restricted to electoral dynamics, the left-wing of Brazil's modernist intelligentsia, take as an unquestionable datum a formally democratic institutional framework that appears to be in a process of total decomposition. Thus, as De Farias has argued, forces on the electoral Left are limited to a nostalgic discourse with a decreasing potential to mobilize the concerns of the working class, particularly the working youth immersed in increasingly precarious urban spaces. This nostalgic rhetoric seems to be enough to garner votes among the layers most affected by the economic crisis and with a vivid memory of recent stability, but a Lula III government will have fewer bargaining chips to play in the game of electoral politics if it cannot – or will not because it would mean abandoning rather than merely reforming the capitalist system – address head on and effectively deal with the multiple contradictions of a capitalist system in crisis. It is evident that neither a return to extractivism and the developmentalism of the neoliberal era, or a neodevelopmentalist strategy of progressive extractivism and poverty reduction favored by Lula's PT government, will work in the current context. The PT regime would pay dearly if it chose to move forward with a program limited to the implementation of minimum mechanisms to reduce inequality and neutralize social conflicts, policies that the party advanced in the 2000s. What is needed but what evidently is nowhere on the political horizon is a pathway toward another world of social and environmental justice, an alternative postcapitalist society in which everyone, including or especially the working class and the communities on the extractive frontier, can "live well" (*vivir bien*).

This is the fundamental challenge faced by progressive forces on the Left: how to bring about a process of structural transformation and systemic change in the context of a double-edged populism on both the Left and the Right. Another challenge for the Brazilian Left, which, according to Sader (2008), has never been as united as in the context of a system in crisis, is to unify the diverse forces of resistance to the advances of extractive capitalism, and in the specific Brazilian context of an assault on one of the world's greatest repositories of resources in the fight against global warming, and restore democracy from the assault of right-wing authoritarian populism, and re-establish a progressive economic policy of a more equitable income distribution. The current context of a system in crisis and a postneoliberal postdevelopment green extractivist transition across the region, it could be argued, is favorable for a pendulum swing back to the Left to consolidate a discernable regional trend in this direction.

Chapter 9

The Politics of Extractive Imperialism

In a recent book on the study of natural resource extraction in resource-rich countries, the former director of development research at the World Bank, Paul Collier, and the director of Oxford Center for the Analysis of Resource Rich Economies, Anthony Venables, conclude that "often plunder, rather than prosperity, has become the norm in the industry" (Collier & Venables, 2011). However, rather than tracing this problem to its all too obvious roots – imperialism and capitalism – they reduce it to a matter of "distortion and dependence" in the "decision-making chains in various [developing country] states." In line with the postneoliberal objectives of improving social outcomes through better governance, Collier and Venables set out improve the management of natural resources in developing countries by "highlight[ing] the key principles that need to be followed to avoid distortion and dependence." But they do this by narrowly focusing on the decision-making process in the management of natural resources and proposing good governance regulatory mechanisms, while ignoring the dynamics of capitalism and imperialism that generate the distortion and dependence in the first place.

Another approach to the economics and politics of natural resource extraction is based on the view that resource extraction has to do with economic growth strategies and the politics of international trade rather than resource pillage and labor exploitation, or environmental degradation and class conflict. In this view, governing regimes in the developing countries (especially in Latin America) responded to the growing demand for primary commodities (i.e., raw materials, food products, minerals) and shifted their economic growth strategies to the extraction of natural resources, given relatively high prices for primary commodities on the world market. The result is a reversion to Latin America's traditional trade structure based on dependence on the export of these commodities, a structure that Latin American theorists in the "structuralist" tradition warn is manifestly disadvantageous for the developing countries on the periphery of the world system, leading as it does to unequal exchange and dependency (Borón, 2008; Kay, 1989).

A third approach to the geopolitics of natural resource extraction is to focus not on the global dynamics of natural resource extraction but instead on the resistance of communities on the extractive frontier, resistance to what we have conceptualized as "extractive imperialism" and neocolonialism, which is characterized by the appropriation by companies of the natural resource wealth of communities on the extractive frontier, together with the violent expropriation and dispossession of the communities from the global commons, and the super-exploitation by Capital of both labor and nature, thereby disrupting the capacity of the communities on the extractive frontier to husband their natural resources and take care of "mother earth" (Girvan, 2014), forcing many families to abandon both agriculture, their traditional way of life and their rural communities, and to take the "development road" out of rural poverty, namely, migration and labor. On these struggle dynamics see Delgado Wise and Veltmeyer (2018).

Congruent with this approach, the chapter will discuss the class struggle dynamics associated with the resistance of the communities on the extractive frontier, dynamics that are often closely associated with mining – the "gran minería," as it is called in Latin America. The chapter explores the politics of this "development" (extractive capitalism and imperialism) along three dimensions. First, it reconstructs the underlying imperialist strategy of natural resource exploitation and its consequences, namely, the pillage of the territory's wealth of natural and human resources, the destruction of the environment and livelihoods of the local communities affected by the resource extraction process, and widespread resistance which has led to a new and virulent form of class struggle and political conflict. On this point, many governments in the region, including those with a progressive regime, have tended to rally to the defense of global capital, taking the side of the companies in their relation of conflict with the communities on the extractive frontier, this in a coincidence of economic interest (profits for the companies, fiscal revenues for the governments). The chapter concludes this discussion with a brief look at the forces of resistance and decolonization that have been built up and mobilized on this front of the class struggle against the advance of extractive capitalism and the machinations of extractive imperialism.

The Limits of Progressive Extractivism (The Cases of Bolivia and Ecuador)

In the current conjuncture of capitalist development, two countries – Bolivia and Ecuador – driven by the political and intellectual activism of both indigenous communities and environmental activists – have sought to go beyond both neoliberalism and the new developmentalism in constructing not an alternative form of (capitalist) development but an alternative to development as such in the construction of a new postdevelopment world based on the indigenous conception of *buen vivir* (Acosta, 2012; Acosta & Martínez, 2014; Huanacuni, 2010; Prada Alcoreza, 2013). This notion of *buen vivir*, or *vivir bien*, in both Bolivia and Ecuador has been entrenched in their constitutions – the constitution of a multiethnic plurinational state that recognizes not only the identity and territorial rights of the indigenous nationalities in the country but also the rights of nature (Gudynas, 2014).

The debate that evolved and continues to surround the notion of *buen vivir* (Acosta & Martínez, 2014) as an alternative form of postdevelopment has several axes. One has to do with the viability of a model and policy regime based on the notion of living in social solidarity and harmony with nature (mother earth, in traditional indigenous culture). Another has to do with the neoliberal policy regime implemented across the region in recent years and the model underlying this regime.

Alberto Acosta (2012), an economist who helped draft the Ecuadorian government's development model and national development plan (*Para Vivir Bien* – but today one of the government's fiercest critics – has argued that the extractivist strategy pursued by the government under the "progressive" policy regime of Rafael Correa, and the policies derived from this strategy, is in irreconcilable contradiction with the concept of "living well," thereby establishing the absolute limits of progressivism.

As Dávalos and Albuja (2014) argue in their discussion of the contradictory features of the Correa government's actual policies regarding economic development, Correa emerged as one of the strongest and ardent supporters of both "new developmentalism" (inclusionary state activism) and "neoextractivism" (the use of resource rents to achieve poverty reduction). Correa's position at the time was that the extraction and exportation of the country's natural resources in a partnership with foreign investors signified an "economic opportunity" that the country and government could not afford to pass by. And this was despite the resistance that this policy had generated in the indigenous movement and in the communities most directly affected by the destructive operations of extractive capital. A manifest form of this resistance is the fight led by CONAIE, an organization of indigenous peoples that has led the opposition to the neoliberal policy agenda of Ecuadorian governments since 1989 and against the government's extractivist policies. In 2015, CONAIE called for an "indigenous and popular uprising" and a "national strike" against the government (CONAIE, 2015).

As Dávalos and Albuja have argued, Correa's policies exemplified the pitfalls of the neoextractivism and submission of the government to the dictates of foreign capital. This includes the enclosure of the commons; the commodification of land, natural resources, and water; and the violation of the territorial rights of indigenous peoples and communities, and their marginalization or integration into the circuits and global dynamics of capital accumulation. It also includes the expansion of the extractive frontier – the exploration and exploitation of the country's oil reserves – in the country's pristine glacial waters and tropical forests as well as the open sea and significantly in nature reserves such as Yasuni-ITT, and in the indigenous territories (the "political ecology of territorial transformation").

The resistance and the struggle against the depredations of extractive capital also encompassed bituminous shale industrialization; opencast mining; corporate agro-extractivism, including the use of pesticides, seeds/genetically modified organisms, and plantation monoculture; the privatization of public services (including water, carbon markets, and the picturesque landscapes of the tourism industry); and the use of biotechnology and geotechnics in the conversion of farmland for the production of biofuels.

In 2007, President Rafael Correa launched the Yasuni-ITT project by means of which the government proposed permanent suspension of oil extraction in the Yasuni Ishpingo-Tambococha-Tiputini National Park (ITT) in exchange for payments of US$3.6 billion by the international community (Gridley, 2018). The project, by all accounts, was received with enthusiasm by environmentalists, postdevelopmentalists, and the indigenous movement and its supporters. The Yasuni-ITT park has around 846 million barrels or 20 percent of the country's proven oil reserves. The aim of the initiative was the conservation of biodiversity, protection of indigenous peoples living in voluntary isolation, and prevention of the release of CO_2 emissions.

Gridley notes that the Yasuni-ITT Trust Fund was officially launched on August 3, 2010, but by 2012 only US$200 million had been committed, prompting a 180° turn in the Yasuní-ITT project. "The world has failed us," Correa announced, and spoke of the rich countries as hypocrites because they emit the most greenhouse gases while expecting poor nations like Ecuador to sacrifice their economic progress to preserve the environment (Bazán Salcedo, 2013).

As with the TIPNIS controversy in Bolivia, Correa's subsequent abandonment of the Yasuni-ITT project shed light on the contradictions of government policy, particularly the contradiction between the government's postdevelopment plan and the government's economic development policies based on capitalism and extractivism.

The plan to extract oil from the Yasuni-ITT reignited a debate on the appropriate development strategy for Ecuador (Chimienti & Matthes, 2013). Many economists and environmentalists, as well as advocates for indigenous territorial rights, have pointed toward a serious defect in the logic of government policy, namely, that the aim is to generate economic growth and reduce poverty through extractivism implies a fatal contradiction with the *Plan Nacional Para Vivir Bien*.

After his election in 2007, Correa embarked on a process of aggressive negotiations with mining companies to obtain for Ecuador a greater share of the market value of the product and thus increase the government's fiscal revenues in service of a strategy aimed at a more equitable distribution of the country's social product. It appeared that Correa's strategy bore fruit. According to the UNDP's 2014 *Human Development Report* from 2003 to 2013, Ecuador's poverty rate was reduced by 50 percent over the course of Correa's administration. This success in meeting the UN's Millennium Development Goal regarding poverty reduction was attributed by the government to the government's policy of expanding expenditures on social welfare programs. But at what cost was this achieved?

This is one of the core issues of the debate stimulated by Correa's policies. Correa's economic development strategy demonstrates the extraordinary importance of the extractive sector in contemporary Ecuador. With the abandonment of banana production for export, oil revenues have come to account for almost one-third of the national budget, although Dávalos and Albuja (2014) argue that resource rents from the extraction of oil contributed next to nothing to the revenues used by the government to reduce poverty. Moreover, under Correa Ecuador experienced not only the negative socioenvironmental impacts of expanded oil production but also an expansion of the palm oil sector and large-scale mining projects that are notoriously destructive of both the environment and livelihoods.

Moreover, in the context of the government's efforts to justify its extractivist policies by reference to the overriding need to combat both underdevelopment and poverty, Correa's concern for the environment and the rights of mother earth had been reduced to vague rhetoric. In this context, Acosta points out, Correa was unable or unwilling to recognize the ecosystem – and political – limits to the dependence on natural resource extraction. In fact, Correa continued to invoke the importance of exploiting the country's wealth of natural sources:

> Our way of life is unsustainable if we do not use our oil and minerals in the next 10 or 15 years while developing alternative energy sources. Those who say that we should not exploit our resources put at risk programs designed to place Ecuador in the forefront of Latin American nations. They would have us return to the status of being a poor nation without a future. (Correa, 2012)

The Struggle Dynamics of Community-based Resistance

Prior to the 1990s, the class struggle in Latin America was basically involved a struggle over land in the countryside and wages and working conditions in the cities. In the 1990s, however, the popular movement, with the agency of class-based and community-based social movements, mobilized against the neoliberal state (and the governing regimes) in resistance against their policies. By the end of the decade a number of these movements – led by proletarianized peasant farmers, rural landless workers, and indigenous communities, in some contexts (Chiapas, Brazil, Ecuador, Bolivia, etc.) – achieved major gains in their struggle, placing the existing neoliberal regimes on the defensive and provoking a legitimation crisis for the neoliberal state. At the turn into the 21st century, to all intents and purposes, neoliberalism was dying if not defunct, no longer able to serve its legitimating function to naturalize and legitimate the social inequalities inherent in the class structure. With the observed – and widely reported – left turn in national politics in 2002 and then again in 2019, the regimes that came to power in the wake of widespread disenchantment with neoliberalism each and all, including overtly neoliberal regimes in Mexico and Colombia (and Peru at the time), sought to move "beyond neoliberalism" – at least rhetorically, in the search for a new form of governance and an alternate path toward national development.

As noted by the establishment (i.e., neoliberal) economist Collier (2003) – an expert in drawing attention to the obvious if not the underlying dynamics of capitalist development and imperialist exploitation – natural resources can, and often do, provoke conflicts within societies as different groups and factions fight for their share. Sometimes, Collier adds, these emerge openly as separatist conflicts in regions where the resources are produced (such as the gas-rich department of Santa Cruz in Bolivia), but often the conflicts occur in more hidden forms, such as fights between different government ministries or departments for access to budgetary allocations. This, Collier notes, tends to erode the government's ability to function effectively.

However, Collier continues, there are several types of relationships between natural resources and class conflicts – and between global capital and the State regarding these conflicts. First, "resource curse effects can undermine the quality of governance and economic performances" (Norman, 2009, pp. 183–207), thereby increasing the vulnerability of countries to conflicts (the "resource curse" argument). Second, conflicts can occur over the control and exploitation of resources and the allocation of their revenues (the "resource war" argument). Third, access to resource revenues by belligerents can prolong conflicts (the "conflict resource" argument) (Le Billon, 2006). According to one study, a country that is otherwise typical but has primary commodity exports around 25 percent of GDP has a 33 percent risk of conflict, but when exports are five percent of GDP the chance of conflict drops to six percent (Bannon & Collier, 2003). While Collier focuses on the internal dynamics of such conflicts, the international dimension is continuously at play, as the imperial state intervenes (and sometimes instigates) into the conflict to gain control of the natural resources by proxy.

The Dynamics of Natural Resource Appropriation and Resistance on the Extractive Frontier

The agency and key agents involved in the politics of resistance against the imperial incursions of capital in the exploitation of "natural resources") – at least in the Latin American context – are the predominantly indigenous communities that populate the areas ceded by the different governments (be they neoliberal or postneoliberal in form) to the foreign mining companies for the exploration and exploitation of the natural resources in their territorial lands.[1] However, they also include a variety of civil society groups and nongovernmental organizations that have been drawn into the conflict between global capital and the local communities.[2] The forces of resistance to resource imperialism include new social movements formed to protest the damage to the environment caused by resource extraction, as well as the effects on the health and the livelihoods of the local

---

[1] Although governments generally acknowledge the rights and ownership of the land in the areas populated by the indigenous communities and also the right of indigenous peoples to be consulted in regard to proposed mining operations and other extractivist "projects" in their "territory," they usually also reserve the right to cede to the mining companies the right to exploit the subsoil resources under a "social license" issued under a regulatory regime (e.g., to protect the environment) and a royalty-tax payment agreement. That is, the indigenous peoples are to be consulted, but the state has the ultimate authority to grant foreign companies the right to explore and produce minerals in their territories.

[2] An example of one of these NGOs is Global Response, which has prepared a manual that can be used by activists to engage the mining companies in the class struggle against imperialist exploitation – to resist the diverse strategies used by these companies to overcome local resistance. See Zorrilla (2009). *Protegiendo a su comunidad contra las empresas mineras y otras industrias extractivas*. Boulder, CO: Global Response.

population – and the miners themselves, who face life-threatening working conditions and health concerns. In other words, many of these movements are rooted in those "affected" by the impacts of resource extraction and mining operations (e.g., REM – Red Mexicana de Afectados por la Minería; and Conacami – Confederación Nacional de Comunidades del Perú Afectadas por la Minería).

According to a forum of peoples, communities and groups "affected" ("negatively impacted") by the operations of mining capital and the resource extraction industry (Foro de los Pueblos Indígenas Minería, Cambio Climático y Buen Vivir) celebrated in Lima on November 2010, the exploitation of the region's mineral resources, and consequently the level of political conflict, by 2009 reached levels hitherto never experienced.[3] Of particular concern here is the Amazon, a broad expanse of space (some 6.7 million sq. km) that encompasses nine countries – Brazil, Colombia, Peru, Bolivia, and Ecuador, as well as Guyana, Peru, Suriname, Venezuela, and French Guiana – whose abundant deposits of gold, bauxite, precious stones, manganese, uranium, etc. are coveted by the multinational companies operating in the mining sector. Another concern was the perceived connection between the multinational corporations in the sector and a host of foundations and NGOs with an alleged humanitarian or religious concern for the environment and the livelihood of the indigenous peoples and communities. In this connection, Eddy Gómez Abreu, President of the *Parlamento Amazónico Internacional*, declared that they had

> incontrovertible evidence of these transnationals and foundations, under the cover of supposed ecological, religious, or humanitarian concerns, collaborated in the effort to "extract diamonds, strategic minerals and genetic" as well as espionage and illegal medical experiments on the indigenous population. (Sena-Fobomade, 2011)

In effect, he alleged that the mining companies regularly used foundations and other NGOs as one of their tactics to secure the consent of the local population to their projects and operations and to manipulate them. If this is true, these foundations and NGOs continue the long sordid history of European missionaries in the Americas of expropriating the lands of the indigenous, but in an updated form.

On the one hand, the forces of resistance use tactics such as marches and demonstrations, road and access blockades, and other forms of direct collective action to impede the mining operations (Zorilla, 2009). On the other hand, the tactics of the mining companies included visiting the community for the purpose

---

[3] According to the forum organizers, who included Fobomade – a Bolivia-based Forum on the Environment and Development that includes all sorts of community-based and nongovernmental organizations concerned with protecting the environment and the country's wealth of natural resources from the depredations of mining capital and capitalist industrialization – 2010 saw the maximum expansion of mining capital in the continent, which dictates a continent-wide mobilization of the forces of resistance.

of gathering information and evaluating the local situation (e.g., the degree of opposition) under false pretexts such as representing themselves as members of an NGO concerned with the welfare of the indigenous; arranging public meetings, with the help of local allies or "friendly" officials; bribing government officials with the promise of jobs and social development funds; manufacturing a "social license" by negotiating with a friendly local group supportive of the project, albeit not representative of the "community"; creating a support group and organization, when a submissive or complaint group does not exist in the community; or seeking support for a proposed mining project by offering gainful employment to unemployed members of the community, work for local contractors or service contracts; purchasing land with access to the concessions; infiltration of the community and spying on the opposition; and strategic litigation against public participation, false accusations, intimidation and death threats, and paramilitary action. Ultimately, the mining companies rely on the direct violence of military, paramilitary, and/or police forces to overcome opposition to their highly lucrative mining operations.

As for the problem at issue in these tactics, and the associated conflict, it was to defeat the forces of resistance against the operations of mining capital and the extraction of resources for the purpose of capital accumulation. From the perspective of the local communities, however, at issue was not only the health of their members and sovereign control over their national territory, but the environment on which their livelihood and way of life and life itself depend. In this regard, Gómez Abreu reported in a sociometabolic analysis of the economy that over a million people in the Amazonian basin suffer from diseases derived from exposure to and ingestion of toxic and carcinogenic substances, such as mercury, which has been demonstrably linked to an increase in the suicide rate in indigenous communities. And the researcher, Edgardo Alarcón, in the same regard, documented the scientific evidence that the Peruvian city of Oroya is one of the 10 most contaminated cities in the world, with high levels of lead and sulfur in the air and high levels of mining-based and related carcinogens such as cadmium, arsenic, and antinomy in the soil, agriculture-based food products, and the water supply – toxins that were also detected in other towns and surrounding communities (Sena-Fobomade, 2011). Thus, what is a source of profit for the transnational mining corporations represents a "death sentence" for local communities.

Conacami, one of the major organizations participating in the Forum, denounced the fact that by the end of 2010 many ancestral sites in its territory were in the hands of the mining and oil companies (the "transnationals"), which have been ceded up to 72 percent of Peru's national territory for the purpose of exploration and the exploitation of the country's natural resources. In this connection, Conacami alerted forum participants of the actions of the government – at that time under the control of Humala's neoliberal predecessor, President Alan García – in declaring 33 mega-projects to be in the "national interest" and thus without the need for the companies to submit environmental impact studies (Sena-Fobomade, 2011).

These and other such reports reflected the fact that Peru, together with Ecuador and Bolivia, is one of the major Latin American sites of class struggle over the extraction and exploitation of natural resources. A major focal point in this struggle was the resistance of the *Aguaruna*, an indigenous people inhabiting the environs of the Marañón River. The rebellion of the Aguaruna (or Awajún, their endonym) against the privatization and expansion of a multinational mining operation in their territory was marked by a massacre on June 5, 2009, that was memorialized and is remembered to this day by the Aguaruna in their continuing mobilizations. "Bagua is not forgotten" has become a rallying cry in the mobilizations and struggles in the Peruvian Amazon against multinational mining operations and against the complicity of the government, which over the years has not only given the companies carte blanche in their operations but has continued to persecute the indigenous leaders (De Echave, 2009b).

Another major and continuing focal point in this struggle relates to the Conga mine, the largest extraction project in the country at the time and one of the largest in the entire region. In March 2012, the entire mine expansion operation was put "on hold," the result of the fierce organized resistance of the local communities in the Cajamarca region. This Conga Project, a joint project between Denver-based Newmont Mining Corporation and Peru's Minas Buenaventura, was designed to help the company (and the government) meet the goal of producing seven million ounces of gold and 400 million pounds of copper by 2017 – expected to provide a major boost to the GDP and company profits, as well as rents (royalties and taxes) collected by the government. But of course, these rents and profits would come at the cost of devastating the land, waterways, and livelihoods of the local indigenous communities contiguous to the mining operations.

The resistance of the local communities made it difficult if not impossible for the stalled project to resume operations. In February 2012, the resistance to the Conga Project took the form of a national march for "water and life," a mobilization that gained broad public support as well as the active participation of diverse social groups and sectors. And if the local communities in their struggle against mining capital and the extractive industry were to succeed in stopping a project that the government declared to be of strategic importance and in the national interest, As it turned out, in 2016 after four more years of class struggle, Newmont Mining, the world's second largest gold mining company, was forced to walk away from the US$5 billion Conga copper mining project, providing a major boost to the forces of resistance throughout the region.

The conga project is worth a closer look as a typical example of the role played by so many governments in the region, including not only neoliberal governments but also progressive governments – as in the case of Rafael Correa – in the relation of conflict between the companies and the communities on the extractive frontier. In the case of the Conga project, the thousands of protesters who packed Lima's downtown core in 2012, one year into the ambiguously "progressive" Humala regime, in the "March for Water and Life," called on the government to cancel the project over fears that the mine's tailing ponds and reservoirs would seep into local water supplies. "We're here because we don't want foreigners taking our water," one of the protesters declared as he marched down a boulevard in central Lima, with the trademark straw hat of a Cajamarca farmer perched atop his head.[4] "It belongs to Peru," he added. The presence of police in riot gear confronting the march was a frightening reminder of the hostility protesters face from mining proponents.

In December 2011, Humala declared a 60-day state of emergency after a series of violent clashes erupted between police and protesters in Cajamarca as a general strike and roadblocks paralyzed the region. Much of the anger at the time stemmed from a perceived flip-flop by Humala, a former left-nationalist and radical populist in the mold of Evo Morales, who spoke out against foreign mining companies during his election campaign for the presidency and even hinted at the possible nationalization of the industry. However, as predicted by some on the Left Humala sided with the mining companies in their conflict with the indigenous communities. The reason for this supposed flip-flop (in fact, Humala's stance was entirely predictable) is clear enough. At issue in the conflict – and in this the Conga mine issue was no different from struggles over the decade and throughout the region – is the capitalist development of the country's natural resources, including the rents and taxes collected by government – which can be considerable, reason enough for a political turn to the right (i.e., a coincidence of economic interests between State and Capital). At this point, there are no end of examples – from Peru and Bolivia to Brazil and Argentina – of an ostensibly anti- or postneoliberal regime spouting nationalist rhetoric regarding ownership and control of the country's natural resources, but then settling all too quickly (or slowly if need be, as in the case of Peru's Conga Project) with global capital in the exploitation of the country's natural resources to a mutual benefit.

In the case of the Conga mine in the Cajamarca region, the company responsible for the project pointed out that the project if allowed to go ahead would have created as many as 7,000 construction jobs and 1,600 operation jobs. Further, the project was expected to pay the government close to US$3 billion in taxes as well as royalties, the proceeds of which Humala promised would be distributed in an equitable fashion in a policy of social inclusion. So, the stakes were high, both for the company and the government. However, as it turned out, the stakes were even higher for the community, namely, *"water and life."*

Antiextractivist Protests and the Global Environmental Justice Movement

Since the late 1990s, across Latin America there has been an increasing incidence of local protests and acts of territorial and environmental resistance against the expansion of extractivism in terms of the agency of large private (privatized)

---

[4]Quoted in a news report ("Peruvians take to the streets in Lima to protest mine developments") posted by Kenyon Wallace of the *Toronto Star* (February 18, 2012). <https://www.thestar.com/news/world/peruvians-take-to-the-streets-in-lima-to-protest-mine-developments/article_fbb12ede-16e7-51de-add1-201762efe893.html>

mining and oil projects financed by foreign capital. With respect to mining, for example, the Observatory of Latin American Mining Conflicts has registered 155 major socio-environmental conflicts in recent years, most of them in Argentina, Brazil, Chile, Colombia, Mexico, and Peru (see Table 9.1).[5] Diverse "stakeholders" (to use the development jargon), especially campesinos, indigenous groups, workers, and small-scale miners, have resisted new investments and projects that give little (few jobs and development) but take and damage a lot (land, water, air – and livelihoods). The numerous mobilizations against extractive activities focus on land and water rights, territorial claims, and the notorious environmental record of extractive industries (North et al., 2006).

While some of these local protests have taken place in marginalized areas and have received little external support or attention, other conflicts have become well-known and achieved online status with the global "antiglobalization movement": the resistance of Peruvian farmers and other local groups against gold mining in Tambogrande and Yanacocha; the massive protests against Barrack Gold's goldmine operations in Argentina's Valle de Huasco, leading to the disappearance of several glaciers, widespread contamination, and drought; the mobilization of Mayan communities against silver and gold mines in Guatemala; and various indigenous protests against extractive activities in the Amazon, including the long history of mobilization against Chevron/Texaco in Ecuador. Many of these local protests have been related to the ecological worldview or growing strength of indigenous movements or the increasing popular resistance to neoliberalism and globalization in the region. However, most of the all-too-abundant reports and studies of this resistance have been linked to the struggle for a more participatory politics and an alternative postneoliberal model of capitalist development and consequently have failed to appreciate its significance regarding the class struggle against capitalism and capitalism.

In this regard, the growing protest movement against mining capital and extractivism (see, e.g., Bebbington, 2007; De Echave et al., 2009a) not only engaged the forces of resistance against neoliberalism and globalization but raised serious questions about the underlying operative capitalist system. Thus, the so-called politics of natural resource extraction could be seen not just a matter of better resource management, a postneoliberal regulatory regime, but as a more socially inclusive development strategy or a new form of governance – securing the participation of local communities and stakeholders in decisions and policies in which they have a vital interest.

Given the interests that they represent, and the coincidence of these interests with those of the "transnational capitalist class," the officials and managers of the postneoliberal state generally side with capital against labor and have not reacted well to the civil society organizations that criticize or resist their mineral policies or extractive projects. The antiextractivist protests in the region have received international activist (and academic) recognition as part of a global environmental justice movement, but the agents and progressive officials of the "postneoliberal"

---

[5]See the Observatory's website [www.olca.cl/ocmal] for details about these conflicts.

states simply ignore them and proceed with their geopolitical project: to advance the exploitation of the country's natural resources by global capital in the public interest. Thus, the politics of natural resource extraction resolves into a matter of class struggle – of combatting the workings of capitalism and imperialism in the economic interests of the dominant class and mobilizing the forces of resistance against these interests.

Conclusion

The recent left turns in Latin American politics revived hopes among progressives that the region might finally have found halting steps toward slaying the twin demons of capitalism and imperialism; that the region is entering a new era of inclusive development and social-environmental justice. However, these hopes are contingent on what might be seen as a benign and overly optimistic scenario regarding the resilience of capitalism and the forces of right-wing reaction that are likely to be mobilized against the forces of progressive change in the current context. In addition, the totally unexpected election of Javier Milei to the presidency of Argentina in 2024 dashed the fragile hope on the Left of another progressive cycle.

A balanced assessment of the forces of capitalist development and the forces of resistance that are still very much at play on the political stage in the region suggests that, as the Zapatistas have determined in their struggle, the capitalist system has not yet exhausted their full potential. Capitalism in this context, as subComandante Marcos once noted, could be viewed as a hydra whose head whenever chopped off gives rise to another.

Chapter 10

What Next for Latin America? The Postextractive Transition

The Los Angeles Times on November 3, 2022, editorialized with the headline: "The left now rules most of Latin America. Will it be able to live up to its promises?" Of course, as we have seen this so-called "rule" is shaky and subject to countervailing forces mobilized from and by the Far Right. And the Left's rule, such as it was or has been in recent decades, has been widely contested, allowing the forces of neoliberal or authoritarian populism in the class struggle to resume for a time their control of the state apparatus. As *The Los Angeles Times* Linthicum and Wilkinson (2022) wrote in their fairly accurate (albeit not too deep) reporting on this issue, the "driving the pendulum [of electoral politics] are voters hungry for change amid rising inequality and frustration with how governments handled the pandemic and its economic fallout." Without digging too deeply into the issue, we can conclude from our review of the dynamics of class struggle that the successive swings of the pendulum of electoral and extra-parliamentary politics to the left and the right are determined in part by the correlation of force in the class struggle, and in part by the capacity of the government or the campaign of a presidential candidate for the presidency, and that of the political party or social movement backing the candidate, to deal with the anger and frustrations of the electorate.

Assessing Latin America's Left Turns

In the first decade of the new millennium, Latin America experienced a series of political, social, ideological, and economic changes that represented a sharp break from the dynamics that had defined Latin American politics since the inception of the neoliberal era in the 1980s. In addition to Argentina, Brazil, and Uruguay, there were other countries that took a clearly marked left turn in national politics in the search for an alternative to the neoliberal policy agenda in the form of neodevelopmentalism – what has been described as a "pink tide" of regime change. Ecuador and Bolivia took an even more radical left turn (a "red" tide?) in the form of a plurinational state on a pathway toward the "socialism of

---

Latin American Politics in the Neoliberal Era:
The Changing Dynamics of Class Struggle, 153–169
Copyright © 2025 by Henry Veltmeyer
Published under exclusive licence by Emerald Publishing Limited
doi:10.1108/978-1-83797-841-020241011

the 21st century"; a project staked out by Hugo Chávez. In addition, Nicaragua and El Salvador joined this left turn against neoliberalism in South America with a cycle of progressive policies.

We can identify two conflicting leftist positions among the progressive governments formed in the "pink tide" that have become increasingly well-defined over the past two decades: One position is favorable, while the other is highly critical to the extent that the progressive regimes – including Venezuela's Nicolás Maduro, Ecuador's Rafael Correa, Bolivia's Evo Morales, and Brazil's Luiz Inácio (Lula) da Silva – are sometimes put in the same category as those on the center-right, even as conservatives in the tradition of social liberalism. On this point, note the trenchant criticisms leveled against the pink tide governments by James Petras (see Chapter 2) and the discussion below on the limitations of neodevelopmentalism, the model used by progressive governments to make policy at the level of economic and social development, and the limitations of social democracy in battling the advances and the onslaught of extractivist capitalism and imperialism.

At the heart of these differences, according to Ellner (2023), is the issue of imperialism. However, a more plausible argument can be advanced regarding extractivism, together with neodevelopmentalism – a pillar of the economic model deployed by the pink tide progressive regimes in the class struggle. Ellner's argument regarding imperialism is that it is the Left's foremost priority worldwide, and given that all the Pink Tide governments have been subjected to and have resisted US interventionism, it is incumbent of the Left to provide steadfast support for them (Ellner, 2023). In this regard, he notes that real progress in halting climate change is contingent on respect for national sovereignty and slashing military spending, fundamental goals of anti-imperialism. However, Ellner himself (2023, pp. 1–2) observes that the number one priority in the world today for the Left and progressive forces is not so much political as ecological. In any case, Ellner's argument reminds one of the noncritical stances taken by many on the Left over the years regarding Cuba and Venezuela. The stance is that the Left should not criticize the shortcomings of the progressive leftist regimes because that would aid and abet the right-wing and reactionary forces in the class struggle. This author rejects this stance.

The New Popular Resistance in Latin America

Notwithstanding the persisting appeal of right-wing populism evidenced by the electoral success of Javier Milei in Argentina the restoration of conservatism has been held back by an upsurge of popular resistance across the region in 2019 (Katz, 2023a). Latin America has long served as a laboratory for an analysis of the dynamics of popular rebellions and transformative political processes and indifferent corners of the region there persists the same tendency toward a restart of the uprisings that signaled widespread rejection of the neoliberal policy agenda in the 1990s, creating conditions that led to a dynamic cycle of progressive policy regimes in the new millennium. These uprisings calmed down over the last decade but recovered in intensity in recent years (Katz, 2023a). The Covid pandemic interrupted this upsurge in popular protest, which neutralized the conservative restoration in 2014–2019, but it did not disable the activism of the popular movements, which experienced an upsurge in 2019, an upsurge that heralded what has turned out to be another left turn in Latin American politics. The 2019 rebellion in Ecuador inaugurated this current phase of protests, which spread to Bolivia, Chile, Colombia, and Peru, the main centers of the recent round of confrontations of class forces.

As Katz among others have documented in recent years, this upsurge of popular uprising has recreated several progressive scenarios that countered the counter-offensive of the right wing, with immediate electoral effects that provoked the departure of right-wing presidents in Bolivia, Chile, Peru, Honduras, and in Colombia. In Mexico, Argentina, and Brazil widespread social discontent did not give rise to similar protests but it did lead to the victory of progressive forces at the polls as in the case of Petro's ascendency to the presidency in Colombia. Also, in Ecuador and Panama important victories were achieved in the streets against the imposition of neoliberal policies (Santos & Cernadas, 2022). As Katz notes, the analysis of these dynamics across the region is often neglected by the studies that are exclusively focused on the dynamics of electoral politics and elite rule. But as Katz argues, an analysis of the upsurge in popular resistance sheds light on the class struggle dynamics involved in both electoral politics and the struggles on the extractive frontier as well as more broadly the prospects of transformative social change.

One dimension of these complex dynamics that warrants a closer look is the effect of the popular uprisings on the concerted efforts of the US government, viewed by the Latin American Left as an agency of imperial power, to interfere in Latin American political affairs, a longstanding historical trend that by several accounts persists in the current conjuncture of political developments in the region. The resurgent popular movement in the region among other results and outcomes has managed to counteract the continuing efforts of Washington to promote an institutional or military coup in any country that opposes or seeks to deviate from US policy and interests. Recent instances of this scenario include US sponsorship of active coup attempts in Honduras (2009), Paraguay (2012), Brazil (2016), and Bolivia (2019). It was the activism of the popular movement in opposing these efforts to bring about change by undemocratic means and impose a neoliberal policy agenda, according to Katz, that held in check the forces of US imperialism and the advance of the far right in the political process. The social rebellion in the streets in 2023 also succeeded in preventing the implementation of the neoliberal policy agenda of conservative governments in Peru, Ecuador, and Panama (Katz, 2023a).

However, these interventions from below have also provoked a more virulent and programmed reaction from the dominant classes, who in the current context exhibited a lack of tolerance to any questioning of their privileges and launched a counteroffensive aimed at resuming, with greater violence if necessary, the failed conservative restoration of the past decade. As Katz argues this complex scenario requires an evaluation of the class forces in dispute.

Alliances in the Class Struggle

Given the complex crosscurrents of the class struggle in these political developments, it is difficult to determine a distinct pattern across the region or to determine the prospects for or the fate of the Left on the road ahead. For one thing, the correlation of force in the class struggle is constantly shifting. On the other hand, the confluence of developments initiated "from above," at the level of national politics, and "from below" by communities on the extractive frontier, appear to prefigure another turn to the left in the direction of a postextractive transition toward a more sustainable and inclusive form of development. For example, the emergence of cross-class coalitions and cross-country regional alliances (Borras, 2023; López y Rivas, 2023) clearly favor the consolidation of left-leaning regimes and the emergence of a new progressive consensus. In addition, the indigenous movement in Mexico, Bolivia, and Ecuador has opened new horizons for a process of revolutionary transformation in the region – a transition to a "development utopia" based on social and environmental justice (Travela, 2018; Pinheiro Barbosa & Rosset, 2023).

In response to the emergence and rise of the radical Right, politicians on the center-left have forged alliances with politicians at the center of the political spectrum in the mold of traditional liberalism. In Brazil, for example, Lula da Silva has built a broad coalition that reaches well beyond his Workers' Party (PT) in engaging forces on both the Left and the Center-Left; and the left-leaning government formed in Colombia by Gustavo Petro has partnered with center-left and even right-of-center politicians, some of whom have been given important positions such as the presidency of the Senate, which is now in the hands of Roy Barreras, previously an ally of the ultra-right-wing former president Álvaro Uribe (Stuenkel, 2022). In Chile, after the decisive defeat of a draft of the proposed new constitution in the referendum of September 2022, Boric announced as ministers representative figures of the former Concertación (a former social democratic) regime) such as Carolina Tohá, formerly mayor of Santiago and minister during the administration of Michelle Bachelet (she was appointed Minister of the Interior, while Ana Lya Uriarte, formerly Bachelet's chief of staff, was appointed Secretary General of the Presidency. However, many critics on the Left argued that while these pacts offered governability, they can also immobilize the transformative energies of the Left and erode its political support base.

For this strategy of strategic broad alliances across the political spectrum to succeed, the new leftist or left-leaning governments will no doubt have to design strategies that break with the political incapacities of the "progressive cycle" of left-wing governments that dominated the political landscape in South America in the years 2002–2012 to bring about the desired "structural transformation" of society. At the same time, these leftist regimes face the challenge of recovering the popular enthusiasm with which the progressive cycle began while also addressing the impact that diverse geopolitical changes have produced in their countries.

After a cycle of a radicalized right-wing regimes that emerged in the second decade of the new millennium, the progressivisms (left-wing regimes) that over the past four years displaced the right-wing regimes have had to make more than ever before important concessions to the liberal political center and the moderate right. This "moderation" shown by the left-leaning regimes currently in control of the state apparatus in a number of countries (see the discussion below), in relation to the radicalism of the first progressive cycle, may allow for some stability (institutional, judicial, and military), but in the long run it can bog down the transformative forces that the Left needs to deploy to meet the expectations of its followers. It also risks being trapped in an emergency management regime without major advances on the front of social change, given that politicians in the political center now have more influence or power.

As for regional alliances forged on the political Left, the call of both the presidents of Mexico and Brazil for a summit of progressive regimes favor the inclusion of both Venezuela and Cuba in a new progressive consensus. This call for a summit of progressive regimes is clearly designed to revive SELA (the *Sistema Económico Latinoamericano y del Caribe*), a regional alliance of Latin American governments that was formed in 1975 in conditions that preceded the neoliberal era of capitalist development, conditions that favored the formation of the Organization of American States (OAS), the US-led regional alliance of "democratic" Latin American countries that excluded both Cuba and Venezuela. The latest turn to the left in 2020 is likely to bring Venezuela and Cuba back into the fold of regional politics as part of an emerging left-leaning consensus and regional alliance.

But it will not be easy sailing across these waters. The hard turn toward the left in Chile by Gabriel Boric, Latin America's youngest head of state ever, revolved around a proposal to create a new constitution that was untainted by the legacy of Augusto Pinochet, the military dictator who initiated Chile's experiment with neoliberal economics in the 1970s after a hard military coup executed against the democratically elected socialist President Salvador Allende on 9/11 in 1973. The failure of this proposal to gather traction or support either in the congress or society at large exposed clear limits to the New Left and a progressivism that is rooted in the class struggle from below. And in Colombia, notwithstanding President Gustavo Petro's broad center-left coalition and his pact (*Pacto Histórico*) with some opposition lawmakers, his health reform program has stalled in Congress amid the biggest challenge yet to the pact struck with diverse forces on the left and center-left, and even elements of the moderate Right (Stuenkel, 2022).

The setbacks experienced by the center-left – the dominant force in the second progressive turn raise questions about the limitations of progressivism and the overall immediate and near future of the Left, and about the prospects for escaping the trap of democratic electoral politics (Dávalos & Albuja, 2014). For example, Petro has urged Congress to give the green light to a number of progressive health, labor, and pension bills, but the lower house had already threatened to shelve the key healthcare reform. In these conditions, Petro warned of the beginnings of another "soft" coup. In fact, *Pacto Histórico* lawmaker and human rights activist Piedad Córdoba warned of a brewing soft coup against Petro back in March. Pointing to cases against other regional leftist leaders like Brazil's Lula da Silva and Argentina's Cristina Fernández de Kirchner; she tweeted out the "steps" of a lawfare campaign, beginning with disinformation. Once an "artificial climate of unsustainable social discontent" is established, she wrote, lawfare campaigns will invent some court case about "whatever – the details don't matter" – in preparing conditions for another soft coup orchestrated by right-wing oppositional forces. And the history of Latin American politics in the dialectic and the see-sawing of electoral politics in the context of the latest turn to the left validates and justifies the concern that Latin America has not yet outgrown and put behind them a sordid history of right-wing coups inspired, financed, and abetted by US imperialism.

The Limitations of Democratic Electoral Politics

In this book, we have reviewed the dynamic and constantly changing situation of the class struggle in different countries across the region. Some of these dynamics have played out, and continue to do so, at the level of electoral politics, what we have described as the first and major front of the class struggle against the advance of capitalism in the development process. However, behind these dynamics can be found an exceedingly complex pattern of crosscutting currents. While it is impossible to trace out the sometimes rapidly changing situations and chart the likely path that the class struggle will soon take, a few guiding principles will help our task: Examining the political dynamics of electoral politics can give us clues as to the underlying forces of change, these forces must be traced out at the level of the class struggle, what we have dubbed the "class struggle from below."

An illustration of this point is the current situation in Colombia, where the pendulum of electoral politics has recently swung to the left. But as in Chile and Peru, this development must be measured against the ever-changing correlation of class forces. For example, most political observers have commented on the internment and burial of the idea of socialism and the project to recreate socialism in a new form – a project popularized by Hugo Chávez and echoed by Evo Morales in the years of the first left turn in Bolivia and by Rafael Correa in his conception of a citizen's revolution. In any case, a relevant datum regarding the current situation in Colombia is the evident survival and reconstruction from below (rather than from above, as in Chávez's Venezuela) of socialism both as an idea used to mobilize action and diverse projects to put it into practice at the grassroots. More on this below.

Another exemplar of this development is Bolivia, where, as we discuss below, the political panorama is riddled with projects to resurrect and put socialism back on the agenda,[1] and Colombia, the one country in the region that until now has

---

[1] An eloquent testimony of this is provided in a series of reports and a webinar organized by Gonzalo Gosalvez Sologuren, a professor of political economy at the Public University of El Alto (La Paz, Bolivia) and the Indigenous University Tupak Katari. Sologuren is an independent journalist and indigenous public intellectual who has traced out many outbreaks in the class struggle initiated from the grassroots; he is also a specialist in community-based solidarity economics, where the forces of community-based resistance from below are concentrated. And this is not just in Bolivia, but all over the region.

always resisted the temptations of the Left – probably because of the long-term survival of the Fuerzas Armadas Revolucionarias de Colombia (FARC), a leftover of leftist politics from the 1960s and 1970s, where the Latin American class struggle took the almost universal form of a national army of liberation led and prosecuted by a rebellious revolutionary peasantry. The survival into the new millennium[2] of FARC, the only revolutionary movement ("army of national liberation") to have survived the "'pogrom" of the 1960s–1970s, a class war orchestrated by a coalition of US imperialism in the form of a program of "integrated rural development" and state repression,[3] explains why the political Left in the neoliberal era was never able to gain a foothold in advancing the class struggle.

Colombia Turns Left. Or Does it?

On August 11, 2022, Colombia began a new chapter in the history of its politics with the inauguration of Gustavo Petro (*The Associated Press*, 2022), the country's first-ever leftist president and a former guerilla commander on August 22, 2022. Observers have differed widely on what Petro's presidency may mean for Colombia and democracy (see, e.g., Stuenkel, 2022, on this). For the political Left and many of Petro's supporters, his inauguration symbolized a historic opportunity for Colombia to finally address its deep-seated challenges. As Stuenkel observed, despite relative economic and political stability over recent decades, Colombia remains one of the most troubled countries in Latin America. Discontent with the government's neoliberal policies and austerity measures reached an all-time high prior to the election, leading to repeated waves of protests between 2019 and 2021 (Albarracín et al., 2020), paralleling developments in neighboring Ecuador (Briscoe, 2022; Sankey, 2022; Stuenkel, 2022).[4]

The conditions driving this discontent and the associated polarization of forces in the class struggle, deepened and accentuated by the Covid pandemic, included crippling socioeconomic inequalities and street violence related to organized crime and narco-capitalism, conditions that led to deteriorating economic conditions as well as the forced internal displacement of almost 80,000 Colombians in 2021 (Briscoe, 2022), high youth unemployment (Turkewitz, 2022), and deforestation in the Colombian Amazon (Stuenkel, 2022).

Many of Petro's political opponents and enemies still associate the Left in Colombia with the country's guerilla movements, such as the now-disbanded

---

[2]On June 2016, FARC signed a ceasefire accord with the President of Colombia, Juan Manuel Santos, in Havana. This accord was seen as an historic step to ending the war waged for some 50 years.
[3]On these class struggle dynamics see Petras and Veltmeyer (2005).
[4]In the case of Ecuador, Collyns (2019) reported that over the weekend of October 12–13, 2019, Ecuador was paralyzed by a national strike as President Moreno refused to heed the demands of protestors, who included indigenous federations as well as unionized workers, for him to step down or repeal the austerity measures that have sparked the worst political unrest in decades.

FARC and expressed fears that Petro will turn out to be a populist – like Mexico's Andrés Manuel Lopez Obrador at best or Venezuela's Nicolás Maduro at worst.

To govern under these conditions Petro had to cobble together a broad coalition of forces on the center-left to obtain a governing majority in Congress. His party, Pacto Histórico, has fewer than 20 percent of seats in both the Senate and the House of Representatives, and his narrow runoff victory gave him a relatively weak mandate. However, as noted by Stuekel, since winning the election Petro has sought to assuage fears that he would govern as a radical. He appointed José Antonio Ocampo – a renowned establishment economist who is known as a defender of a more progressive taxation – as his minister of finance. Currently, only five percent of Colombians pay personal income tax, and Petro plans to increase taxes on the rich. Petro also picked conservative political veteran Álvaro Leyva as foreign minister and Alejandro Gaviria, who has worked for center-right governments, to head the ministry of education, clear signs that he seeks to project himself as a pragmatist capable of reaching across the aisle.

However, the capacity of Petro to stay in power in a context of democratic politics while turning toward the left will depend not on his parliamentary coalition but on extending the networks and coalitions forged in Colombia's civil society, coalitions that had propelled him into the presidency in the first place. These networks and coalitions included rural–urban coalitions, environmentalists, and indigenous groups concerned with weaning the country off of fossil fuels,[5] militant industrial trade unions concerned with the drastic fall in the value of wages in an inflationary and crisis environment, indigenous communities seeking the support of the government in its fight with the companies over their territorial rights and in defense of the environment, and peasant organizations and agrarian movements pushing for authentic agrarian reform if not revolutionary change.

One particularly sensitive area for Petro – and for Colombian democracy – will be the government's relations with the military. Petro has been a longtime, leading critic of the armed forces, accusing them of collaborating with paramilitaries and participating in drug trafficking (Agence France-Presse – AFP, 2022). As Stuenkel (2022) has pointed out, the military have made little secret of its concerns about a leftist electoral victory.

Another sensitive issue is Colombia's relationship to the United States, which has long served as the United States' greatest ally in the war on communism and against what Washington deems to be terrorism and terrorist states, which, in the contemporary context, includes Venezuela as well as Cuba. Petro may have the greatest impact on United States–Latin America relations by mobilizing regional

---

[5] Petro differs from Latin American Left populists in projecting himself as a more modern and progressive leftist. While both the Mexico's and Venezuela's leaders embrace fossil fuels and often describe environmental concerns as a fig leaf of Western imperialism, Petro has established strong ties to grassroots environmentalism, even promising to ban fracking and announcing that he would wean Colombia off of fossil fuel exploration (Moloney, 2022; Stuenke, 2022).

leaders to question the wisdom of coca eradication and the militarization of the fight against drugs (Longley, 2021). However, Washington's stance on Venezuela and Cuba will undoubtedly constitute for Petro a red line in Colombia–United States relations. Also, Petro is expected to join Mexico and Bolivia in a broad regional coalition in both progressive politics and the fight against US imperialism.

Extractivism as a Postdevelopment Pathway: Mexico Weighs in[6]

At issue in the recent swing of the pendulum politics, first to the Left and then to the Far Right, is the most effective strategy for bringing about progressive change: whether progressive forces would focus on gaining state power "from above" (via elections) or "from below" (via social movement mobilization from within civil society). In this context, the authors argue that those social movements that supported electoral transitions were demobilized or coopted by the social assistance policies of the state, while autonomist movements that refused to engage with the state were mostly marginalized. In effect, both strategies failed their popular constituencies. The authors conclude that the way forward for progressive social movements is to engage with the state while mobilizing the forces of resistance for movements to retain their independence from the state and autonomy from political parties. In the case of Mexico, for example, the challenge for AMLO and supportive or sympathizer social movements in Mexico is how can they support each other while advancing in a popular-democratic agenda of sustainable development?

In Mexico, this challenge has been confronted by politicians and policymakers in the context of an extended debate on the role of extractivism in the design of a new industrial and energy policy (Moreno-Brid et al., 2023). In the phase of state-led development from the 1950 to the 1970s, national development was equated with industrialization and an endogenous industrial policy was deemed to be an essential drive of the engine of economic growth. However, the installation in the 1980s of a "new world order" based on the principles of neoliberal globalization radically changed the prospects for further industrial development of countries and regions on the periphery of the world capitalist system. In the forced compliance to the rules of the new neoliberal world order, and the dictates of global capital and the governments and international organizations that advanced these dictates (integration into the globalization agenda), these countries were prevented or deprived of their capacity to pursue an active independent industrial policy and become "a global manufacturing power."

This was a turning point in the capitalist development process on the periphery of the system – a turn toward the advance of extractive capital in the development

---

[6]This section reproduces some material in Chapter 1 of one of the author's earlier works published by Routledge in 2020 (Veltmeyer & Zayago Lau, 2020). Permission from Francis & Taylor (Routledge) to use this material is gratefully acknowledged.

process. Many, if not most development theorists, in response either argue or assume that both extractivism (the extraction of natural resources) and industrialization (industrial development) are required conditions for expanding the forces of production and bringing about a modern form of capitalist development or modernization. The problem, however, is how to combine industrialization and extractivism in a way that avoids the destructive socioenvironmental impacts of both – a problem that has surfaced and taken form in the notion of neoextractivism and, according to the authors, in the revival of the search and efforts to construct a new industrial policy. The problem, it is argued, is that in the context of the new (neoliberal) world order, Mexico, together with other governments in the region, has been prevented from implementing an independent and endogenous industrial policy, resulting in the destruction of forces of production built up over several decades of state-led industrial development based on an industrial policy designed to build up domestic industries.

Rather than building up an industrial sector to process the region's wealth of natural resources, the neoliberal macroeconomic agenda of the governments formed within the institutional and policy framework of this agenda favored and promoted the advance of extractive capital, leading to an affluence of resource-seeking extractive investments that reinforced the orientation of the economies in the region toward a reliance on natural resource extraction and the export of these resources in primary commodity form, with all of the attendant contradictions and conflicts.

In this context, it is important to understand that the 1980s provided a major turning point for developing countries, moving away from a state-led approach to development based on a strategy of import-substitution industrialization toward (re)primarization and an associated return to extractivism as a national development strategy. This turn toward primarization and extractivism had its origins in several trends. One was the advance of resource-seeking "extractive" capital (investments in the extraction of natural resources) to meet and satisfy the strong demand for "primary commodities" on capitalist markets. Another is the long commodities boom of 2002–2014, which spurred the interest of those governments formed in the search for a more inclusive form of development in the extraction of natural resources in the region as a source of fiscal resources to finance their social development (poverty reduction) programs. This concern for additional fiscal resources led these governments to open the economy to foreign investment and provide the bearers of this investment, the large multinational corporations in the extractive sector, greater access to long-term contracts, and concessions to explore for oil and gas.

Solidarity Economics and Communal Socialism (Bolivia, Venezuela)

Many groups and communities across Latin America today, in resisting the advance of capitalism and extractivism in the development process, have organized and are organizing alternative ways of securing their livelihoods and the protection of their communities from the forces of capitalist "development." In this regard, there are numerous examples today in both urban and rural areas of people promoting local activities and organizing cooperatives and markets for local exchanges (through barter or use of local currencies or national monies) within and among communities. But, as Barkin (2021) has documented, in most of Latin America these alternative strategies are now emerging predominantly among peasants and indigenous groups, organized collectively to resist the advance of capitalism by forging an economy that reflects a commitment to a variety of alternative models of a popular economy (Gago et al., 2023), or solidarity economics, what Barkin terms "ecological economics from below" but indigenous thinkers and leaders in the Andean region describe as *buen vivir* or *vivir bien*.

The proliferation of these initiatives, he argues, reflects a recognition of the importance of human development and the view that capitalism in any form (but particularly in the form of neoliberalism, extractivism, and colonialism) is inimical to human development and the possibility of living well in social solidarity and harmony with nature (Acosta, 2012; Gudynas, 2013, 2014). In effect, these ideas, initiatives, and experiments in the construction of a postdevelopment alternative to capitalism are part of the class struggle from below.

In all of these diverse collective actions and experiments there appear two fundamentally different conceptions of a social and solidarity economy: one advanced as part of a strategy to manage the complex dynamics of urban and rural development, the other as part of a grassroots and social movement strategy for confronting what the Zapatistas term "the capitalist hydra" and finding alternatives that offer more opportunities and a better quality of life than offered by today's capitalist economy. The idea here is that the various strategies devised by the organizations of international cooperation and development – and this includes the strategy of community-based local development based on the "empowerment of the poor" (mobilizing their social capital for their own development) – are designed as mechanisms of adjustment that are functional for the continuation of capitalism. From a leftist perspective, however, this strategy is viewed as a neoliberal ploy to defend the system from the forces of resistance mobilized by the anticapitalist movement.

The idea of a social economy based on the progressive principles of social solidarity (fraternity) and harmony with nature, as well as cooperativism, workers self-management, and local development, has a long pedigree that can be traced back to the 18th and 19th centuries. However, in its current form (represented most clearly and forcefully by the Zapatistas in Chiapas), in the current context of capitalist development, it is the product of initiatives associated with the resistance movement erupting predominantly on the extractive frontier.

The plethora and diversity of experiments in the construction of a social and solidarity economy can best be understood as an outcome of the class struggle from below – a struggle to demand access to the global commons and to recover territorial autonomy, a struggle that notably implicates the indigenous communities on the extractive frontier. However, the idea of an alternative form of society and development (communal socialism) based on the progressive principles of social solidarity, cooperativism, and autonomous local development has also emerged among the political class on the front of democratic electoral politics in the specific context of Hugo Chávez's ascension to state power in Venezuela (Azzellini, 2023; Gilbert, 2023).

From the year 2000 onward in Venezuela, with the proactive support of President Hugo Chávez and his government, diverse popular organizations, communities, and even the government itself advanced various local self-government initiatives and promoted the formation of worker-managed cooperatives and commune socialism. In 1998, when Chávez was first elected to state power, there existed fewer than 800 cooperatives; by August 2005, there were almost 84,000. Because of this development and associated initiatives and experiences, the Communal Council was formed in 2005 as a form of self-administration at the neighborhood level; this was followed in 2007 by the construction of the commune as a tier of self-government above that. Both institutions were formed with substantive grassroots organizations although their rapid expansion was undoubtedly due to formal support by the state under the project "The Socialism of the 21st Century" championed by Chávez in the context of his re-election in December 2006 (Chávez Frías, 2007).

In January 2005 at the World Social Forum, Chávez explicitly called for the reinventing of socialism in a form that was different from what had existed in the Soviet Union. "We must reclaim socialism as a thesis, a project and a path, but a new type of socialism, a humanist one which puts humans and not machines or the state ahead of everything." Six months later, Chávez argued the importance of building a new communal system of production and consumption in which there is an exchange of activities determined by communal needs and communal purposes not just what Marx described as the cash nexus or the profit motive, the incentive to make money, accumulate capital. "We have to help to create it, from the popular bases, with the participation of the communities, through the community organizations, the cooperatives, self-management and different ways to create this system."

Out of the different experiences and initiatives advanced with reference to this project, there emerged what Chávez termed "the communal state," which subsequently became the political and social project of both the government and the popular movements in Venezuela. At the base of this state, as Chávez understood and tried to construct it, were the communal councils that were identified as the fundamental cell of Bolivarian socialism. As Chávez declared: "All power to the communal councils," which would bring about an "explosion in communal power," designated as the fifth of "five motors" driving the path toward socialism.

Chávez's project of reconstructing socialism in the context of the 21st century provoked not only virulent opposition of politicians on the near- (center-right) and the Far Right of the ideological spectrum but also the opposition of the US government, which over the past two decades engaged extensive resources in a campaign and diverse strategies and efforts to topple the regime. This included sanctions and the freezing of funds generated by Petróleos de Venezuela, S.A. (PDVSA), the Venezuelan state-owned oil and natural gas company and held by US banks and US-controlled financial institutions, and generous financial support of center- and far-right-opposition politicians and their campaigns and coup attempts, and orchestrating the isolation and exclusion of Venezuela from access to international financial institutions and regional alliances.

On this class struggle and the imperialist war waged by the US administration against Venezuela and Cuba, and the complex political dynamics associated with the effort to advance at the level of the state the Chavista project of direct democracy based on communist, anarcho-syndicalist, indigenous and afro-Venezuelan ideas and experiences, see Azzellini (2023).

Indigenous Resistance and Class Struggle on the Extractive Frontier

> As Indians they subjugated us and as Indians we will free ourselves. (Ujuy, Pueblos Originarios, *Resumen Latinamericano*, July 4, 2023)

On June 17, 2023, *Resumen Latinamericano* – an observatory of the popular movement and class struggles across Latin America – reported on the violent police repression of community members from the highlands of *Purmamarca* (Argentina), a repression that was on par with countless such confrontations over years of anticolonial and anti-imperialist struggles, but, it was pointed out, one of the worst seen in recent years of invisibility, denial and violence, adding to the violent and systematic repression of the indigenous peoples across the region, and closer to home (the province of Jujyu), members of the Qom, Wichis, Mapuches, and now the Kollas de la Puna. This repression and these struggles can be traced out over 500 years of anticolonial and anti-imperialist struggle, accentuating the fact that the indigenous peoples of the Americas have been, and remain, the primary object and major victims of both capitalism and imperialism, the histories of which are closely intertwined.

A review of the recent history of class struggle in the region shows that the advance of extractive capital and extractivism in the countryside, particularly over the past two decades, points toward an extension and deepening of the class struggle on the frontier of extractive capital, and the incidence of violent confrontations and conflicts with each advance. Currently, Latin America is home to the largest volume of environmental conflicts, all based on the resistance of indigenous communities to the advance of extractive capital, in the world (Torres Wong, 2019; Veltmeyer, 2016, pp. 27–44). According to the Environmental Justice Atlas, there are currently 960 ongoing environmental and territorial conflicts in the region (https://ejatlas.org).

However, such a review would also disclose the important role of the indigenous communities in advancing the resistance against both capitalism and imperialism in their extractive form. Not only are the communities in the vanguard of the forces of resistance, but this resistance has increasingly taken, and is taking, the form of a search for alternative, more sustainable ways of living and forms of "development" – or rather, "postdevelopment," given the fundamental link between development and capitalism.

The political ecologist David Barkin (Barkin, 2021; Barkin & Sánchez, 2019) has conceived of the indigenous peoples and communities on the extractive frontier of the world capitalist system – recognized as the most marginalized, discriminated against, ignored, vilified, and exploited sector of humanity – as a revolutionary or socially transformative force. This is with reference not so much to their political power or achievements as to the empowerment achieved by indigenous peoples in recent decades, a power evidently derived from the close relationship between regions inhabited by indigenous peoples and areas of biological wealth,[7] as well as the synergy created between the knowledge generated in academia and the powerful forces of indigenous resistance and the rebellion movements and their organizations (Toledo, 2023).

However, the most tangible manifestation of this new emerging global power of indigenous peoples is the success achieved in the construction of alternative ways of living and governance (as per the *juntas de buen gobierno*) established by the Zapatistas in Chiapas) guided by the principles of *buen vivir* – respect for and the care of nature, solidarity based on the respect of all cultures and diverse ways of thinking and being, and autonomous local development; ways of being and forms of organization that "promote and connect diverse territories of life conceived as a source of identity and culture, of autonomy and self-management, in an openly political perspective" (Toledo, 2023).[8]

Where is Latin America Heading? Some Considerations and Tentative Conclusions

The big question is whether Latin America will tilt further to the left under the impact of the diverse forces of resistance on the three major fronts of the class struggle – electoral politics, peasant movements, the extractive frontier – or whether the correlation of forces in the class struggle will pull or push the region back to the future, toward the right in a deepening of the class struggle from above.

On the front of electoral politics, apart from the unsettled issue regarding the correlation of forces on the Left and the Right in the class struggle, there is the contentious issue that surrounds the relationship of Latin America with the United States in the context of what is widely understood as the projection

---

[7]On this point, see Toledo in a chapter written for the *Encyclopedia of Biodiversity* (https://rb.gy/ipzdj) re: data collected by G. Oviedo and his team for the *Global 2000 Project* of the World Wildlife Fund. Oviedo and his team identified 136 terrestrial ecological regions that by their characteristics were defined as priority areas for conservation, 80 percent of which are inhabited by indigenous peoples (https://acortar.link/hOAwY8).

[8]This way of looking at the world is eloquently captured in the words of David Choquehuanca, a peasant leader and trade unionist, Evo Morales' Chancellor (2006–2017) and currently the vice-president of Bolivia. Choquehuanca is also a renowned philosopher of *buen vivir:* "The [global] movement to care for life and brotherhood, to bring about integration and renewal, grows. Our grandparents have told us that the last battle of capitalism and imperialism will be against the indigenous peoples, and they will lose. The culture of life will overcome the culture of death" (*La Jornada*, 29/7/23).

of state power and the hegemony of the United States, or US imperialism. One consequence of the several recent turns to the Left on the political front is the increased questioning and rejection of US hegemony, and the assertion of independence from policies advocated, and in some contexts imposed, by the US State Department. US hegemony in the region was established early in the 19th century in the form of the Monroe Doctrine, but in the 20th century it was entrenched in the form of a policy of intervention in the affairs of countries in the region wherever and whenever US economic and political interests are at stake (Gordon & Webber, 2008).

In the current context, this interventionist policy and the power and capacity of the US government to impose its will and dictate policy have been severely curtailed, reduced to a matter of influence exercised at the level of diplomacy and a regional alliance in the form of the OAS. However, even this mechanism has its limitations in the ability of the US government to dictate or even influence policymaking by other governments in the region. First, in the context of the progressive cycle and a second left turn in Latin American politics, the US government has surrendered its capacity to dictate macroeconomic policy in terms of the neoliberal policy agenda. This agenda, originally imposed by the United States via the World Bank and the IMF's structural adjustment program, thanks to the activism of the popular movement, is not only on the defensive but also is in obvious decline, its demise on the horizon. Second, in the current context of regional politics and international relations, the capacity of the US government to intervene militarily in the affairs of other governments in the region is zero. Even the OAS, which has served the US government well as a means of imposing its will and dictating policy, no longer does so. This is reflected in the impotence of the United States, in the context of the OAS, in regard to taking collective action against the governments of Nicaragua, Venezuela, and Cuba, the three countries that are currently in the crosshairs of US imperialism. Both Colombia and Chile, countries that have long been aligned with the United States but that turned toward the left in recent presidential elections, have joined Bolivia and Brazil in straying well outside the sphere of US influence, deepening an opening in the region to new trading partners, most significantly, China. Regarding China, in the current context of capitalist development even right-wing governments such as Uruguay, Ecuador, and Panama have joined Chile, Costa Rica, and Peru in negotiating a free trade agreement with China, a growing global power that is challenging US hegemony in the region. Already it is Latin America's second-largest trading partner after the United States, and in South America. Apart from Brazil, China is already the largest trading partner for Argentina, Bolivia, Brazil Chile, Paraguay, Uruguay, and Venezuela.[9] This economic realignment toward

---

[9]Some background on this. https://www.scmp.com/news/china/diplomacy/article/3245805/china-reportedly-suspends-us65-billion-currency-swap-agreement-argentina_ https://www.peoplesworld.org/article/china-cancels-line-of-credit-pulling-the-plug-on-argentinas-anarcho-capitalist-president/_https://thediplomat.com/2024/01/the-patagonian-enigma-chinas-deep-space-station-in-argentina/_

China, initiated by the governments formed in the pink tide, is already having foreign policy consequences that will strengthen growing demands for regional autonomy and a new more inclusive regional alliance vis-á-vis the governments of Cuba, Venezuela, and Nicaragua. Both Presidents Lula da Silva and López Obrador have promoted an alternative regional Alliance (an alternative to the OAS) that incorporates Cuba, Venezuela, and Nicaragua.

In 2022, at the Summit of the Americas, Biden proposed an Alliance for Economic Prosperity in the Americas to boost economic growth in the hemisphere and counter growing Chinese influence. However, the summit was overshadowed by Washington's decision to exclude Cuba, Nicaragua, and Venezuela, which prompted criticism and boycotts from heads of state such as López Obrador, highlighting regional discontent with US foreign policy. AMLO reiterated his criticism at the "Three Amigos" meeting between Mexico, Canada, and the United States in January 2023, calling on Biden to change the United States' hegemonic stance toward Latin America. Latin America, he lectured Biden, is no longer a subjugated vassal at the beck and call of the United States. Indeed, the days of US imperialism, like the neoliberal era, seem to be drawing to an end.

...

The development and resistance dynamics of the class struggle, at least as we have reconstructed them in this book, can be traced out along three fronts. One of these fronts is formed by and relates to the contradictions inherent in the capital-labor relation of economic exploitation and political conflict, a struggle waged by the working class but taken up by the political class as a battle over the direction of social change in the political arena. This struggle and associated battles have taken diverse changing forms in the current context of capitalist development, most notably as a struggle by the working class for higher wages – a fair share in the proceeds of social production – and improved working conditions. In this book, we have traced out the dynamics of this struggle as they have unfolded in the political development of a progressive cycle formed in response to the advance and changing form of capital in the development process and a series of left and right swings of the pendulum of electoral politics.

A second front of the class struggle can be traced out in a protracted struggle over land and access to the global commons in the context of the capitalist development of agriculture and industry. In the current context, this struggle has taken diverse forms, notably as collective actions taken by a semiproletariat of rural landless workers, the remnants of what once was a vibrant peasantry of small-scale agricultural producers, against the advance of capitalism in the countryside and the neoliberal policy agenda of many governments in the region. The political activism of this peasant movement in its diverse permutations and iterations in the 1990s generated conditions – a generalized discontent with the neoliberal policy agenda and rejection of neoliberalism in policy circles – that allowed the political left in the new millennium to take state power. In the current context of capitalist development in the region, this peasant movement has assumed the leadership of the popular movement of resistance to the advance of capitalism and the elaboration of a systemic alternative to capitalism in its current form, that is, monopoly capital and agribusiness, neoliberalism, and extractivism.

The epicenter of the resistance and the associated class war and the third front in the resistance against the advance of capitalism in the development process – and in what has been described as "the construction of social power from below" – has been forged by the activism of the indigenous and peasant communities on the extractive frontier. By several accounts, and this accords with our own observations and tentative conclusions, the activism of these communities in the struggle for their territorial rights and access to the commons constitutes the most formidable force of social transformative social change in the current context of a transition toward another world of social and environmental justice.

However this is one of the two conclusions that we draw from our review and analysis of the changing dynamics of resistance in the Latin American class struggle – transformative or revolutionary social change requires and is predicated on uniting the diverse forces of resistance generated in the current conjuncture of the capitalist development process on all the fronts of the class struggle. These include the indigenous communities on the extractive frontier, militant trade unions, the displaced and semiproletarianized rural landless workers, the urban precariat of impoverished and low-income or unemployed informal workers in the urban centers, and the peasant-based and-led agrarian movements. These forces of resistance offer a potential for an alternative more inclusive form of noncapitalist or postcapitalist development based on the agency of a popular movement constructed from below.

A second conclusion is the need for the political and social Left to come together and unite in a class struggle against the forces of capitalist development and construction of a broad interclass social movement as well as a political instrument or party capable of advancing the struggle.

References

Acosta, A. (2012). *Buen Vivir/Sumak Kawsay: Una oportunidad de imaginar otros mundos*. Ediciones Abaya-Yala.
Acosta, A., & Machado, D. (2012). Movimientos comprometidos con la vida. Ambientalismos y conflictos actuales en América Latina. *Revista Colección OSAL, 32*, 67–94. http://lalineadefuego.info/2012/10/01/ambientalismos-y-conflictos-actuales-en-america-latinamovimientos-comprometidos-con-la-vida-por-alberto-acosta-y-decio-machado
Acosta, A., & Martínez, E. (2014). *Desarrollo, postcrecimiento y buen vivir. Debates e interrogantes*. Ediciones Abya-Yala.
Agence France-Presse – AFP. (2022, May 6). *Colombia military bristles at rise of leftist presidential hopeful*. France 24. https://www.france24.com/en/live-news/20220506-colombia-military-bristles-at-rise-of-leftist-presidential-hopeful
Albarracín, J., Botero, S., & Gamboa, L. (2020, June 30). Colombia's new president aims to swing his country left. It won't be easy. *Washington Post*. https://www.washingtonpost.com/politics/2022/06/30/petro-president-leftist-colombia-coalition/
Almeyra, G. (2016, February 28). Bolivia: Un tiro en la pie. *La Jornada*.
Altieri, M. A., & Toledo, V. M. (2011). The agroecological revolution in Latin America: Rescuing nature, ensuring food sovereignty and empowering peasants. *Journal of Peasant Studies, 38*(3), 587–612. http://dx.doi.org/10.1080/03066150.2011.582947
Andrade, D. (2022). Neoliberal extractivism: Brazil in the twenty-first century. *The Journal of Peasant Studies, 49*(4), 793–816.
Araghi, F. (2010). Accumulation by displacement, global enclosures, food crisis and the economic contradictions of capitalism. *Review, 32*(1), 113–146.
Arbix, G., & Martin, S. (2010, March 12–13). *Beyond developmentalism and market fundamentalism in Brazil: Inclusionary state activism without statism* [Paper presentation]. Presented at the Workshop States, Development and Global Governance, University of Wisconsin-Madison.
Avila Nieto, C. (2017). Comunicación de gobierno en el populismo latinoamericano: El caso de Rafael Correa, *Ecuador* [Thesis, Pontificia Universidad Católica de Chile]. https://doi.org/10.7764/tesisUC/COM/21604
Aznárez, C. (2016, de Enero 9). El peligro de minimizar el poder letal de Mauricio Macri. *Resumen Latinoamericano*. https://www.resumenlatinoamericano.org/2016/01/08/argentina-el-peligro-de-minimizar-el-poder-letal-de-mauricio-macri/
Azzellini, D. (2023). Chapter 14: Commune socialism: Self-management, popular power and autonomy in Venezuela. In H. Veltmeyer & A. Ezquerro-Cañete (Eds.), *From extractivism to sustainability: Scenarios and lessons from Latin America*. Routledge.
Bannon, I., & Collier, P. (Eds.). (2003). *Natural resources and violent conflict: Options and actions*. World Bank.
Bárcenas, F. (2012, February 28). Detener el saqueo minero en México. *La Jornada*. https://www.jornada.com.mx/2012/02/28/opinion/023a1pol
Barkin, D. (2021). The community as a collective revolutionary subject. In H. Veltmeyer & P. Bowles (Eds.), *The essential guide to critical development studies* (pp. 420–428). Routledge.
Barkin, D., & Sánchez, A. (2019). The communitarian revolutionary subject: New forms of social transformation. *Third World Quarterly, 41*(8), 1421–1441. https://doi.org/10.1080/01436597.2019.1636370

Bazán Salcedo, C. (2013). La 'correísta' Luisa González y el empresario Daniel Noboa disputarán la segunda vuelta presidencial en Ecuador. *El Diario.Es.* August 21. https://www.eldiario.es/internacional/luisa-gonzalez-daniel-noboa-disputaran-presidencia-ecuador-segunda-vuelta_1_10455574.html

Bebbington, A. (2007). *La glocalización de la gobernanza ambiental: Relaciones de escala en los movimientos socioambientales y sus implicaciones para la gobernanza ambiental en zonas de influencia minera en Perú y Ecuador.* Universidad de Manchester, Escuela de Medio Ambiente y Desarrollo.

Bebbington, A. (2009). The new extraction: Rewriting the political ecology of the Andes? *NACLA Report on the Americas, 42*(5), 12–21.

Bebbington, A., & Bury, J. (Eds.). (2013). *Subterranean struggles: New dynamics of mining, oil and gas in Latin America.* University of Texas Press.

Béjar, T. (2023). Herencia colonial, capitalismo racista y estallido social. In G. Montoya & H. Quiroz (Eds.), *Estallido popular. Protesta y masacre en el Perú, 2022–2023* (pp. 39–50). Editorial Horizonte.

Benjamin, T. (1989). *A rich land, a poor people: Politics and society in modern Chiapas.* University of New Mexico.

Berberoglu, B. (Ed.). (2020). *The global rise of authoritarianism in the early 21st century.* Routledge.

Bernstein, H. (2010). *Class dynamics of agrarian change.* Fernwood Publications.

Berry, B. (2010). The natural resource curse in 21st century Latin America. *Canada Watch,* Fall, 23–24. https://cwatch.journals.yorku.ca/index.php/cwatch/article/view/35993

Blas, J. (2013, April 14). Commodity traders reap $250bn harvest. *Financial Times.* https://www.ft.com/content/9f6f541e-a397-11e2-ac00-00144feabdc0

Bollier, D., & Silke, H. (2012). *The wealth of the commons: A world beyond market and state.* Levelers Press.

Borón, A. (2008, Agosto–Septiembre). Teorías de la dependencia. *Realidad Económica,* 238. https://www.iade.org.ar/system/files/ediciones/realidad_economica_238.pdf

Borón, A. (2012). *América Latina en la geopolítica del imperialismo.* Ediciones Luxemburg.

Borras, S. M. (2018, March 17–18). Understanding and subverting contemporary right-wing populism: Preliminary notes from a critical agrarian perspective. In *Conference chapter no. 147 – International conference authoritarian populism and the rural world.* ISS.

Borras, S. M. (2023). Contemporary Agrarian, rural and rural–urban movements and alliances. *Journal of Agrarian Change, 23*(3), 453–476.

Bresser-Pereira, L. C. (2006). El nuevo desarrollismo y la ortodoxia convencional. *Economía UNAM, 4*(10), 7–29.

Bresser-Pereira, L. C. (2007, Julio–Agosto). Estado y mercado en el nuevo desarrollismo. *Nueva Sociedad,* 210. https://nuso.org/articulo/estado-y-mercado-en-el-nuevo-desarrollismo/

Bresser-Pereira, L. C. (2009). *Developing Brazil: Overcoming the failure of the Washington consensus.* Lynne Rienner.

Bretón, V., González, M., & Rubio, B. (2022). Peasant and indigenous autonomy before and after the pink tide in Latin America. *Journal of Agrarian Change, 22*(3), 547–575. https://doi.org/10.1111/joac.12483

Briscoe, I. (2022, June 19). Gustavo Petro's big win. Colombia's first leftist president could transform the region. *Foreign Affairs.* https://www.foreignaffairs.com/articles/colombia/2022-06-19/gustavo-petros-big-win

Bunker, S. (1984). Modes of extraction, unequal exchange, and the progressive underdevelopment of an extreme periphery: The Brazilian Amazon, 1600–1980. *American Journal of Sociology, 89*(5), 1017–1064.

Burchardt, H.-J., & Dietz, K. (2014). (Neo-)extractivism – A new challenge for development theory from Latin America. *Third World Quarterly, 35*(3), 468–486.

Burdick, J., Oxhorn, P., & Roberts, K. (Eds.). (2009). *Beyond neoliberalism in Latin America? Societies and politics at the crossroads.* Palgrave Macmillan.

Burgwal, G. (1990). Chapter 3: An introduction to the literature on urban movements in Latin America. In W. Assies, G. Burgwal, & T. Salman (Eds.), *Structures of power, movements of resistance: An introduction to the theories of urban movements in Latin America*. (pp. 163–175) Center for Latin American Research and Documentation.

Caballero, V. (2023). *Castillo. Breve historia del gobierno del pueblo*. Penguin Random House Grupo Editorial.

Chávez Frías, H. (2007, January 8). *Palabras del presidente reelecto*. ABN—Agencia Bolivariana de Noticias. https://web.archive.org/web/20080828015718/http://www.abn.info.ve/discurso_presidente.php

Chiasson, T. (2016). Neo-extractivism in Venezuela and Ecuador: A weapon of class conflict. *The Extractive Industries and Society*, 3(4), 888–901.

Chimienti, A., & Matthes, S. (2016). Ecuador: Extractivism for the twenty-first century? *NACLA Report on the Americas*, 46(4), 59–61. https://doi.org/10.1080/10714839.2013.11721895

Chossudovsky, M. (1997). *The globalisation of poverty: Impacts of IMF and World Bank reforms*. Zed Books.

Collier, P. (2003, April 28). *Natural resources, development and conflict: Channels of causation and policy interventions*. World Bank.

Collier, D. (2014, April). *The commons as a template for transformation*. Great Transformation Initiative. http://www.greattransition.org/publication/thecommons-as-a-template-for-transformation

Collier, P., & Venables, A. J. (2011). *Plundered nations? Successes and failures in natural resource extraction*. Palgrave Macmillan.

Collyns, D. (2019, October 10). Ecuador paralyzed by national strike as Moreno refuses to step down. *The Guardian*. https://www.theguardian.com/world/2019/oct/09/ecuador-strike-lenin-moreno-latest

Correa, R. (2012). Ecuador's path. *New Left Review*, 77, 88–104.

Cypher, J. (2010). South America's commodities boom. Developmental opportunity or path dependent reversion? *Canadian Journal of Development Studies*, 30(3–4), 635–662.

Dancourt, Ó. (2016). *Las vacas flacas en la economía peruana* [Working Chapter 428]. PUCP, Departamento de Economía.

Dangl, B. (2007). *The price of fire: Resource wars and social movements in Bolivia*. AK Press.

Dávalos, P., & Albuja, V. (2014). Ecuador: Extractivist dynamics, politics, and discourse. In H. Veltmeyer & J. Petras (Eds.), *The new extractivism: A model for Latin America or the New Imperialism?* (pp. 143–171). Zed Books.

De Echave, J. (2009a). *Minería y conflicto social*. IEP, CIPCA, CIES.

De Echave, J. (2009b). Bagua, un punto de inflexión en el escenario social del Perú. In H. Alimonda, R. Hoetmer, & D. Saavedra Celestino (Eds.), *La amazonía rebelde. Perú 2009*. (pp. 23–28). CLACSO.

De Farias, L. F. (2022, de Julio 27). Brasil. Bolsonarismo más allá de las elecciones. *Resumen Latinoamericano*. https://www.resumenlatinoamericano.org/2022/07/27/brasil-bolsonarismo-mas-alla-de-las-elecciones/

Delgado Wise, R., & Veltmeyer, H. (2018). Chapter 12: Development and social change in Latin America. In G. H. Fagan & R. Munck (Eds.), *Handbook on development and social change* (pp. 228–247). Edward Elgar.

Desmarais, A. (2007). *La Vía Campesina: Globalization and the power of peasants*. Fernwood Publications.

Dos Santos, T. (1986). *Imperialismo y dependencia*. Ediciones Era S.A.

Durand, J. (2022, December 18). Perú fragmentado. *La Jornada*. https://www.jornada.com.mx/notas/2022/12/18/politica/peru-fragmentado-20221218/

ECLAC – Economic Commission for Latin America and the Caribbean. (2012). *Capital flows to Latin America and the Caribbean. Recent developments*. ECLAC.

ECLAC – Economic Commission for Latin America and the Caribbean. (2015). *Economic survey of Latin America and the Caribbean 2015*. ECLAC.

References

ECLAC – Economic Commission for Latin America and the Caribbean. (2023). *Economic survey of Latin America and the Caribbean 2023*. ECLAC.

Edelman, M. (2021). Hollowed out Heartland, USA: How capital sacrificed communities and paved the way for authoritarian populism. *Journal of Rural Studies, 82*, 505–517.

Edwards, S. (2010). *Left behind: Latin America and the false promise of populism*. University of Chicago Press.

El Pais. (2024, March 4). *Desterrar la perspectiva de género: Milei y Bukele encabezan la última cruzada de la ultraderecha latinoamericana*. https://elpais.com/america/2024-03-04/desterrar-la-perspectiva-de-genero-milei-y-bukele-encabezan-la-ultima-cruzada-de-la-ultraderecha-latinoamericana.html

Ellner, S. (2023, October 27). Prioritizing U.S. imperialism in evaluating Latin America's Pink Tide. *Monthly Review, 74*(10). https://monthlyreview.org/2023/03/01/prioritizing-u-s-imperialism-in-evaluating-latin-americas-pink-tide/

Estes, N. (2021, September 17). Indigenous people of Brazil fight for their future. *Counterpunch*. https://www.counterpunch.org/2021/09/17/indigenous-people-of-brazil-fight-for-their-future/

Farthing, L. (2018). An opportunity squandered? Elites, social movements, and the government of Evo Morales. *Latin American Perspectives, 30*(20), 1–18.

Farthing, L. (2023). Latin America's new left surge. *NACLA Report on the Americas, 55*(1), 1–4. https://doi.org/10.1080/10714839.2023.2184065

Fearnside, P. (2005). Deforestation in Brazilian Amazonia: History, rates and consequences. *Conservation Biology, 19*(3), 680–688.

Freeman, W., & Perello, L. (2024, February 8). The drop in crime in El Salvador is stunning, but it has a dark side. *The New York Times*. https://www.nytimes.com/2024/02/08/opinion/el-salvador-bukele-election.html

Gago, V., Cielo, C., & Tassi, N. (Eds.). (2023). *Economías populares. Una cartografía crítica latinoamericana*. CLACSO.

Galeano, E. (1973). *Open veins of Latin America: Five centuries of the pillage of a continent*. Monthly Review Press.

García Aguilera, J. A., & Mantilla Monsalve, C. O. (2018). Cumbre agraria, campesina, étnica y popular. Transformaciones de lo público desde los movimientos sociales rurales en Colombia. In *Las disputas por lo público en América Latina y el Caribe* (pp. 357–392). CLACSO.

Garcia de Leon. (1995). *Prologo. EZLN. Documentos y Comunicados. 2 De Octubre 1995/24 De Enero 1997 (Problemas De Mexico)*. Ediciones Era S.A. De C.V.

García Linera, A. (2012). *Geopolítica de la Amazonia: Poder hacendal-patrimonial y acumulación capitalista*. Vicepresidencia del Estado Plurinacional.

García, A., & Borba de Sá, M. (2022). Brazil: Development strategies and peripheral conditions. In H. Veltmeyer & P. Bowles (Eds.), *The essential guide to critical development studies* (2nd ed., pp. 147–157). Routledge.

Gaudichaud, F. (2016, February 7). Reality can't be radically transformed only through institutions. *Resumen Latinoamericano/The Dawn*. https://www.cadtm.org/Franck-Gaudichaud-Reality-can-t-be

Gaudichaud, F., Webber, J., & Oodonesi, M. (2019). *Los gobiernos progresistas latinoamericanos del siglo XI*. UNAM.

Giarracca, N., & Teubal, M. (2014). Argentina: Extractivist dynamics of soy production and open-pit mining. In H. Veltmeyer & J. Petras (Eds.), *The new extractivism* (pp. 47–79). Zed Books.

Gilbert, C. (2023). *Commune or nothing! Venezuela's communal movement and its socialist project*. Monthly Review Press.

Girvan, N. (2014). Extractive imperialism in historical perspective. In J. Petras & H. Veltmeyer (Eds.), *Extractive imperialism in the Americas* (pp. 49ff). Brill Books.

References 175

Gonzales de Olarte, E. (2016). *Una economía incompleta. Perú 1950–2007. Análisis structural*. Fondo Editorial de la Pontificia Universidad Católica del Perú and Instituto de Estudios Peruanos.

Gordon, T., & Webber, J. (2008). Imperialism and resistance: Canadian mining companies in Latin America. *Third World Quarterly, 29*, 63–87.

Gridley, M. (2018). *The Yasuní ITT initiative and the creation of global green sovereignty* [Honors Thesis, University of Mississippi-Sally McDonald Barksdale Honors College]. https://egrove.olemiss.edu/hon_thesis

Grugel, J., & Riggirozzi, P. (2009). *Governance after neoliberalism in Latin America*. Palgrave Macmillan.

Gudynas, E. (2010). *The new extractivism in South America: Ten urgent theses about extractivism in relation to current South American progressivism*. Bank Information Center. http://www.bicusa.org/en/Article.11769.aspx

Gudynas, E. (2011). Más allá del nuevo extractivismo: Transiciones sostenibles y alternativas al desarrollo. In F. Wanderley (Ed.), *El desarrollo en cuestión. Reflexiones desde América Latina* (pp. 379–410). Oxfam/CIDES-UMSA.

Gudynas, E. (2013). El malestar Moderno con el Buen Vivir: reacciones y resistencias frente a una alternativa al desarrollo. In *Ecuador Debate. Identidades y diferencias* (no 88, pp. 183–205). CAAP.

Gudynas, E. (2014). *Derechos de la Naturaleza: Etica biocéntrica y políticas ambientales*. PTDG, RedGE, CooperAcción and CLAES.

Gudynas, E. (2018). Development and nature. Modes of appropriation and Latin American extractivisms. In J. Cupples, M. Palomino-Schalscha, & M. Prieto (Eds.), *The Routledge handbook of Latin American development* (pp. 389–399). Routledge.

Gunderson, C. (2013). *The provocative cocktail: Intellectual origins of the Zapatista uprising, 1960–1994* [Ph.D. dissertation, City University of New York]. ProQuest 1430904296.

Gutierrez, E. (2021). *The paradox of illicit economies: How opium and coca transform agrarian markets, violence, and state formation in the developing world* [Ph.D. dissertation, Erasmus University]. Erasmus University Rotterdam's International Institute of Social Studies (EUR-ISS).

Hall, D. (2013). Primitive accumulation, accumulation by dispossession and the global land grab. *Third World Quarterly, 34*(9), 1582–1604.

Harrup, A. (2019, May 17). South America suffers from the end of commodities boom. *The Wall Street Journal*. https://www.wsj.com/articles/south-america-suffers-from-end-of-commodities-boom-1460487125#

Harvey, D. (2003). *A brief history of neoliberalism*. Oxford University Press.

Hernandez, M. (2018). Argentina: The return of the right. In J. F. Petras & H. Veltmeyer (Eds.), *Class struggle in Latin America: Making history today*. (pp. 79–104) Routledge.

Hernandez Navarro, L. (1994). *Chiapas: la Rebelión de los pobres*. Gakoa Liburuak.

Huanacuni, F. (2010). *Vivir Bien/Buen Vivir Filosofía, Políticas, Estrategias y Experiencias Regionales*. (1st ed.). Coordinadora Andina de Organizaciones Indígenas—CAOI. https://dhls.hegoa.ehu.eus/uploads/resources/5888/resource_files/Buen_vivir_Vivir_bien.pdf?v=63741889204

Human Rights Watch. (2023). *World report 2023 (Events of 2023)*. https://www.hrw.org/world-report/2023/country-chapters/ecuador

Indigenous Missionary Center. (2021). *Violence against indigenous peoples in Brazil: Data from 2020*. https://cimi.org.br/wp-content/uploads/2021/11/relatorio-violencia-povos-indigenas-2020-cimi.pdf

Kay, C. (1989). *Latin American theories of development and underdevelopment*. Routledge.

Kay, C. (2008). Reflections on Latin American rural studies in the neoliberal globalization period: A new rurality? *Development and Change, 39*(6), 915–943.

Katz, C. (2023a). La nueva Resistencia popular en América Latina (The new popular Resistance in Latin America). *Revista Libertas Juiz de Fora, 23*(1), 23–24.

References

Katz, C. (2023b, April 3). El desconcierto del neoliberalismo latinoamericano – Sumario. *Rebelión.* https://rebelion.org/el-desconcierto-del-neoliberalismo-latinoamericano/

Kotze, C. (2012, June 15). South American mining sector to continue as resource-based economy. *Mining Weekly.* http://www.mining weekly.com/article/south american-mining-sector-to-continue-as-resource-based-economy-2012-06-15

La Jornada. (2011, de Noviembre 14). *500 años de saqueo, Suplemento Especial.* https://www.jornada.com.mx/2011/11/14/minera.pdf

Lalander, R., & Lembke, M. (2018). The Andean Catch-22: Ethnicity, class and resource governance in Bolivia and Ecuador. *Globalizations, 15*(5), 636–654.

Le Billon, P. (2006). *Fuelling war: Natural resources and armed conflicts.* Routledge.

Leiva, F. I. (2008). *Latin American structuralism: The contradictions of post-neoliberal development.* University of Minnesota Press.

Leiva, F., & Petras, J. (1994). *Poverty and democracy in Chile.* Westview Press.

Levitsky, S., & Roberts, K. (Eds.). (2011). *The resurgence of the Latin American Left.* Johns Hopkins University Press.

Lewis, P., Clarke, S., & Barr, C. (2019, March 7). Revealed: Populist leaders linked to reduced inequality. *The Guardian Weekly.* https://www.theguardian.com/world/2019/mar/07/revealed-populist-leaders-linked-to-reduced-inequality

Linthicum, K., & Wilkinson, T. (2022, November 3). The left now rules most of Latin America. Will it be able to live up to its promises? *The Los Angeles Times.* https://www.latimes.com/world-nation/story/2022-11-03/the-left-has-swept-intopower-across-latin-america

Linz, J., & Stepan, A. (Eds.). (1978). *The breakdown of democratic regimes.* Johns Hopkins University Press.

Lomeli, E. (2013). Conditional cash transfers as a social policy. In H. Veltmeyer & D. Tetreault (Eds.), *Poverty and development in Latin America* (pp. 163–188). Stylus.

Longley, K. (2021, June 8). The U.S. war on drugs helped unleash the violence in Colombia today. *Washington Post.* https://www.washingtonpost.com/outlook/2021/06/08/us-war-drugs-helped-unleash-violence-colombia-today/

López Segrera, F. (2016). *América Latina: Crisis del posneoliberalismo y ascenso de la nueva derecha.* CLACSO.

Lopéz, G. y Rivas. (2023, February 14). México: La oposición al Tren Maya. *Nodal.* https://www.nodal.am/2023/02/mexico-la-oposicion-al-tren-maya-por-gilberto-lopez-y-rivas

Lust, J. (2019a). Objective and subjective conditions for the continuity of the Peruvian extractive development model. *Globalizations, 16*(7), 1232–1246.

Lust, J. (2019b). *Capitalism, class and revolution in Peru, 1980–2016.* Palgrave MacMillan.

Lust, J. (2019c). The rise of a capitalist subsistence economy in Peru. *Third World Quarterly, 40*(4), 780–795.

Lust, J. (2023). *Underdevelopment in Peru. A profile of peripheral capitalism.* Routledge.

Lust, J., & Cypher, J. M. (2021). Bordeando el precipicio. Puede el nuevo presidente izquierdista del Perú, Pedro Castillo, mantenerse en el poder? *Observatorio del Desarrollo, 10*(29), 23–31.

Macas, L. (2000, Diciembre). Movimiento indígena ecuatoriano: Una evaluación necesaria. *Boletín ICCI 'RIMAY,' 3*(21), 1–5.

Macdonald, L., & Ruckert, A. (2009). *Post-neoliberalism in the Americas.* Palgrave Macmillan.

Machado, D., & Zibechi, R. (2016). *Cambiar el mundo desde arriba. Los límites del progresismo.* Centro de Estudios para el Desarrollo Laboral y Agrario (CEDLA).

Marcos, S. (1994). Tourist guide to Chiapas. *Monthly Review, 46*(1), 8–18.

Martins, C. E. (2011). *Globalização, dependencia e neoliberalismo na América Latina.* Boitempo.

Marx, K. (1975). *Capital: A critique of political economy* (Vol. 1). Marxists Internet Archive. Progress Publishers. (Original work published 1867). https://www.marxists.org/archive/marx/works/1867-c1/

References

McClintock, C., & Vallas, F. (2005). *La democracia negociada: Las relaciones Perú-Estados Unidos*. Instituto de Estudios Peruanos.

Mendes Pereira, J. M. (2005). El MST en una perspectiva historica. *Revista Argumentos, 48/49*, 9–26 (Número especial). https://argumentos.xoc.uam.mx/index.php/argumentos/issue/view/38

Milei, J. (2024). *Davos 2024: Special address*. World Economic Forum. https://www.weforum.org/agenda/2024/01/special-address-by-javier-milei-president-of-argentina/

Milhorance, E. (2021, September 11). Deforestation in Brazilian Amazon hits highest annual level in a decade. *The Guardian*. https://www.theguardian.com/environment/2021/aug/20/brazil-amazon-deforestation-report-bolsonaro-climate

Moloney, A. (2022, August 4). Can President Petro crack Colombia's reliance on oil and coal? *Reuters*. https://www.reuters.com/article/colombia-climate-politics/analysis-can-president-petro-crack-colombias-reliance-on-oil-and-coal-idUSL8N2ZD5F8/

Montaño, P., & Carlos Tornel, C. (2022). Balance de la política climática de AMLO. *Análisis Plural, 1*(1), 1–18.

Moreno-Brid, J. C., Puyana Mutis, A., & Garry, S. (2023). Is there a role for extractivism in a post-development transition towards sustainability. In H. Veltmeyer & A. Ezquerro-Cañete (Eds.), *From extractivism to sustainability* (pp. 107–118). Routledge.

Morris, L. (2023, May 23). 'A megaproject of death': Fury as Maya train nears completion in Mexico. *The Guardian Weekly*. https://www.theguardian.com/global-development/2023/may/23/fury-as-maya-train-nears-completion-mexico

Motta Villegas, J. D. (2023). Estallido: Crisis, golpe de Estado y lucha de clases en el Perú. Herencia colonial, capitalismo racista y estallido social. In G. Montoya & H. Quiroz (Eds.), *Estallido popular. Protesta y masacre en el Perú, 2022–2023* (pp. 67–82). Editorial Horizonte.

Moyo, S., & Yeros, P. (Eds.). (2005). *reclaiming the land: The resurgence of rural movements in Africa, Asia, and Latin America*. Zed Books.

Munck, R., & O'Hearn, D. (1999). *Critical development theory: Contributions to a new paradigm*. Zed Books.

Norman, C. S. (2009). Rule of law and the resource curse. *Environmental and Resource Economics, 43*(2), 183–207.

North, L., Clark, T. D., & Patroni, V. (Eds.). (2006). *Community rights and corporate responsibility: Canadian mining and oil companies in Latin America*. Between the Lines.

O'Connor, J. (1998). *Natural causes: Essays in ecological Marxism*. Guilford Press.

Ocampo, J. A. (2007, December). The macroeconomics of Latin America's economic boom. *CEPAL Review, 93*, 7–28.

OCMAL—Observatorio de Conflictos Mineros en América Latina. (2017). *Conflictos Mineros en América Latina: Extracción, Saqueo y Agresión. Estado de situación en 2017*. https://www.ocmal.org/informe_2017-3/

O'Donnell, G. (1973). *Modernization and bureaucratic-authoritarianism: Studies in South American politics*. Institute of International Studies, University of California.

O'Neill, A. (2024, February 1). *Latin American & Caribbean: Urbanization from 2012 to 2022*. Statista. https://www.statista.com/statistics/699089/urbanization-in-latin-america-and-caribbean/

Ospina, P., & Ramírez Gallegos, F. (2023, Agosto). Ecuador, al borde del precipicio. *Nueva Sociedad*.

Osborn, C. (2022). A far-right huddle in São Paulo. *Foreign Policy Magazine*. https://staging05.foreignpolicy.com/2022/06/17/cpac-brazil-far-right-south-america-bolsonaro-kast-milei-trump

Oviedo Freire, A. (2017). *Sumak Kamsay: Arte de vivir en armonía*. Global Sur Editores.

Paige, J. (2020). *Indigenous revolution in Ecuador and Bolivia*. University of Arizona Press.

Paley, D., & Granovsky-Larsen, S. (2019). *Organized violence: Capitalist warfare in Latin America*. University of Regina Press.

Perú Libre. (2020). *Ideario y Programa*. https://perulibre.pe/wp-content/uploads/2020/03/ideario-peru-libre.pdf
Petras, J. (2013a, December 30). *The most radical conservative regime: Bolivia under Evo Morales*. http://petras.lahaine.org/?p=1968
Petras, J. (2013b, November 2). *Ecuador: Left-center political regimes versus radical social movements*. Retrieved August 13 from http://petras.lahaine.org/?p=1926
Petras, J. (2016, July 8). *Washington's 'New Managers' in Latin America: Oligarchs, bankers and swindlers*. Global Research. https://www.globalresearch.ca/washingtons-new-managers-in-latin-america-oligarchs-bankers-and-swindlers/5534790
Petras, J. (2017). The return of the right. In J. Petras & H. Veltmeyer (Eds.), *Class struggle in Latin America: Making history today* (pp. 250–265). Routledge.
Petras, J. (2020). The Latin American politics of neoliberal authoritarianism. In B. Berberoglu (Ed.), *The global rise of authoritarianism in the early 21st century* (pp. 91–114). Routledge.
Petras, J., & Leiva, F. (1994). *Poverty and democracy in Chile*. Westview Press.
Petras, J., & Veltmeyer, H. (2005). *Social movements and state power: Argentina, Brazil, Bolivia, Ecuador*. Pluto Press.
Petras, J., & Veltmeyer, H. (2017). *The class struggle in Latin America* (1st ed.). London: Routledge. https://doi.org/10.4324/9781315195124
Petras, J., & Veltmeyer, H. (2018). *Class struggle in Latin America: Making history today*. Routledge.
Petras, J., & Veltmeyer, H. (2019). *Latin America in the vortex of social change*. Routledge.
Pinheiro Barbosa, L., & Rosset, P. (2023). *Aprendizajes del Movimiento Zapatista. De la insurgencia armada a la autonomía popular* (Lessons of the Zapatista Movement). CLACSO.
Porter, E. (2023, August 23). *AMLO's anti-poverty success in Mexico has a dark side*. Bloomberg. https://www.bloomberg.com/opinion/articles/2023-08-23/amlo-s-anti-poverty-success-in-mexico-has-a-dark-side
Prada Alcoreza, R. (2013). Buen Vivir as a model for state and economy. In M. Lang, L. Fernando, & N. Buxton (Coords.), *Beyond development alternative visions from Latin America* (pp. 145–158). The Transnational Institute and Quito: Fundación Rosa Luxemburg. https://www.tni.org/files/download/beyonddevelopment_buenvivir.pdf
Quiroz, H., & Beraun, E. (2023). Insurrección y nueva utopía andina. In G. Montoya & H. Quiroz (Eds.), *Estallido popular. Protesta y masacre en el Perú, 2022–2023* (pp. 173–177). Editorial Horizonte.
Ramírez, G. F. (2023). Guillermo Lasso y la "muerte cruzada" en Ecuador. *Opinión, Nueva Sociedad*, mayo. https://nuso.org/articulo/ecuador-lasso-muertecruzada/
Rathbone, P. (2013, May 12). Doubts come to surface about 'the decade of Latin America'. *Financial Times*. https://www.ft.com/content/b622f752-b967-11e2-9a9f-00144feabdc0
Redclift, M. (1987). *Sustainable development: Exploring the contradictions*. Methuen.
REM—Red Mexicana de Afectados por la Minería. (2010, de Febrero 10). *Blackfire demandará al gobierno de Chiapas. El cinismo de las mineras canadienses*. https://www.remamx.org/2010/02/rema-blackfire-demandara-al-gobierno-de-chiapas-el-cinismo-de-las-mineras-canadienses/
Resumen Latinoamericano. (2019, de Octubre 8). *Ecuador. La fuerza política de los indígenas tiene historia y es imponente*. https://www.resumenlatinoamericano.org/2019/10/08/ecuador-la-fuerza-politica-de-los-indigenas-tiene-historia-y-es-imponente/
Rivera-Batiz, A. (2000). *Currency boards, credibility, and macroeconomic behavior* [Working Paper No. 2000/097]. IMF. https://www.imf.org/external/pubs/ft/wp/2000/wp0097.pdf
Rivas Molina, F. (2023, Agosto 10). Quién era Fernando Villavicencio, el candidato presidencial asesinado en Ecuador? *El País* (Mexico). https://elpais.com/internacional/2023-08-10/quien-era-fernando-villavicencio-el-candidato-presidencial-asesinado-en-ecuador.html

Roberts, K. (1996). Economic crisis and the demise of the legal left in Peru. *Comparative Politics, 29*(1), 69–92.
Roberts, K. (1998). *Deepening democracy? The modern left and social movements in Chile and Peru*. Stanford University Press.
Robles, W., & Veltmeyer, H. (2015). *The politics of Agrarian reform in Brazil: The landless rural workers movement*. Palgrave Macmillan.
Roman, R., & Velasco Arregui, E. (1997). Zapatismo and the workers' movement in Mexico. *Monthly Review, 49* (July–August), 98–116.
Rojas, C. (2015). García Linera identifica a cuatro ONG y advierte con expulsarlas. *Oxigeno.bo*. August 10. https://oxigeno.bo/node/10540
Ross, J. (1994). *Rebellion from the roots: Indian uprising in Chiapas*. Common Courage.
Rosset, P., & Martínez-Torres, M. E. (2012). Rural social movements and agroecology: Context, theory, and process. *Ecology and Society, 17*(3), 17. http://doi.org/10.5751/ES-05000-170317
Sader, E. (2008). The weakest link: Neoliberalism in Latin America. *New Left Review, 52*(July–August). https://newleftreview.org/issues/ii52/articles/emir-sader-the-weakest-link-neoliberalism-in-latin-america
Sader, E. (2011). *The new mole: Paths of the Latin America left*. Verso.
Salcedo, L., Pinzón, R., & Duarte, C. (2013). *El paro agrario: Análisis de los actores agrarios y los procesos organizativos del campesinado*. Centro de Estudios Interculturales, Universidad Javeriana de Cali.
Sanahuja, J. A., & López Burian, C. (2021). Latin American neo-patriot far-right: Between the crisis of globalisation and regional political processes. In G. P. Doval & G. Souroujon (Eds.), *Global resurgence of the right: Conceptual and regional perspectives* (pp. 98–122). Routledge.
Santos, M., & Cerrnadas, G. (2022, June 7). Es possible una segunda ola de protesta en América Latina? *Nodal*. http://www.nodal.am/2022/06/es-posible-una-segunda-ola-progresista-en-America-Latina-por-monolo-de-los-santos-y-gisela-cernadas
Sauer, S. (2020). Interview with João Pedro Stédile, national leader of the MST-Brazil. *The Journal of Peasant Studies, 47*(5), 927–943. https://doi.org/10.1080/03066150.2020.1782892
Saxe-Fernandez, J., & Nuñez, O. (2001). Globalización e imperialismo: La transferencia de Excedentes de América Latina. In J. Saxe-Fernández, J. Petras, H. Veltmeyer, & O. Nuñez (Eds.), *Globalización, imperialismo y Clase social* (pp. 87–166). Lúmen Humanitas.
Wager, S. J., & Schultz, D. (1995). Civil–military relations in Mexico: The Zapatista revolt and its implications. *Journal of Interamerican Studies and World Affairs, 37*(1), 1–42. https://doi.org/10.2307/166215
Schuster, M., & Stefanoni, P. (2023, Agosto 16). La derecha dura cautiva al electorado argentino. *Nueva Sociedad*.
Schuurman, F. (Ed.). (1993). *Beyond the impasse: New directions in development theory*. Zed Books.
Scoones, I., Edelman, M., Borras, S. M., Forero, L. F., Hall, R., Wolford, W., & White B. (2022). *Authoritarian populism and the rural world*. Routledge.
Sena-Fobomade. (2011). *Se intensifica el extractivismo minero en América Latina*. Foro Boliviano sobre Medio Ambiente y Desarrollo, 03-02. http://fobomade.org.bo/art-1109
Smith, J. (2016). *Imperialism in the twenty-first century. Globalization, super-exploitation, and capitalism's final crisis*. Monthly Review Press.
Solón, P. (2014). *Vivir Bien: Notes for the debate*. Focus on the global south. Systemic Alternatives.org. https://systemicalternatives.org/2014/08/20/notes-for-the-debate-the-rights-of-mother-earth/
Sosa, M., & Zwarteveen, M. (2009). Accumulation by dispossession: The case of large mining industry in Cajamarca [Water Justice Workshop and Conference]. Organized by the Irrigation and Water Engineering Group from Wageningen University in Cusco, Peru.

References

https://research.wur.nl/en/publications/accumulation-by-dispossession-the-case-of-large-mining-industry-i

Sotelo, A. (2000). Globalización: Estancamiento o crisis en América Latina? *Problemas de Desarrollo, 31*(120 enero-marzo), 31–53.

Sotelo, A. (2009). *Neo-imperialismo, dependencia e novas periferias. A América Latina e os desafios da globalizaca.* Boitempo.

Standing, G. (2011). *The Precariat – The new dangerous class.* Bloomsbury.

Stijns, J.-P. (2006). Natural resource abundance and human capital accumulation. *World Development, 34*(6), 1060–1083.

Stédile, J. P., & Frei, S. (1993). *A Luta pela Terra no Brasil.* Scrita.

Stuenkel, O. (2022). *The greatest risk facing Colombia and its new leftist president. Carnegie endowment for international peace.* https://staging.carnegieendowment.org/2022/08/11/greatest-risk-facing-colombia-and-its-new-leftist-president-pub-87663

Svampa, M. (2011). Neo-developmentalist extractivism and social movements: An eco-territorial turn towards new alternatives? In M. Lang & D. Mokrani (Eds.), *Beyond development* (pp. 185–217). Abya Yala.

Svampa, M. (2015). Commodities consensus: Neoextractivism and enclosure of the commons in Latin America. *The South Atlantic Quarterly, 114*(1), 65–82.

Svampa, M. (2017). *Del cambio de época al fin de ciclo: Gobiernos progresistas, extractivismo, y movimientos sociales en América Latina.* Edhasa.

Svampa, M. (2019). *Neo-extractivism in Latin America. Socio-environmental conflicts, the territorial turn, and new political narratives. Elements in politics and society in Latin America.* Cambridge University Press. https://www.memoria.fahce.unlp.edu.ar/libros/mpm.5180/pm.5180.pdf

Svampa, M. (2021). *Del cambio de época al fin de ciclo: Gobiernos progresistas, extractivismo y movimientos sociales en América Latina.* Edhasa.

Svampa, M., & Antonelli, M. (2009). *Minería transnacional, narrativas del desarrollo y resistencias sociales.* Editorial Biblos.

Svampa, M., & Sola Alvarez, M. (2011, Abril). Modelo minero, resistencias sociales y estilos de desarrollo: los Marcos de la discusión en la Argentina. *Debate Ecuador*, 105–126. http://hdl.handle.net/10469/3526

Tejera Gaona, H. (1996). Las causas del conflicto en Chiapas. In H. Grammont & H. Tejera Gaona (Eds.), *Los nuevos actores sociales y procesos politicos en el campo* (pp. 299–332). UAM/UNAMIPlaza y Valdes de C.V.

Tetreault, D. (2020). The new extractivism in Mexico: Rent redistribution and resistance to mining and petroleum activities. *World Development, 126*, 104714.

Tetreault, D., Lucio, C., & McCulligh, C. (2023). *Extractivismo, contaminación y luchas socioambientales en México: Extractivismo, contaminación y luchas socioambientales en México.* Editorial Itaca.

The Associated Press – AP. (2022). *Ex-rebel sworn in as Colombia's president in historic shift.* https://www.npr.org/2022/08/07/1116215977/ex-rebel-sworn-in-as-colombias-president-in-historic-shift

Toledo, V. (2023, de Agosto 1). El nuevo poder global de los pueblos indígenas. *La Jornada*. https://www.jornada.com.mx/2023/08/01/opinion/016a2pol

Tornel, C. (2023a, September 26). AMLO's neoliberalism in Mexico: Extractivism, militarism and climate breakdown. *The Bullet.* https://socialistproject.ca/2023/09/amlo-neoliberalism-mexico/

Tornel, C. (2023b). Energy justice in the context of green extractivism: Perpetuating ontological and epistemological violence in the Yucatan Peninsula. *Journal of Political Ecology, 30*(1). https://doi.org/10.2458/jpe.5485.

Torres Wong, M. (2019). *Natural resources, extraction and indigenous rights in Latin America: Exploring the boundaries of environmental and state-corporate crime in Bolivia, Peru and Mexico.* Routledge.

References

Toye, J. (1987). *Dilemmas of development: Reflections on the counter-revolution in development theory and policy*. Basil Blackwell.
Travela, J. C. (2018). The development Utopia. Contributions to think viable alternatives, *Divulgatio. Perfiles Académicos de Posgrado*, 2(6), 104–121.
Turkewitz, J. (2022, June 19). Gustavo Petro wins the election, becoming Colombia's first leftist leader. *The New York Times*. https://www.nytimes.com/2022/06/19/world/americas/gustavo-petro-colombia-presidential-election.html
UNCTAD – United Nations Conference on Trade and Development. (2007). *World investment report 2007: Transnational corporations, extractive industries and development*. United Nations.
UNCTAD – United Nations Conference on Trade and Development. (2011). *World investment report. Non-equity modes of international production and development*. United Nations.
UNCTAD – United Nations Conference on Trade and Development. (2012, January 24). *Investment trend monitor, No. 8*. United Nations.
UNDESA – United Nations Department of Economic and Social Affairs. (2005). *The Inequality predicament: Report on the world social situation*. United Nations.
UNDP – United Nations Development Program. (2010). *Regional human development report for Latin America and the Caribbean 2010*. UNDP.
Valencia Lomeli, E. (2013). CCTs as social policy: A critical assessment. In H. Veltmeyer & D. Tetreault (Eds.), *Poverty and development in Latin America: Public policies and development pathways* (pp. 163–188). Kumarian Press.
Veltmeyer, H. (1992). New social movements in Latin America. In J. Dominguez (Ed.), *Mexico, Central, and South America: New perspectives: Social movements* (pp. 159–190). Routledge.
Veltmeyer, H. (1997, October). New social movements in Latin America: The dynamics of class and identity. *The Journal of Peasant Studies*, 25(1), 139–169.
Veltmeyer, H. (2000). The dynamics of social change in Mexico. *Latin American Perspectives*, 27(5), 88–110.
Veltmeyer, H. (2005). Development and globalization as imperialism. *Canadian Journal of Development Studies*, XXVI(1), 89–106.
Veltmeyer, H. (2010, April 27). The global crisis and Latin America. *Globalizations*, 7(1–2), 217–233. https://doi.org/10.1080/14747731003593596
Veltmeyer, H. (2012). The natural resource dynamics of post-neoliberalism in Latin America: New developmentalism or extractivist imperialism? *Studies in Political Economy*, 90, 57–86.
Veltmeyer, H. (2013). The political economy of natural resource extraction: A new model or extractive imperialism? *Canadian Journal of Development Studies*, 34(1), 79–95.
Veltmeyer, H. (2016). Investment, governance and resistance in the new extractive economies of Latin America. In K. Deonandan & M. Dougherty (Eds.), *Mining in Latin America: Critical approaches to the new extraction* (pp. 27–44). Routledge.
Veltmeyer, H. (2017). Resistance, class struggle and social movements in Latin America: contemporary dynamics. *Revista Theomai*, 35, 52–71.
Veltmeyer, H., & Petras, J. (2014). *The new extractivism: A post-neoliberal development model, or imperialism of the twenty-first century?* Zed Books.
Veltmeyer, H., & Záyago Lau, E. (Eds.). (2020). *Buen Vivir and the challenges to capitalism in Latin America*. Routledge.
Vergara-Camus, L. (2009). The MST and the EZLN struggle for land: New forms of peasant rebellions. *Journal of Agrarian Change*, 9(3), 365–391.
Vergara-Camus, L. (2023). *Resistencia colectiva al neoliberalismo*. CLACSO.
Vergara-Camus, L., & Kay, C. (2017a). Agribusiness, peasants, left-wing governments, and the state in Latin America: An overview and theoretical reflections. *Journal of Agrarian Change*, 17(2), 239–257.

Vergara-Camus, L., & Kay, C. (2017b). The Agrarian political economy of left-wing governments in Latin America: Agribusiness, peasants, and the limits of neo-developmentalism. *Journal of Agrarian Change*, *17*(2), 415–437.

Webber, J. (2008). Rebellion to reform in Bolivia. Part I: Domestic class structure, Latin-American trends, and capitalist imperialism. *Historical Materialism*, *16*, 23–58.

Webber, J. (2010, July 13). Indigenous struggle, ecology, and capitalist resource extraction in Ecuador. *The Bullet*, 391. https://socialistproject.ca/2010/07/b391/

Weizenmann, P. P. (2019). 'Tropical Trump'? Bolsonaro's threat to Brazilian democracy. *Harvard International Review*, *40*(1), 12–14.

Wheatley, J. (2014, October 5). Emerging markets adapt to 'new normal' as markets adapt to the new normal as commodities cycle. *Financial Times*. https://www.ft.com/content/27a1b0d8-4b09-11e4-839a-00144feab7de

Williamson, J. (1990). What Washington means by policy reform. In J. Williamson (Ed.), *Latin American adjustment: How much has happened?* Peterson Institute for International Economics. https://www.piie.com/commentary/speeches-papers/what-washington-means-policy-reform

Wolf, E. (1971). *Peasant wars of the 20th century*. Faber & Faber.

World Bank. (2005). *Extractive industries and sustainable development. An evaluation of World Bank group experience*. The World Bank, IFC/MIGA.

World Bank. (2007). *World development report 2008: Agriculture for development*. Oxford University Press.

Yashar, D. (2005). *Contesting citizenship in Latin America: The rise of indigenous movements and the postliberal challenge*. Cambridge University Press.

Zacatecas Online. (2012, de Marzo 12). *Cientos de empleos en minería tras visita de MAR a Canada*. https://zacatecasonline.com.mx/noticias/local/20784-mineria-mar-canada

Zanotti, L., & Roberts, K. M. (2021). (Aún) la excepción y no la regla: la Derecha populista radical en américa latina. *Revista Uruguaya de Ciencia Política*, *30*(1), 23–48.

Zermefio, S. (Ed.). (1997). *Movimientos sociales e identidades colectivas: México en la década de los noventa*. La Jornada Ediciones.

Zermeño, S. (Comp.). (1997). *Movimientos sociales e identidad colectiva. México en la década de los noventa*. CIICH/UNAM.

Zibechi, R. (2012, Abril 19). La nueva geopolítica del capital. ALAI, América Latina en Movimiento. *Le Monde Diplomatique Colombia*. https://www.eldiplo.info/la-nueva-geopolitica-del-capital/

Zorrilla, C. (2009). *Protegiendo a su comunidad contra las empresas mineras y otras industrias extractivas*. Global Response.

Index

Accumulation, 14
Activism of popular movement, 155
Administrative decentralization, 30
Agrarian, Peasant, Ethnic, and Popular Summit (CACEP), 63
Agrarian change, 8, 55–56, 63
Agrarian movements, 53
 Agrarian social movements as force of social transformation, 62–63
 in class struggle, 56–62
 classes of labor in rural society, 54–55
 politics of Agrarian change, 55–56
Agribusiness, 116
Agro-mineral and export bourgeoisie, 68
Agro-mineral extractive model, 39
Agroecological revolution, 63
Agroextractivism, 136
Alianza Bolivariana para los Pueblos de Nuestra América (ALBA), 66
Alianza Popular Revolucionaria Americana (APRA), 83
Alliances in class struggle, 156–158
Alternative development, 32
Amazon, 133
 Bolsonaro's war on, 136–139
Andean capitalism, 72–74
Andrés Manuel López Obrador (AMLO), 3
Anti-imperialist resistance, 19, 31
Anticapitalist, 11, 56, 163
Antiextractivist Protests, 150–152
Argentina
 class struggle, 70–71
 political earthquake in general elections, 126–127

Argentine Armed Forces, 70
Armed Forces, 45
Armies of national liberation, 62
Asociación Campesina Popular (Asocampo), 63*n*3
Asociación Nacional Agraria y Campesina (Asonalcam), 63*n*3
Asociación Nacional de Zonas de Reserva Campesina (Anzorc), 63*n*3
Authoritarian neoliberalism, 24
Authoritarian populism, 4*n*4
Autoridad Nacional Afrocolombiana (Anafro), 63*n*3

Biofuels, 32
Bolivia, popular uprisings, 72–74
Bolsa Familia, 38, 135
Bolsillos de olvido ("forgotten pockets"), 60–61
Bolsonarism, 129
Bolsonaro, 120
 war on Amazon, 136–139
Brazil, class struggle, 68–70
Brazilian Institute of Geography and Statistics (IBGE), 133
Brazilian Social Democracy Party (PSDB), 35, 135
BRICS, 14
"Broad Front" government, 40
Buen vivir concept, 36–37*n*2, 92, 142
Bukele, 5
"Bull, bullet, and bible" bloc, 137*n*7
"Bureaucratic authoritarian" regimes, 31
Bureaucratic authoritarianism, 6, 30

Cabildo Abierto (CA), 4
CACEP, 63

Index

Capital, 6n6, 13
  accumulation, 15, 67, 132–133, 137, 148
  flows, 32
Capitalism, 13
  contradictions of, 18–20
  extractive, 7, 14
Capitalist class, 1n1
Capitalist development, 7, 34, 77
Capitalist hydra, 163
Capitalist markets, 1, 7–8, 10, 22, 37, 64, 162
Capitalist warfare, 123
Capital–labor relation, 10, 18
Cartographies of Violence in the Amazon Region, 138
Casa Rosada (Pink House), 6
Castillo government, 91–95
Center-left, 1, 5, 40, 80–81, 160
Center-periphery, 7, 17, 35
Central Independiente de Obreros Agrícolas y Campesinos (CIOAC), 107
Central Única dos Trabalhadores (CUT), 68
Chávez, 11, 80, 120, 164
Chavista Venezuelan United Socialist Party (PSUV), 81
Chiapas, 105
Chicago Boys, 7, 30
"Chicago School" of neoliberal, 7
Chile, 2, 4, 31, 158
Citizen Revolution, 40, 47, 76
Citizen's Revolution movement, 2
Citizens movement, 75
Civil society, 31, 111
Class, 1n1
  class-ethnic alliances, 79
  consciousness, 58
  of labor in rural society, 54–55
Class Position of Political Right, 91–95
Class struggle, 1n1, 7–11, 53, 68–70
  Agrarian movements in, 56–62
  alliances in, 156–158
  changing dynamics of, 120
  on extractive frontier, 165–166
  in Latin America, 77
  three decades of, 67–68
Coalición de Movimientos y Organizaciones Sociales de Colombia (Comosoc), 63n3
Colombia, 159–161
Colombia Humana, 42
Colombian peace accords, 123
Comité de Defensa Popular de Durango (CDP), 112
Commodities boom, 1, 8, 15–16, 66, 84, 135, 162
Commodities consensus, 19
Communal socialism, 72–74, 162–165
Communal state, 164
Communities, 9, 11, 20, 54, 76, 98, 108, 164, 169
Community-based resistance, struggle dynamics of, 145–146
Community-based resistance movements, 116
Comprehensive development, 67
Conga copper mining project, 149
Congreso de los Pueblos (CDP), 63n3
Conservatism, 40
Conservative Lollapalooza, 120–122
Conservative restoration, 51, 155–156
Constitutional Reform (2013), 115
Consulta Popular, 58
Contradictions, 18–20
Coordinador Nacional Agrario (CNA), 63n3
"Corporate social responsibility" program, 116
Corporatism, 68–70
Correa, 3, 20, 76, 144–145
Correism, 3
Crisis, 6, 18, 45, 140
Cuban Revolution, 56
Cultural war, 50n9

Democratic electoral politics, limitations of, 158–159
"Democratic electoral" transition, 38

Democratic Unity Movement (MUD), 81
"Demonstrations for Peace" in Lima, 99
Dependency, 19, 37
Deregulation of markets, 7, 15
Development
  assistance, 67
  of underdevelopment, 15*n*5
Developmentalism, 62
Developmentalist model, 67
Dual power, 70
Dutch disease, 19

Economic dynamics, 13
Economic model, 14–15, 21–22*n*11
Economic opportunity, 143
Economic sabotage, 66–67, 91–95
"Economically backwards" countries, 67
Economics of exploitation and inequality, 84–87
Ecuador
  electoral pendulum, 122–124
  middle-class radicalism, 74–79
Ejército Zapatista de Liberación Nacional (EZLN), 75, 111
Electoral politics, 119–120
Environmental terrorists, 37
Environmentalists, 160
Ethno-class struggle in Ecuador, 75
Euro-Bolivian rulers, 74
Evo Morales, 2, 22, 73, 78–79, 93, 158
Exploitation, 7, 14, 61, 141, 146–147
Export primarization pattern, 35
Extractive capital, 8, 34
  geoeconomics of, 32–34
  political economy of, 15–18
Extractive capitalism, 7, 14
Extractive export strategy, 73
Extractive frontier, 11, 20, 146–150
Extractive imperialism
  Antiextractivist Protests and Global Environmental Justice Movement, 150–152
  dynamics of natural resource appropriation and resistance, 146–150
  limits of progressive extractivism, 142–145
  politics of, 141
  struggle dynamics of community-based resistance, 145–146
Extractivism, 1, 11, 16–17, 36, 65, 131
  development dynamics of, 34–35
  as postdevelopment pathway, 161–162

Far Right, 3–5, 10, 23, 43–44, 47, 49, 121–122, 161, 164
Federación Nacional Sindical Unitaria Agropecuaria (Fensuagro), 63*n*3
Feminist ideology, 50*n*9
Fiscal stability pacts, 92
Fobomade, 147*n*3
Foreign direct investment (FDI), 15, 32, 84
  exponential increase and sectoral distribution, 34–35
Formal sector, 109
Fossil fuels, 32
Fourth revolution, 115
Fourth transformation, 41–42
Free market capitalism, 7
"Free market" regimes, 46
Free Trade Area of the Americas (FTAA), 78
"Free-market" neoliberal policies, 81
Frente Amplio, 43
Frente Zapatista de Liberación Nacional (FZLN), 109, 111
Fuerzas Armadas Revolucionarias de Colombia (FARC), 159
Fuerzas Armadas Revolucionarias de Colombia–Ejército del Pueblo (FARC–EP), 56
Fuerzas de Liberación Nacional (FLN), 107

Geoeconomics of extractive capital, 32–34
Geopolitics of capital, 13–15

Global Environmental Justice Movement, 150–152
Global financial crisis, 16
Global Response, 146*n*2
Global value chains, 86
Globalization process, 7, 135
Golden age of US imperialism, 77
Governmental power, 95
Gross domestic product (GDP), 84
Guayaquil, 124

High-intensity class struggle, 70–71

IMF Reforms, 31
Imperialism, 15*n*5, 35, 134, 154 (*see also* Extractive imperialism)
Inclusionary activism, 38
Inclusionary state activism, 36
Inclusive development, 8, 67
"Inclusive economic growth" policy agenda and strategy, 68
Indigenous groups, 160
Indigenous Missionary Council (CIMI), 139
Indigenous Nationalities of Ecuador, 75
Indigenous resistance, 165–166
Industrial capital(ism), 14
Industrial policy, new, 162
Informal sector, 109
Institutional Revolutionary Party (PRI), 106
Intentional violent deaths (IVMs), 138
International relations, center–periphery structure of, 35
International Tribunal of the Right of Nature, 41
Intra-agrarian class dynamic, 55
Izquierda Unida (IU), 89, 125

Junta of National Salvation, 57

Kirchner regime, 71
Kleptocracy, 39

Lacandon region, 106
Land reform, 73
Land sovereignty, 55
Land struggle, 8, 31, 53, 55–56, 77, 107
Landgrabbing, 8
Landless Workers Movement, 56
Latin America
 left turns, 153–154
 new popular resistance in, 154–156
Latin American class struggle, setting agenda for, 6–7
Latin American dependency theory, 103
Latin American politics, 29
 setting stage for progressive cycle in, 30–32
Latin American social movements, 104
Left turns, 10, 130*n*2
Left-wing populism, 20–23
Leftist academics, 39
Leftist progressivism to rightist populism, 135–136
Liberalization, 7, 15
Lima Group, 92
"Living well" concept, 143
Low-intensity class struggle, 71
Lula, 2–3, 35, 44–45, 47, 50, 69, 117, 129, 156, 158, 168

Macri, 1–2, 24, 48, 82, 121
Manta, 124
Marcos, 106
"Market-led land reform" model, 34
Marx's theory of capital, 18
Marxist political economy, 103
"Mayan Train" project, 41, 115
Mesa de Unidad Agraria (MUA), 63*n*3
Mestizo, 73
Metals, 32
Metals Economics Group, 16
Mexico, 103
 development dynamics of extractive capitalism in, 112–114
 New Social Movement, 104–108

policy dynamics of neoextractivism in Mexico, 114–116
struggle for social change in neoliberal era, 108–112
Mexico, Argentina, Brazil (MBA), 7
Middle-class radicalism, 74–79
Milei, 4, 6, 49, 126–127
Minerals, 32
Minga, 121*n*3
Mining, 16, 46, 72, 76, 113, 124, 147–148, 151
Modernization theory, 103
Mont Pelerin Society (MPS), 7*n*7
Morales-Linera regime, 74
Morales' MAS regime, 47
Movement of National Regeneration (MORENA), 119
Movement Toward Socialism (MAS), 2, 72, 78
Movimento dos Trabalhadores Rurais Sem Terra (MST), 56
Movimiento por la Constituyente Popular (MCP), 63*n*3
Movimiento Social y Político Colombiano Marcha Patriótica (MAPA), 63*n*3
Muerte cruzada (impeachment), 122

NAFTA on Steroids, 65
National Agrarian and Popular Strike (PNAP), 62
National Confederation of Indigenous Nationalities (CONAIE), 57, 59–60, 75–76
National Consultation on Labor and Union Freedom (*Trabajo y Libertad Sindical*), 111
National Democratic Alliance (AND), 3*n*3
National Democratic Convention (CND), 111
National income, 6
National Security Doctrine, 30
Natural resource appropriation and resistance, 146–150

extraction, 11
Neocolonialism, 142
Neodevelopmentalism, 8, 17, 35–37, 65, 130*n*2
politics of, 37–38
Neoextractivism, 14, 16, 35–38
policy dynamics in Mexico, 114–116
Neoliberal "structural reforms", 7, 31
Neoliberal authoritarianism
development dynamics of extractivism, 34–35
geoeconomics of extractive capital, 32–34
neodevelopmentalism or neoextractivism, 35–37
politics of, 29
politics of neodevelopmentalism, 37–38
progressive cycle, 42–45
right-wing interlude or demise of neoliberalism, 45–48
right-wing neoliberal authoritarianism, 39–42
setting stage for progressive cycle in Latin American politics, 30–32
Tragedy of the Left, 38–39
Neoliberal era, 168
peasant-based agrarian movements in, 8
social change in, 108–112
Neoliberal extractivist development model, 84
Neoliberal policy agenda, 32
Neoliberal regimes, 46
Neoliberal wave, 46
Neoliberalism, 1, 7, 130*n*1
demise of, 45–48, 65
to neodevelopmentalism, 132–135
New Brazil, 132–135
New class-based unionism, 68
New conservatism, 6
New economic model, 67
New FUNAI, 139
New geoeconomics, 13–15

New popular resistance in Latin
America, 154–156
New Republic, 134
New rurality, 32
New Social Movement, 31, 96–98,
104–108
New social policy, 67
New unionism, 68
New world order, 19
Nexo, 138
Nongovernmental organizations
(NGOs), 31
North American Free Trade
Agreement (NAFTA), 57
Nueva Sociedad, 123

Observatory of Mining Conflicts in Latin
America (OCMAL), 37*n*3
Oligarchs, 39
Organización Nacional Indígena de
Colombia (ONIC), 63*n*3
Organization of American States
(OAS), 157
Organized violence, 123

Pachakutik, 75–76
Pachamama (Mother Earth), 73, 79
Pacific Alliance, 43
Pacto Histórico lawmaker, 158
PAIS Alliance, 40
Partido Comunista Mexicana
(PCM), 107
*Partido Revolucionario Clandestino Union
del Pueblo* (Procup), 108
Peace agreement, 123
Peasant movements, 29, 32, 37, 56, 62,
64, 131
Pellerin Society, 7
Peru, 83
Castillo government, class position
of political right, and
economic sabotage, 91–95
economics of exploitation and
inequality, 84–87
fall of Castillo and weakness of
left, 95–96

return of the right, 99–101
social protests and new social
movement, 96–98
Victory of the Left in the
Presidential Elections of
2021, 88–91
weakness of political left, lack
of class consciousness,
and failure of leadership,
124–126
Perú Libre program, 88, 92–93, 96, 124
Peruvian economy, 85
business structure, 86
Petro, 42–43, 158, 160–161
Petróleos de Venezuela, S. A.
(PDVSA), 164
Pink tide, 14, 16, 154
of regime change, 3–4
Pink wave, 130*n*2
Policy dynamics of neoextractivism in
Mexico, 114–116
Political dynamics, 13
Political earthquake in general
elections, 126–127
Political economy of extractive
capital, 15–18
Political state power, 95
Politics
of Agrarian change, 55–56
of neodevelopmentalism, 37–38
Popular Defense Committee of
Durango, 112
Populist authoritarianism, 56
(*see also* Neoliberal
authoritarianism)
Bolsonaro's war on Amazon,
136–139
leftist progressivism to rightist
populism, 135–136
New Brazil, 132–135
proletarianization process, 130
Postcapitalist transition, 11
Postdevelopment, 38, 66, 135, 165
Postextractive transition, 153
alliances in class struggle,
156–158

Colombia, 159–161
considerations, 166–169
extractivism as postdevelopment pathway, 161–162
indigenous resistance and class struggle on extractive frontier, 165–166
Latin America's left turns, 153–154
limitations of democratic electoral politics, 158–159
new popular resistance in Latin America, 154–156
solidarity economics and communal socialism, 162–165
Postmodernist/development perspective, 104
Poverty, 73
reduction, 20–23
Power bloc, 137n7
Primary commodities, 162
Primitive accumulation, 137, 139
Privatization, 30
of means of production, 15
of state enterprises, 7
Proceso de Comunidades Negras (PCN), 63n3
Productive Community Social Economic Model (MESCP), 22n11
Productivist neoextractivism, 94
Progressive cycle, 1–2, 8, 42–45, 66
Argentina, 70–71
Bolivia, 72–74
Brazil, 68–70
Ecuador, 74–79
end of, 24–25
end of, 79–81
in Latin American politics, 30–32
of macroeconomic and social policies, 53
three decades of class struggle, 67–68
Progressive extractivism, limits of, 142–145

Progressive governments, 4, 16, 20, 36, 38, 154
Progressive regimes, 8, 20, 24, 43
Progressives, 43
Proletarianization process, 130
Propertyless rural workers, 58
Public lands, 73, 138
Pueblo Unido, 107

Radical right authoritarianism, 5
Radical right populism (RRP), 4n4
Radicalism, 74
Regime change, 3–4, 10, 13, 20, 68, 78
Regional grassroot organizations, 9
"Republican austerity" program, 115
Republican Proposal (PRO) party, 1
Resistance, 10, 20, 53, 111, 119, 145, 169
Resource curse effects, 19, 146
Resource nationalism, 20–23
Resource-seeking "extractive" capital, 15, 29, 34, 129–130
Restored democracy, 30
Resumen Latinamericano, 165
Revolutionary transformation, 66
Right turns, 10
Right-wing coup, 76
Right-wing interlude, 45–48
Right-wing neoliberal authoritarianism, 39–42
Right-wing opposition, 66–67
Right-wing populism, 6, 21
Right-wing populist authoritarianism, 10
Right-wing wave, 46
Rightwing huddle, 120–121
Rightwing parties, 39
Rural Landless Workers Movement (MST), 58–59, 130n3
Rural poor, 8, 31–32, 55, 105
Rural–urban coalitions, 160

Second Agrarian Reform, 94
Semiproletariat, 8, 31, 54, 119, 131
Shared economic interest, 34
Shining Path, 83

Sistema Económico Latinoamericano y del Caribe (SELA), 157
Social and environmental justice, 11, 135, 140, 156, 169
Social change
  contradictions of capitalism, 18–20
  end of progressive cycle, 24–25
  in neoliberal era, 108–112
  new geoeconomics and geopolitics of capital, 13–15
  political economy of extractive capital, 15–18
  resource nationalism, left-wing populism, and poverty reduction, 20–23
  structure of Latin American exports, 17
Social inclusion, 150
Social mobilizations for rurality, 62
Social movements for agrarian reform, 34
Social protests, 96–98
Social solidarity, 11, 92, 143, 163
Social transformation, Agrarian social movements as force of, 62–63
Socialism, 164
Socioenvironmental conflicts, 18, 20, 36, 105, 139, 144, 162
Soft coup, 120
Solidarity economics, 162–165
Structural adjustment program, 67
Structural reforms, 15, 19, 67
Sustainable development, 10, 19–20, 36, 161

Terra Research Group of Emerging Territories and Resistance Networks in the Amazon (*TERRA*), 138
Territorial restructuring, 34
Trade unions, 76
Tragedy of the Left, 38–39
Trans-Pacific Free Trade regime, 67
Trans-Pacific Partnership agreement, 65
Transnational capitalist class, 151

"Trojan Horse" ploy, 46
Tropical Trump, 5

UN Economic Commission for Latin America (ECLAC), 35–36
United Plurinational Pachakutik Movement–New Country (MUPP-NP), 60
United Workers Front, 76
US Conservative Political Action Conference (CPAC), 121
US imperialism, 23, 30, 32, 77, 155, 159, 161, 167–168
US intervention, 66–67

Vaca Muerta (Dead Cow) complex, 79
Venezuela, 4, 24, 66, 80–81, 157, 164, 168
Via Campesina, 63
Victory of the Left in the Presidential Elections of 2021, 88–91
Violence against Indigenous Peoples in Brazil, 139
Vivir bien, 142
Vulture funds, 23

War on gangs, 51
Washington Consensus, 67–68, 131
Water war, 72
Workers Party (PT), 35, 69, 129, 135, 156
  in Brazil, 38
Working class, 1n1, 53
  movements of, 55
World Bank, 11, 17, 54, 67, 94, 141
World capitalist system, 7, 11, 17, 34, 53, 77, 85, 104, 134, 161, 165

Yasuni Ishpingo-Tambococha-Tiputini National Park (ITT), 143–144
Yucatán home, 115

Zapatista Army of National Liberation (EZLN), 57, 60–62
Zapatista insurrection, 105
Zapatista Rebellion, 104–108
Zapatistas, 57, 61–62, 106

Printed and bound by CPI Group (UK) Ltd, Croydon, CR0 4YY
05/02/2025
14638924-0001